Accession no.
36022123

KU-302-485

Sport and the English, 1918–1939

WITHDRAWN

Sport and the English, 1918–1939 is a comprehensive, accessible and innovative analysis of sport as an expression of the values and social relations of a nation. Bringing the central place of sport in English life between the wars into sharp focus, this insightful history provides us with a fresh perspective on issues of gender, class, religion and identity, and ideas of morality, continuity and change.

Themes include:

- the nature of sport and its place in national life
- how sport was portrayed in the media and through the sports stars of the age
- tradition and change in sport and in society
- gaining meaning from sport: the pursuit of pleasure, moral codes, and ideas of Englishness
- class, social conflict and social cohesion.

This original and lucid study is ideal for students of sport and social history, and anyone interested in the social role of sport.

Mike Huggins lectures in History and Sports Studies at St Martin's College, Lancaster, UK. His *Flat Racing and British Society 1790–1914* was awarded the Sports History Book of 2000 Award by the North American Society of Sports Historians.

Jack Williams was Reader in Cultural History at Liverpool John Moores University, UK. His *Cricket and England: A Cultural and Social History of the Inter-War Years* and *Cricket and Race* were each awarded the Lord Aberdare Prize by the British Society of Sport History.

Sport and the English, 1918–1939

Mike Huggins and Jack Williams

1789855

LIBRARY	
ACC. No. 3602223	DEPT.
CLASS No.	
UNIVERSITY OF CHESTER	

Routledge
Taylor & Francis Group

LONDON AND NEW YORK

First published 2006 by Routledge
2 Park Square, Milton Park, Abingdon, Oxon OX14 4RN

Simultaneously published in the USA and Canada
by Routledge
270 Madison Ave, New York, NY 10016

Routledge is an imprint of the Taylor & Francis Group

© 2006 Mike Huggins and Jack Williams

Typeset in Bembo by GreenGate Publishing Services, Tonbridge, Kent
Printed and bound in Great Britain by The Cromwell Press, Trowbridge,
Wiltshire

All rights reserved. No part of this book may be reprinted or reproduced
or utilised in any form or by any electronic, mechanical, or other means,
now known or hereafter invented, including photocopying and recording,
or in any information storage or retrieval system, without permission in
writing from the publishers.

British Library Cataloguing in Publication Data
A catalogue record for this book is available from the British Library

Library of Congress Cataloging in Publication Data
A catalog record for this book has been requested

ISBN 10: 0–415–33184-6 (hbk)
ISBN 10: 0–415–33185-4 (pbk)

ISBN 13: 978-0-415-33184-5 (hbk)
ISBN 13: 978-0-415-33185-2 (pbk)

Contents

Introduction

This book focuses on a deceptively simple question – what did sport mean to the English between the wars? This was a time when watching or participating in sports had become major leisure interests. The English were regularly presented as a sport-loving people, an image which visiting foreigners immediately identified. Rudolf Kircher, a German visitor, believed that sport was 'immediately and inseparably bound up with the whole life of the people … none of the great modern nations has built it up in quite the same way into a rule of life and a national code' (Kircher 1928: 3–6). Newspapers usually devoted more space to sports than to all other forms of leisure. Sport was often a focus in leisure settings from pub conversations to the cinema, where, by the 1930s, it regularly formed between 20 and 25 per cent of most newsreel features. Sport was given enormous ideological significance. It received far more approval from the political and social establishment than most other forms of leisure. The monarchy attended national sporting events, and politicians were often keen to benefit by associating themselves with sport. There was sufficient élite interest in cricket to attract the prime minister and many of the cabinet to watch the fifth test against Australia at the Oval which gave England the Ashes in August 1926. Ramsay MacDonald, as a Labour leader, was among those bidding farewell to the touring Australian rugby league team after the Ashes match at Rochdale in 1930. Stanley Baldwin, by contrast, was a fan of the Oxford versus Cambridge athletics meetings. Betting on sport and cheating in sport often provoked controversy, but criticism of such practices rarely resulted in condemnations of sport itself. Discourses surrounding sport often argued that besides promoting physical health, sports encouraged moral qualities such as honesty, selflessness, courage or resolution which could be transferred to other areas of life. Apologists for sport often pointed out that sportsmanship was application of Christian morality.

By examining why sport was held in such high esteem in England between the wars this book sheds much light on English cultural values and social relations. Its concentration on the inter-war years permits deeper analysis than would a longer period of time. For the same reason it focuses on England rather than Britain, although many in England used the terms 'English' and

'British' interchangeably, particularly when talking about the Empire, but the conflation of England with Britain requires more research. Although useful work has been carried out on south Wales soccer by Martin Johnes (2002), inter-war sports in Scotland still await their historian. Separate international teams reflected divided loyalties within Britain.

Deciding the boundaries of sport is never easy and for the purposes of this book, we have taken sport to include those physical and competitive activities widely accepted as sport between the wars. In practice this has meant that 'sports' were those covered on newspaper sports pages, though we also include aeroplane racing, often described as a sport, but not featured on the sport pages. We have excluded activities such as card games and dominoes, which, while competitive and included in the sport pages of many local weekly newspapers, were not physical; and ballroom dancing, since it was not seen as a sport between the wars.

In order to uncover how sport was regarded in England, the book first explores the forms and extent of interest in sport, how these compared with other leisure interests and how far involvement with sport differed between social groups and between sports. It then turns to the representations of sport between the wars. Reactions to sport were very much responses to how sport was represented and its multiple meanings diffused. But those who followed sport also helped to shape such representations. The representations of sport are examined through analyses first of the media and their images of sport and second of sport star celebrity, the status of sport stars, and what these reveal about the qualities and dilemmas that were imagined to surround sport. The variety of meanings that were attached to sport is further explored through the pleasures associated with sport, notions of correct behaviour in sport and the assumptions that sport in England was morally superior to that in other countries. The continuities and changes in sport, including the introduction of new sports and the responses to them and the changes in playing techniques of established sports, are discussed to determine how far sport was characterised by conservatism and an acceptance of tradition. In the concluding section of the book, we explore how far sport expressed and may have deepened social conflict and cohesion in England, sport's gender and class dimensions and how far sports reflected and promoted senses of local, regional and national identity that transcended these.

Ignoring sport can lead to inadequate treatments of social and cultural history. The prime justification for this book is that the numbers following sport and the importance accorded to sport between the wars were so extensive that they demand more attention. Hundreds of thousands paid to play or watch sport each week. Far more were interested in sport than the high arts. Almost all gambling took place on sporting events. The physicality of sport meant that it expressed much about the cultural assumptions surrounding the legitimate uses of the body and because of this was intertwined with notions of femininity and masculinity. Common beliefs that sports in England were pervaded by 'sportsmanship' and that this was a distinctively English quality which other peoples should emulate were connected with notions of English moral worth. Analysing the social contexts of sport can tell us much about the social role of institutions such as the churches, pubs, the workplace and schools. Study of government involvement with sport helps delineate the nature and extent of government activity. The expression of gender, class and regional identities through sport adds a further dimension to what can be learned about social conflict and cohesion from politics, industrial relations, responses to the emancipation of women and religious animosities. The breadth of interest in sport and the ideological baggage associated with it mean that it should be in the mainstream, and not at the margins, of social history.

This book takes the view that how people choose to spend leisure provides vital insights into their cultural values and into socially acceptable behaviour. The historical significance of sport lies in its cultural production and reproduction. So this book sets out to make a substantive contribution to our understanding of leisure in inter-war England. We recognise the difficulties of defining leisure. We accept that in many respects any distinction between work and leisure is a false dichotomy, and especially so for many women. Income from work often determined what activities could be pursued outside working hours. Leisure could be seen as part of the labour process because it provided time to recuperate from the demands of work and so enabled work to be resumed with revitalised minds and bodies. Skills developed in sport, such as physical co-ordination and working in groups, could be applied in the workplace. The pursuit of sporting success, so often dependent on speed and using time more efficiently, may have encouraged acceptance of the time and motion techniques of modern industrial production. An increasing number of firms provided sport facilities for their employees between the wars, perhaps in the hope that this would promote co-operation between management and labour. Some leisure interests, such as talking about sport, could be pursued while working and may have combated workplace boredom. Much betting on sport took place in factories. Between the wars work and leisure were often intermingled in sport. Spectators at Football League matches, county cricket, horseracing and rugby league, for instance, were paying to use their 'free' time watching paid sports players, while press attention concentrated on the latter. Even sports which resisted professionalism among players usually had some paid administrators and stadiums required groundsmen, trainers, painters and joiners. Sport provided a livelihood for journalists, and for those involved in the manufacture and selling of sports equipment and clothing. Meeting the needs of sports players and spectators made up part of the business of many building, transport and drink concerns.

This book is not an economic and social study. Its emphasis is on the meanings associated with sport and the narratives through which these were articulated. To a degree this follows the agenda for sport historians articulated by Jeffrey Hill in his *Sport, Leisure and Culture in Twentieth-Century Britain* (2002). Hill argues that sports should be examined as

cultural agencies with a power to work on their participants and consumers ideologically. In other words, they are processes from which we
derive *meanings*. In their manifold activities are inscribed and structured
habits of thought and behaviour which contribute to our ways of seeing
ourselves and others, to a making sense of our social relationships, and to
the piecing together of some notion of what we call 'society'.

(Hill 2002: 2)

The book also reflects the contention of Clifford Geertz that social groups
imagine who they are through the stories they tell about themselves (1973).
Sport was a narrative, or rather a series of narratives, through which those living in England shaped their senses of self, of how they differed from others and
of what was important to them. The narratives surrounding sport in England in
the 1920s and 1930s, of course, were sometimes inconsistent. Different meanings were associated with different sports and not all social groups derived
identical messages from the same sports. With its emphasis on narrative, this
book can be regarded as part of the 'linguistic turn' in historical study. It accepts
that languages can be encoded in many forms. Not all sport narratives were
verbal. In some circumstances it is likely that a narrative delivered through
visual images was more powerful than one expressed through words. Habitual
forms of behaviour connected with sport, sporting rituals, notions of sporting
decorum and sporting costume can all be viewed as sport narratives. While this
book is related to the 'linguistic turn', it is not an example of what has been
called linguistic determinism or the belief that all culture and social relationships are shaped by language. We recognise that economics did much to shape
the playing and watching of sport in the 1920s and 1930s.

Much of how sport was regarded arose from the experience of playing and
watching sport but the values that were associated with sport, and also its excitements and pleasures, often stemmed from how it was represented. Historians of
sport have been reluctant to evaluate these representations, which is surprising
when one considers that newspapers are probably the primary source used most
often. More attention still needs to be paid to how language was used in writings
about sport and to its visual narratives. Media representations of sport provoke
the further questions of how far they presented sport in the same fashion, how far
their consumers accepted the messages connected with sport and whether, or to
what extent, the attitudes of the consumers of the mass media influenced sporting representations. It is almost impossible to discuss narrative and representations
of sport without considering reception theory and Barthes' (1977) contention
that meaning is imparted to a text by readers rather than authors, which implies
that there can be as many interpretations of a text as there are readers and that all
are equally valid. We acknowledge that different, and often contradictory, meanings can be attributed to a text or narrative, that a narrative can have different
layers of meaning and that even the same reader can attribute different readings
to a text in different social situations. But while audiences had to engage with

texts whose meanings were potentially fluid, slippery and contestable, we suspect that that there was often fairly widespread shared agreement about the associations and meaning of most sports texts between the wars.

This book is also a result of the growing interest in the inter-war period among historians of sport, although attempts at overviews have been limited. Sir Derek Birley's *Playing the Game* (1995), is a narrative history of sport in inter-war Britain which traces the major developments in most sports and discusses how these were related to broader cultural and social changes. Birley's approach of breaking the inter-war period into two decades, with each decade exploring topics which consider different sports in turn, means that his book has little more than incidental comment on the nature of sportsmanship, the representations of sport or the varieties of sporting celebrity. Stephen Jones, *Workers at Play: A Social and Economic History of Leisure 1918–1939* (1986), incorporated much sport into a wider study of working-class life. Ross McKibbin, in *Classes and Cultures: England 1918–1951* (1998) included an appraisal of England's sporting life, and Peter Beck (2003) has recently contributed a short but perceptive analysis.

Nicholas Fishwick's *English Football and Society, 1910–1950* (1989), was one of the first academic monographs devoted to a single sport in the inter-war period. Peter Beck's *Scoring for Britain: International Football and International Politics, 1900–1939* (1999) examined the Football Association's relations with soccer overseas and uncovered how far governments between the wars tried to use soccer as an adjunct to diplomacy. In the same year Jack Williams' *Cricket and England: A Cultural and Social History of the Inter-war Years* (revised edition, 2003) discussed how cricket had become a symbol of Englishness and investigated what could be deduced from cricket about gender and class relations, the social role of the churches and attitudes to commercialism in England. Mike Huggins' *Horseracing and the British 1919–39* (2003) explored the culture of horse-racing, the structure of the sport, the conflicts surrounding it and its connections with gambling. No similar volumes have yet been published on sports with a large following in the inter-war period such as golf, tennis, athletics, boxing, either rugby code or the new sports of greyhound racing and speedway but some valuable articles have appeared. Although knowledge of the social and economic determinants of sport in inter-war England is still not exhaustive, enough is now known for us to provide tentative answers to questions about the cultural significance of sport in general at this time.

One stress of the book is on sport as a source of pleasure. Historians of sport have often stressed that pleasure was a reason for playing or watching sport but few have analysed the range of pleasures associated with sport and how far these varied between social groups. Very little has been written about the pleasures of the sociability of team sports and of watching sports or about success in sport as consolation for failure in other areas of life. While evidence about sexual behaviour is notoriously unreliable, the prudishness of the inter-war period and the censorship of sexual material raise the unanswerable question of whether the energies devoted to sport may have stemmed from sexual frustration. Watching the opposite sex playing sports may have been a form of voyeurism, although sexual attraction was rarely mentioned as a cause of sporting stardom. Psychoanalytical musings about the connections between blood and sexuality prompt questions about the pleasures associated with hunting and shooting. Barthes's (1977) notion of *jouissance*, often translated in English as bliss or ecstasy that goes beyond pleasure, which argues for the variety of pleasures, is clearly relevant to discussion of a hierarchy of pleasures surrounding sport and whether these had a sexual component. As Bakhtin (1984) argued, in the past festivals had traditionally been accompanied by the temporary reversal of social roles and utopian indulgence in forms of behaviour not usually permitted in the everyday round. Such festivity, including a release from the daily round of work, was an important part of the pleasures of inter-war sport.

Hopefully this book will go some way to answering those questions that perplex students of English social history for whom sport is not a major interest. Political historians have long examined nationalism, especially because of its links with fascism and with decolonisation movements, but until recently little attention has focused on non-political expressions of nationalism and on Englishness in particular. The collection of essays by Colls and Dodd (1987) stressed how in the late nineteenth and early twentieth centuries artistic expressions of England and Englishness often stressed the rural and castigated the town as the site of social dislocation, disease and unEnglish money-grubbing. Georgina Boyes (1993) also showed how at that time the pastoral was taken by those from the political left as well as the right to represent the essence of England and that this was expressed in the revival of traditional folk song and dance, the move to suburbia and architectural styles that drew on what was imagined to be an indigenous English rustic building tradition. Such approaches to Englishness have tended to concentrate on artistic expression and more needs to be learned of what the English imagined distinguished them from other nations between 1918 and 1939. Examining the discourses of moral worth surrounding sport and responses to international sporting contests can add interesting perspectives to how Englishness was imagined. Support for amateurism in sport and the attempts to restrict players' earnings in sports where payment was permitted are clearly relevant to the debate initiated by Martin Wiener (1981) and Corelli Barnett (1986) about how far English culture, and particularly that of the public schools, with its disdain for aggressive commercialism and manufacturing, had led to Britain's relative decline as an international economic power in the twentieth century.

Compared with the Edwardian period and the years since the 1960s, the 1920s to the 1950s appear to be a time when demands for female liberation were relatively muted. The extension of women's rights was rarely seen as a political priority between the wars. Women were granted electoral equality with men in 1928 and more women, though few in number, took up higher education and entered the professions. In the 1920s and 1930s the emphasis in what has been called the 'new feminism' was not so much on women gaining access to spheres traditionally dominated by men but on more recognition being granted to areas of feminine expertise such as mothering, nursing and other forms of caring. In her *Sporting Females: Critical Issues in the History and Sociology of Women's Sports* (1994), Jennifer Hargreaves showed how the growth of sports playing by women between the wars was related to the widening of women's social horizons during the First World War but by establishing their own sports organisations rather than demanding a larger role in those controlled by men, women sport players were acting very much in keeping with the spirit of the new feminism. The relationship of sport with women's other leisure interests, and its age-specific nature, given that most women perceived that 'leisure' stopped with marriage, are explored in Claire Langhamer's *Women's Leisure in England 1920–60* (2000). Richard Holt (1996b), in one of the few explorations into sport and the construction of masculinity in England between the wars, has claimed that men learned what it was to be a man through the examples of sporting heroes. It is hoped that this book, through its discussion of how levels and forms of involvement with sport differed between men and women, female sporting heroes and the gendered identities associated with sport, will deepen understanding of why a less confrontational form of feminism was so dominant in England at that time.

Examining the nature of class relations in sport will further extend the historiography of English social class. There seems little doubt that in the first half of the twentieth century, most people in England recognised that they lived in a highly stratified society, where wealth was distributed unequally, and were aware of their place and that of others in the social hierarchy (see Cannadine 1998; McKibbin 1998). The term 'class' was used frequently to categorise social status. Most people knew to which class they belonged. But this awareness of class does not seem to have been accompanied by a very strong sense of class antagonism. The Labour Party, largely financed by trade unions, won a decisive majority at only one general election in the first half of the twentieth century. The strength of identities based on gender, ethnicity, religion and location undermined class solidarity. One can argue that the high level of national unity shown at the start of the two world wars would not have occurred had the classes been fiercely suspicious of each other. Involvement with sport was often a means of expressing social distinction and class affiliation, but the following for sport often crossed class boundaries. Sport can help to explain why social and economic inequalities in England were not accompanied by a stronger sense of class antagonism.

The study of class and sport in inter-war England has so far been approached largely from the perspective of the working class. There is no equivalent to John Lowerson's *Sport and the English Middle Classes, 1878–1914* (1993). To date no monograph has discussed the role of the landed aristocracy across sport although there are studies of their involvement with individual sports such as Mike Huggins' discussion of their support for horseracing. Class and participation in sport after the Second World War have been explored by Martin Polley (1998) and by Holt and Mason (2000). *Sport, Politics and the Working Class* (1988) by Stephen Jones is the only monograph concerned specifically with sport, and class between the wars and provides much detail about working-class involvement with sport, the extent of popular support for commercialised sport and sport organisations set up by trade unions, the Labour Party and other socialist groups. Jones says little, however, about how far bourgeois attitudes to sport influenced working-class association with sport. John Hargreaves' *Sport, Power and Culture: A Social and Historical Analysis of Popular Sport in England* (1986) discusses the role of sport in bolstering bourgeois cultural hegemony from the 1880s to the 1980s but says very little about the inter-war years. Because it considers the involvement of all classes with sport, this book examines class distinctions in sport and how far different classes ascribed the same values to sport. By looking across the classes, this book is the first to assess the nature of class relationships in sport between the wars and what these reveal about class co-operation and conflict in society at large.

The place of sport in national life

In inter-war England there was a shared love of and pride in sport. Few leisure interests received so much respectful approval and so little criticism. In 1933 Sir John Foster Fraser, the journalist, travel writer and political commentator, wrote that 'Most of us would prefer having inscribed on our tombstones "He was a good sportsman" to anything else. A lad going up to the university would rather have the prospect of a Blue than becoming a Cabinet Minister.'[1] Sports were thought to demonstrate English superiority over other nations and to validate its imperial mission. Sport promoted physical well-being and had moral and social benefits. Yet at the same time, much of the discourse surrounding sport stressed that for the English, games were only games. A visiting American student of sport at British universities and public schools found in 1924 that 'The English insist on playing at their games' (Savage 1926: 27). The moral benefits of sport, it was often imagined, derived from sports being a form of fun. Many maintained that taking sports too seriously undermined their value.

The esteem of sport

Approbation of sport approached veneration, and stressed its tradition. Racing was 'the sport of kings'. Golf was a 'good and venerable' sport.[2] Cricket was 'an institution'(Cardus 1930: 7). When novel commercialised forms of greyhound racing, speedway and ice hockey were introduced, their promoters made clear their sporting nature, so as to restrict opposition to them. An apologist for ice hockey described it as an 'exciting, clean, healthy sport' and emphasised player sportsmanship.[3] In 1936 the *Speedway News* worried that having a parade of elephants at a speedway meeting would raise questions over whether speedway was sport 'of a serious sort', as such 'variety turns' could damage its prestige by causing it to be regarded as a 'circus'.[4] In 1927 a *Times* editorial argued that it was essential for 'the fair fame of English sport' for greyhound racing to establish a governing body without financial interests in the sport.[5] Ruling bodies were largely amateur and high status.

Royal involvement underlined sport's importance in England's national life. The monarchy had long been associated with field sports and horseracing but after 1918 attending sport events became an increasingly important royal function. In June and July 1930, for instance, George V and Queen Mary went to Epsom on Derby Day, spent four days with other members of the royal family at Royal Ascot and attended one day of the Wimbledon tennis championship. On Saturday 28 June the King went to the Lord's test match against Australia while the Queen visited Wimbledon again. At the end of July both were at Cowes for the regatta. The King also received the Australian test cricketers, the steward of Ascot and the Maharaja Jam Sahib of Nawanagar, formerly Prince Ranjitsinhji, one of the leading batsmen for England at the turn of the century. The Prince of Wales was represented at the funeral of Sir Henry Segrave, the world land speed record holder, received members of the British Arctic Air-Route Expedition and attended the Police Athletic Association annual championship. The Duke of York visited the Richmond Royal Horse Show. George V, Edward VIII and George VI were all Patrons of the Rugby Union. King George V attended the FA Cup Final for the first time in 1914, and was present in the recently constructed 'Royal Box' at the first Wembley final in 1923, with its potentially disastrous crowd incursions. When he arrived the good-humoured crowd sang the National Anthem while the police and staff were still trying to clear the huge crowds forced onto the pitch. Thereafter the King regularly attended the cup finals and England v. Scotland matches at Wembley except for illness in 1929 and on two wet afternoons. The teams were ceremonially presented to him before the start. One member of the FA Council later boasted that 'once we had the King, Queen, Princess Royal and Duke and Duchess of York all together. The Prince of Wales (later Duke of Windsor) came twice. In 1937, shortly after his succession to the throne, King George VI came, and Queen Elizabeth presented the Cup to Sunderland' (Pickford n. d: 240).

The Duke of York, the future George VI, was president of the National Playing Fields Association, to which George V donated two paddocks at Hampton Court.[6] The King George V Jubilee Fund and the King George V Memorial Funds made grants for local authority acquisition of playing fields. Although English political support for republicanism was negligible, association with sport probably helped to sustain English acceptance of monarchy while emphasising sport's social respectability. By contrast no senior member of the royal family attended speedway or greyhound racing.

Regard for sport was often entwined with assumptions about sportsmanship's moral qualities, issues dealt with in more detail in Chapter 6. The acquisition of such values was often put forward as the key justification for playing. In 1929, for instance, the headmaster of Harrow accepted that by playing 'games as they ought to be played it is exceedingly possible that we shall lose most of the championships all the time' but added that 'it would be a pity for the sake of a game to lose all the true reasons for playing games'.[7] Much of the approval for sport assumed that sport in England was permeated with sportsmanship. Even though instances of cheating existed, these did not weaken the belief that sportsmanship was a distinctive feature of English sport. Bishop Welldon, who had been head-master of Harrow, wrote in 1923 that

> no game can be played unless the players play it in a right spirit. Sport is, or was, a synonym for honour. A sportsman was a man who would not, and could not, do a shabby act. The sporting spirit was the spirit of sensitive honour. To 'play the game' was to do, and to do only, the upright thing.[8]

Press coverage of sport also suggested that sport was held in high esteem. National and local press coverage increased, though largely in terms of results, an easy way of filling space. Yet while one can never be sure how far newspapers reflected readers' attitudes, the extent of sports coverage suggests that it was thought to boost circulation. Newspapers were sometimes critical of aspects they disliked but hardly ever condemned sport in general, and usually took the line that extending the playing of sport was in the national interest. Given the emphasis of the BBC on broadcasting as a form of mental and moral cultivation, the expansion of radio coverage also shows the general approbation of sport in England.

Reasons for the approbation of sport

J.A. Mangan (2001) has shown the centrality of sports to public-school educa-tion in late Victorian and Edwardian England. Support for sport among the political and social élite, many of whom had been educated at public schools, helped explain the status of English sport, especially cricket, rugby and field sports. Criticising sport was tantamount to criticising public schools, since their apologists often assumed that the moral qualities and character development supposedly encouraged by playing sport were as important as, and often more important than, academic attainment. Even some younger English writers, such as Robert Graves or Edmund Blunden, were keen to play or watch, and both were captains of their local village football teams in 1922 (O'Prey 1982: 144). Only a minority of public schoolmasters recognised that the emphasis on sport had become excessive and called for more stress on intellectual training. At Haileybury's speech day in 1938, Canon E. F. Bonhote argued that 'discipline, pluck, endurance and playing the game' had 'certainly won the War' but that the problems of the modern world called for 'clearness of mind to see what ought to be done for the future'. The 'coming generation needed to be a bet-ter one intellectually'.[9] In 1938, W.H. Davies, the retiring chairman of the Assistant Masters' Association, warned of undervaluing the intellect while 'belauding athleticism and physical prowess'.[10]

Sport was an important source of prestige at Oxbridge while the 'new' uni-versities increased their provision for sport, partly through pressure from the National Union of Students. It was increasingly taken for granted that grammar schools needed playing fields. Many even felt that the benefits of playing sports should be spread more widely still. The BMA stressed the health-giving benefits of sport, and Sir George Newman, the first Board of Education Chief Medical Officer, encouraged the introduction of games in schools. Much favourable publicity was given to an Oxford scheme where the university colleges allowed local elementary schoolboys to play cricket on their grounds.[11] Clifton, Cheltenham, Fettes, Mill Hill, Taunton, Weymouth, Reading and Downside schools operated similar schemes as early as 1926. In 1935 the Associated Schools Games Club was set up to allow elementary schoolchildren to use public school playing fields during school holidays.[12]

Sport's reputation had been boosted by the First World War, when almost all sports organisations supported the war effort. Many professional sportsmen enlisted. No prominent sports player became a conscientious objector. Initially, the playing or watching of sport by civilians was condemned as unseemly and a discouragement to recruitment. Yet by 1917 sporting spectacles and playing sport were portrayed as vital for keeping up civilian morale. Sport kept soldiers fit and instilled regimental loyalties. Apologists for sport argued that sportsmen made better soldiers. In 1920 the editor of the *Field* claimed that 'it was admitted on all sides, by friends and foes alike, that the men who had been players of team games made much better soldiers and officers'. Sir Eric Geddes, a postwar Minister of Transport, believed that the war would have ended much sooner had more drafts been games players. In March 1918, Lord Hawke, a former Yorkshire and England cricket captain, claimed that sportsmen had 'done their duty in the war'. If more had played sport, 'there would not have been so many men lagging behind, and perhaps no conscientious objectors'.[13]

Approbation for sport, and particularly team ball games, also owed much to the association of sport with the churches, where 'sportsmanship' and 'team spirit' were presented as analogous to Christian ethics and social teaching. Church teams and church-based leagues dominated the lowest levels of recreational soccer and cricket in much of the industrial North, where numbers of urban church-affiliated sport teams often peaked in the 1920s. Church teams were less common in southern England but clerics were often presidents of village sports clubs. In most towns the YMCA ran sports teams, though few churches had rugby union or rugby league teams. Church involvement helped create a respectable image for sport, and explains why relatively few clubs playing recreational soccer and cricket had formal links with pubs. The strength of sport at the public schools, which were virtually all regarded as Christian institutions producing Christian gentlemen, reinforced assumptions about the concordance of sport and Christian morality. Home Office files suggest that strong lobbying from the Nonconformist sects against sports with betting associations was a major reason why neither the 1923 Select Committee nor the 1932 Royal Commission recommended the legalisation of prepaid off-course betting.

An imperial dimension added to the general approval of sport. Sports such as cricket and rugby union, with their amateur, public-school influences, supposedly strengthened the ties of Empire. English international matches were played only against teams from the dominions or colonies. Rugby union matches against France ceased in 1931. Horseracing abroad was often modelled on British racing. By contrast, soccer, the team sport with most players and spectators in England between the wars, had a far weaker imperial presence. While a powerful case can be made for seeing economic considerations as the driving force of imperial expansion, imperial discourses stressed the morality of Empire. The British, and in such contexts the terms 'British' and 'English' were used interchangeably, were regarded as having a duty to take the benefits of British civilisation to less fortunate parts of the globe. The ideologies of sport and Empire were mutually supporting and reinforced notions of the other's moral worth. As challenges to imperialism, such as the creation of the Irish Free State and growing support for independence in India, became stronger, it seems plausible that imperialism's supposed morality was emphasised to justify its continuation. The selflessness of English sport was regarded as proof of Britain's right to exercise imperial power.

There was also an English belief that playing team sports reflected and helped to consolidate an idealised form of social relations. Enthusiasm for sport crossed class boundaries. The rise of the Labour party, more militant trade unionism in the early 1920s, the support for communism and fascism in Europe, the difficulties Britain's older industries experienced in harsher world trading conditions and the growing American influence on much popular culture were seen by many as socially disruptive. Social relations in sport, on the other hand, were believed to be characterised by harmony and cohesion even if many sports were riddled with social exclusion and snobbery. In many sports the cult of amateurism helped to retain an upper- and middle-class presence. In cricket, it was accepted that amateurs should captain county and England teams. Association football, where virtually all performers at the highest level were professional, was regarded more disdainfully by the social and political élite. In the 1920s many grammar schools started to play rugby union instead of soccer, often claiming that professionalism had driven sportsmanship out of soccer. Nearly all sports, including those with high numbers of professional players, were controlled and administered by those from the middle and upper classes.

Apologists from the wealthier classes imagined that the social relations of sport could resist cultural and political change. Certainly there was little criticism of traditional power relationships. Trade unionism made little headway among professional sports players. Horseracing was praised for uniting monarchy, aristocracy and populace. Sport stimulated national, regional and town loyalties which often transcended class and economic divisions. Although the numbers of women participating in sport increased between the wars, sport was very much a male social sphere. But male involvement was very much dependent on the support, or exploitation, of women. Yet between the wars, feminists rarely complained about male privilege in sport, perhaps because they saw the promotion of women in other areas as more important. Where women did take up sport, they usually accepted the male values ascribed to it. Sport was a cultural space where male social power was rarely challenged.

The economically privileged saw themselves as the guardians of sportsmanship but imagined that its values could be, and often were, more widely accepted. Sportsmanship was considered to encourage acceptance of the social order through its expectations of agreement with the decisions of umpires and referees. They could be seen as representatives of established authority. R.L. Hodgson, an Anglican cleric who had a regular column in the *Cricketer*, wrote in 1932 that 'The umpire gives you out: out you must go. The man in the white coat is a symbol of constitutional government.'[14] The promotion of friendliness and understanding between classes was seen as an essential dimension to sport. Much of the exaltation of village cricket rested on beliefs that it brought together the local community. In 1922 Pelham Warner, a former amateur captain of England and Middlesex, wrote that village cricket represented 'the essence of the game; for a village match is the truest democracy' which encouraged 'feelings of freemasonry, camaraderie, and *esprit de corps*. I cannot imagine a man who has been bowled out by the village blacksmith not having a fellow feeling towards him afterwards. Can you imagine a cricketer becoming a Lenin?'[15] Apologists for company provision of sports facilities often stressed that this promoted social harmony between management and workers.

It was also widely assumed that playing sport provided an antidote to antisocial behaviour. Basil Holmes, secretary of the Metropolitan Public Gardens Association, claimed in 1924 that sports were important for 'health ... good manners' and 'alertness in business'. He thought that for London youth the way out of 'acquiescence in a perpetual imprisonment in bricks and mortar' would be through physical exercise and that their 'sanity and their self-respect demand it'.[16] In 1928 a speaker at the annual conference of the National Association of Head Teachers declared that youth was 'like cordite – quite innocuous in free air but highly explosive in confinement. Sport is a preventive of hooliganism'.[17] For the sons of the wealthier, according to Howard Marshall (quoted in Matthews and Harrison 2004: 36, 848)), the sports writer, in 1927, rugby bred 'hardiness, which in these days of cocktails and lounge-lizards, is a quality to be encouraged'.

The economy and sport

Sport between the wars provided employment and opportunities for investment and profit between the wars but even crude estimates of the scale of its contribution to the economy are not possible. Part of the activity of a very large number of firms in the drink, catering, printing, publishing, building, clothing trades and transport was related to sport but the proportion of this cannot be disaggregated from the rest of their business. Much betting on sport was illegal. Few attempts were made between the wars to analyse the economic structures of different sports or to examine how sports could promote economic expansion in other sectors of the economy though company sports provision was advocated as means of achieving labour co-operation with management. The economic dimension of sport was hardly ever celebrated but the cult of amateurism and resistance to commercialisation in many sports were a source of pride. Chapter 4 discusses what sport reveals about English cultural assumptions surrounding commercialisation and profit maximisation.

Economic fluctuations influenced involvement with sport. After peace in 1918 England entered a short-lived economic boom and crowds returned to spectator sports. Racing attendances peaked in 1919 and 1920 before dropping, but remained well above pre-1914 levels. Despite the beginnings of slump in 1920, cricket attendances reached their inter-war peak in 1921. Gate receipts at Lancashire Cricket Club, for example, reached twice their inter-war average that year. The gross receipts for the All-England Lawn Tennis Club in June 1919 were almost double those of 1914, even though the finals were domi- nated by foreigners. There was so much demand for tickets that for the first time the All-England Lawn Tennis Club had to hold a ballot.

Initial economic confidence and optimism were short-lived. Many traditional industries such as coal and cotton were losing market share, and they faced new trading patterns and increased competition from overseas. Much of the industrial North experienced periods of heavy unemployment in 1926 and first half of the 1930s. Horseracing's attendances fell steeply in the mid-1920s, with particularly poor attendances in 1926, the year of the General Strike. Strikes in the transport industry hit some sport hard and caused the abandonment of race meetings. Sport's increased impact on absenteeism and production schedules led one con- tributor to *Textile Weekly* to complain in 1928 that 'I sometimes wonder if we haven't all got pleasure on the brain, from bosses of mills and works down to the lads straight from school. Pleasure never built a business up, but it can easily knock one down' (quoted in Jones 1988: 59). For those in work, however, real wages grew over the period, allowing a rise in disposable income. This created a wider spread of involvement in sport, but in a context of widening choices such as more spacious houses, home improvements, electrical goods, cinemas and dance halls, or even the motor cycle and car (McKibbin 1990: Ch. 5; Walton 2000: 725–44). Many new forms of manufacturing, such as the motor industry, were situated in the Midlands and South-east, and sports in these areas attracted generally bigger crowds. Lord's had more spectators in 1926, the year of the General Strike, than in any year between 1922 and 1939, and for several sports the period was one of growth in attendances, though with much short-term fluctuation. Average attendance at first division Football League matches increased from 23,115 in 1913–14 to 30,659 in 1938–9.

At the height of the depression, in the early 1930s, many sports experienced loss of revenue. In horseracing, average prices paid for yearlings were poor from 1930, reflecting economic retrenchment by wealthy owners, with 1931 a par- ticularly bad year. It was also a year of particularly poor gate receipts for county cricket, while soccer clubs in towns heavily reliant on a single industry, such as Middlesbrough or Blackburn, similarly found themselves at risk. The Annual Report of the Amateur Rowing Association for 1931 stated that 'the unem- ployment rife throughout the country, the heavier taxation, the salary and wage cuts, the economy that has been made necessary by these and other causes – all have contributed to make the past year one of great anxiety' (Halladay 1990).

The unemployed found watching sport difficult, though the Pilgrim Trust noted how the unemployed lined the streets of Liverpool on match days just to watch spectators going to Goodison Park or Anfield. Even so, some clubs were able to sustain support. Sunderland, despite a very high unemployment rate, managed average gates of 23,000 in 1931–2. Crowds and income could also vary with the weather and club success. After 1931 Somerset Cricket Club had its next lowest gate receipts in 1933, Derbyshire in 1935, Surrey, Northampton and Lancashire in 1936, and Kent in 1937. Unemployment may have deterred some from playing, but in the Bolton area the numbers of cricket teams were greatest in the first half of the 1930s when unemployment was highest. Oral evidence does not record that players stopped playing if they became unemployed. Some unemployed players have been remembered as passing time in summer working on the pitches of their clubs. But sporting hobbies could be hit hard. In Bolton, the responses men gave to Mass-Observation as to why pigeon racing was on the decline included 'bad trade and depression', 't'pits not doin' so well, thee geet short o' money', 'the buggers were aw skint wi' being' out o' work' (Mass-Observation 1987: 290).

Sports professionals

It is impossible to establish how many earned a living from sport but only a relatively small number were paid to play or were employed by clubs or sports organisations. Census returns from 1921 and 1931 are certainly underestimates. Many played part-time, semi-professionally, and we lack 1941 census figures. The 1921 and 1931 published census tables aggregate England and Wales. In 1921, 9,367 gamekeepers were employed, indicating the continued importance of field sports to the wealthy. Golf and racing, catering for the middle and upper classes, were the next highest employers of labour. Of the three only golf showed significant growth by 1931. In 1921 there were 8,116 involved full-time with golf, of whom 4,226 were professionals, green-keepers, caddies, etc. By 1931 there were 13,007 full-timers. In 1921 racing employed 4,485 full-time, of whom 3,424 were trainers, jockeys, stable attendants, grooms, and labourers. Racing employed 5,429 in 1931.

Football and cricket employed far fewer. In 1921 there were 2,041 working in football, of whom 1,577 were footballers, trainers and groundsmen. There were 1,492 recorded working in cricket, of whom 1,046 were professionals or groundsmen. Neither sport had experienced much change by 1931, and both were overtaken by dog racing, which employed 2,369. It was the betting industry which increased most. Even though the census figures omit many illegal cash bookmakers and part-time 'runners', lookouts, etc., the figures rose from 2,824 male bookmakers and 73 females in 1921 to 9,330 male and 425 female bookmakers in 1931.

The playing of sport

Participatory sport was an important leisure activity in inter-war England, but we have a sketchy knowledge of how many played regularly. Club membership lists are of limited help. Sports such as bowls, tennis and golf could be played outside club auspices. In 1921 for example, in Tyne and Wear over 2,600 were members of affiliated tennis clubs, but some members no longer played, some clubs, such as Ashbrooke, had 'far too many … for its number of courts', while others, such as Gateshead Fell, had a 'huge waiting list' (Patterson 1921).

The statistics kept by some towns of the numbers using municipal facilities usually only record the total numbers using them each month or year. Whilst these reveal fluctuations in the numbers using such facilities, they do not establish, for instance, whether higher use of sport facilities was due to larger numbers playing or a smaller number playing more often. Little is known about the numbers who played indoor sports such as darts, billiards and snooker. Only guesses can be made about the extent of sea bathing, swimming in rivers and canals, or knockabout games of football and cricket. Records kept by governing bodies about the numbers playing sports are patchy. The Marylebone Cricket Club (MCC) universally accepted as cricket's supreme authority, had no formalised powers over the sport and made no attempt to calculate how many played cricket each week.

Far more men than women played sport regularly. Age, of course, limited the extent to which some sports were played. All social classes played sport although some sports were more socially exclusive than others. Sport was differentiated on class lines. The majority of those who played association football, the team ball game with most players, were working-class, but the wealthier classes also played it. Public and grammar schools which played soccer usually had old boys teams. All classes played cricket, the team ball sport with the second highest number of players. Almost all areas would have at least one cricket club whose members belonged predominantly to the local economic and social élite. In most sports, socially exclusive clubs tended to play against teams with similar backgrounds. Village cricket teams were often praised for including members from the full range of local society though fragmentary evidence from Sussex, Kent and Surrey suggests that most players were working-class. In Bolton, and presumably in most other industrial districts, the great majority who played belonged to the lower middle and working classes. The working-class presence tended to be strongest at the lowest level of recreational cricket. Some sports, such as polo, fox hunting or yachting tended to be played only by the wealthy. Only the very rich could race motorcars or aeroplanes. In most of England rugby union and golf seem to have been played mainly by the middle classes. Mass-Observation found that in Bolton in 1938 tennis clubs had a more middle-class ambience than cricket clubs. Costs meant that fishing in some rivers was restricted to the very wealthy but angling was also a pastime of many working men.

Evidence about the social class of women sport players is patchy. Many tennis clubs and golf clubs with women members were predominantly middle-class. Those playing cricket under the auspices of the Women's Cricket Association tended to be from the upper or middle classes whereas in the 1930s, the Women's Cricket Federation, confined to Lancashire and Yorkshire, had many working-class players. In Bolton the number of mill teams suggests that rounders had a higher proportion of working-class players than hockey.

There are some figures for participation. In 1937, 35,000 clubs were affiliated to the Football Association. If each of these fielded one team, 385,000 would have played soccer each week. If half of them had two teams, 580,000 would have played each week. How many clubs played regularly without being affiliated is unknown (Fishwick 1989: 1). The numbers playing cricket are hard to calculate even to the nearest 100,000. Using local data as proxies for the national picture suggests that in 1931 the numbers playing cricket each week would have been somewhere between 100,000 and 400,000 (Williams 2003: 45–48). There were 2,874 tennis clubs with over 75,000 members by the mid 1930s, and there were over 1,200 golf clubs by the late 1930s. The numbers playing sports varied between regions and also within regions. In 1939 some boroughs and urban districts had one football pitch for every 900 inhabitants. Others had one for every 4,800 inhabitants. The number of cricket pitches varied from one for every 5,000 inhabitants to one for every 14,000. Eight Northern industrial towns – five in Lancashire, two in the West Riding and one in County Durham – had in total 1,213 teams playing football each week in 1922, 840 in 1930 and 612 in 1939. In 1922 they had 732 cricket teams, 914 in 1930 and 727 in 1939. For all three sample years Sunderland and its surroundings always had more football than cricket teams whereas Halifax always had more cricket than football teams (Williams 1996: 115). Between 1933 and 1939 the number of Surrey cricket clubs affiliated to the Club Cricket Conference rose from 208 to 344 and Essex clubs from 112 to 159.[18] Coverage of cricket in the *Sussex Express* shows that the number of teams playing in Sussex rose from 83 in 1930 to more than 170 in 1939. In Birmingham, the number of cricket teams playing regularly, excluding those taking part in the inter-departmental competitions of firms, was 200 in 1922, 300 in 1930 and 320 in 1939 (Williams 2003: 45–49). By 1939 swimming clubs had over one million active members but 50 towns with a combined population of over two millions had no swimming baths.[19]

The playing of sport by women increased between the wars, although in the early 1920s the playing of sport by women was hit by the reversal of the social and economic gains that women had made during the war. By 1938 there were over a thousand women's hockey clubs, twice the number of those for men, and 160,000 women played netball for clubs affiliated to the All-England Women's Association for Netball. The number of women playing cricket rose after the formation of Women's Cricket Association in 1926. In 1927 only ten clubs affiliated, but by 1938 women's cricket clubs were thought to have over 6,000 members. Sixty thousand belonged to the Women's League of Health and Beauty.[20] The following for sports varied significantly at local levels. In Bolton and its surroundings, for instance, the number of women's rounders teams rose from 20 in 1920 to 59 in 1939 while the number of women's hockey teams fell from 38 to 18. Although Bolton was a stronghold for the playing of men's cricket it only had one women's cricket club (Williams 2003: Ch. 5).

Sports ground availability influenced local patterns of play. By 1939 over £6,000,000 had been spent on providing playing fields but the National Fitness Council feared with 'good reason' that

> the spread of housing and of industry has involved more than a corresponding loss of facilities. Reports which we have received from all parts of the country indicate that hundreds of small football and cricket clubs have disappeared, through the loss of their grounds and their inability to find other grounds'.[21]

In 1933 the National Playing Fields Association claimed that each year 1,700 acres of the 13,000 acres of land available for sport within ten miles of Bermondsey were being lost.[22] In the late 1930s house building around six towns in the West Riding took ground which had accommodated 130 football pitches.[23]

To an extent losses were made good. The National Fitness Council provided grants between 1937 and 1939 for 283 football pitches, 197 cricket pitches, 73 hockey pitches, 96 netball courts, 152 pavilions and 37 athletic tracks, but probably no more than 20,000 could have used these facilities at any one time.[24] Some local authority-owned estates obtained better facilities. Wimbledon's corporation-owned Park Estate had twenty tennis courts, bowling greens, putting greens and playing fields by the early 1930s. More firms introduced welfare schemes which included sport facilities for their employees. Usually they bought and equipped a sports ground, maintaining it by deductions of a few pence from weekly wages. By the late 1930s Rowntrees in York had more than fourteen acres with three soccer pitches, three hockey pitches, three cricket squares, a baseball pitch and seven tennis courts.[25] In the midlands a golf course was provided by GEC, and a first-class cricket ground by Courtauld. In the eight industrial towns and their surroundings already mentioned, the number of works-based teams playing cricket rose from 45 in 1922 to 135 in 1939 and those for football from 78 to 167. By January 1938, 102 firms were members of the Sheffield and District Works Sports Association. Railways were also in the vanguard of provision. The GER provided seven football pitches and a running track near their Stratford works in 1920. For the wealthier, private estates also increasingly provided more exclusive facilities. Wentworth Country Club estate, for example, had three full-size golf courses, 26 tennis courts, swimming baths, and putting courses.[26]

Sabbatarianism restricted the playing of sport. Games could be played on privately owned sports grounds on Sundays, but until the Second World War,

week to every house in York, and there is nothing to suggest that this was untypical of other towns. Most who bet regularly, and particularly those who made prepaid off-course bets, were working-class but gambling on sport was also common among some sections of the middle and upper classes. The social acceptability of betting by working-class women seems to have varied between localities. Betting probably increased betters' sporting knowledge, but opponents argued that gambling degraded sport.

The popularity of sport in relation to other leisure interests

Sport never dominated English leisure, and only a small fraction of the adult population actually participated. In Bolton and its surroundings relatively high numbers of males played football and cricket but in 1931 only one in 35 of those aged between 15 and 44 would have played soccer each week and only one in 40 cricket. The proportion of women taking part in sport would have been even smaller. No sport approached cinema's popularity. For the years ending in March 1937, 1938 and 1939, the cinema provided more than half of all entertainment duty revenue in the United Kingdom. For the year ending in March 1939, cinema payments were £5.6 million, theatres and music halls just over one million, football £470,000, horseracing £240,000 and cricket £30,000.[32] The *Kinematograph Yearbook* estimated that weekly cinema attendances in Great Britain averaged ten million in 1934 and 23 million in 1937.[33] Annual admissions reached 987 million by 1938 (Beck 2003: 459). In England alone, 19 million attended every week by 1939 (Reid 2000: 776). Even on Saturdays more people probably visited the cinema than paid to watch sport. *The Social Survey of Merseyside* estimated that 576,000 cinema admissions were made each week in Liverpool in 1930. Even if only a sixth of these had been made on Saturdays, the number of Saturday cinema admissions would have been over 90,000, when the average league attendances for the Liverpool and Everton football clubs were both less than 30,000 (Jones 1934: 281).

Per capita spending on sport cannot be calculated with confidence but if gambling on sport is included, it would certainly have exceeded 6.5 per cent of consumer expenditure in 1938 spent on alcohol. But more went to the pub than played or watched sport. For pubs, like cinemas, Saturdays were peak days. In York in 1938, over 35,000 visits were made to pubs on Saturdays, and even though some would have visited pubs more than once, it would still seem that more would have gone to the pub than would have played or watched Saturday sport. Some would have visited a pub and played or watched sport on the same day. Some sports, such as darts and dominoes, were often played in pubs, but this varied between localities. Liverpool magistrates tried to discourage games in pubs. In 1937 darts was played in only two of the 250 pubs in Huddersfield (Mass-Observation 1987: 300–1, 306–7). Observers from Mass-Observation found that sport was a frequent topic of Bolton pub conversation.

Over two million radio licences were bought in 1927 and just over 9 million by the start of the Second World War. If two people had listened to each radio for two hours every day in 1939, probably more man-hours would have been spent each week listening to radio than on watching sport or playing organised sport, although Saturday sports broadcasts allowed those unable to attend events to participate vicariously.

Nationally more people probably attended church or Sunday school than played or watched sport, but with significant local variation. For a sample Sunday at York in 1935, Rowntree calculated that the total number of those aged over 17 attending churches, chapels, Bible classes and Sunday schools was close to a quarter of York's total population, higher than the number who would have played or watched sport on the previous Saturday (Rowntree 1941: 422). By contrast, Bolton Wanderers were believed in 1938 to draw 'each Saturday more people than go into pubs or churches' (Mass-Observation 1987: 19).

Opposition to and criticism of sport

Those who disliked sport, or who were indifferent, usually kept their opinions to themselves. Outright condemnations of sport in general are hard to find. In 1926 W.R. Lethaby, the Surveyor of Westminster Abbey who had been Professor of Design at the Royal College of Art, described interest in sport as 'a disease caused by the divorce of art from labour'. In his view, many turned to sport and other distractions because their work was not artistically fulfilling.[34] In 1932 H. Ramsbottom, the Parliamentary Secretary to the Board of Education, speaking at the International Congress of Secondary Education, while recognising that team games could strengthen unselfishness, argued that the 'effect on character which is caused by individual excellence at games is very dubious and individual excellence at games leads directly to the cult of athletic hero worship'. The task of educators was to demonstrate that 'the cricketer at the top of the batting averages is not really so great a man as the Prime Minister'.[35]

Criticisms of particular sports or of aspects of them were more common. Many found cricket too slow. Enthusiasts for some sports disliked others. In 1930 Graham W. Walker, a former motorcycle road racing champion, claimed that 'devotees of the older forms of motor-cycle sport' looked on speedway with 'contempt, jealousy, amazement and distrust ... they regard dirt-track racing as a species of circus stunt riding, and this impression is heightened by the knowledge that many ... who perform really well on the cinders are quite hopeless on more orthodox surfaces' (Walker 1930: 94). Criticisms were usually of specific aspects thought to be undermining a sport's moral and social worth. The National Anti-Gambling League was the most active of the organisations in England that campaigned against betting, condemning it as contrary to Christian values and as a cause of poverty by wasting income that could have been spent on family welfare. Greyhound racing and horseracing were often attacked as having betting as their *raison d'être,* but there were few successes in stopping developments. In November and December 1927, the trustees of the Crystal Palace agreed to allow it to be used for greyhound racing by a vote of thirteen to nine. There were opposing majorities on a number of local authorities, including Croydon and Wandsworth Borough Council, and, a little later, the City Corporation and London County Council. There was a letter campaign in the press, and Protestant churches in south London organised petitions, with some 43,434 signatures finally obtained. The National Anti-Gambling League took legal action against the trustees for breach of their trust, arguing that dog racing was 'a serious menace to the social and moral well-being of the nation', and the development failed.[36] In 1931 protests from neighbours and Christian groups led to the rejection of a proposal from the Duchy of Cornwall to allow greyhound racing at the Oval, even though any income would have been devoted to home improvements in the Kennington area. Anti-betting opposition weakened between the wars but not sufficiently to allow the legalisation of prepaid off-course betting (Huggins 2003: Ch. 4). The growth of 'pools' betting did not cause similar attacks on football, because gambling was not the major reason for football's existence. The Football Association and the Football League tried to prevent football coupon betting and publicly opposed the pools promoters, but with little success. Many sports tried to avoid any association with betting. Although many speedway meetings were held at greyhound stadiums, the Auto-Cycle Union, the supreme governing body for English motorcycle sport, was always keen to ensure that no bookmaking took place during meetings. In 1927 the Rugby Union expressed its hopes that rugby clubs would not permit greyhound racing on their grounds.[37] In 1932 an emergency committee of the Football Association recommended that no affiliated club should let its ground for greyhound or speedway racing, though the resolution was later withdrawn.[38]

There was continued hostility to professional sport by the English élite, a carry-over from pre-war years. Amateurism in sport was defended strongly as helping to preserve sportsmanship. Amateurs argued that where a man's livelihood depended on sport, he sometimes put his own performance before that of the team. This could lead to cheating. Because amateurs were not financially dependent on sport, it was suggested they had less temptation to cheat and could be more sportsmanlike. Because it was almost entirely professional, league football was often condemned as unsporting. In 1922 a *Times* editorial declared that 'sportsmanship in professional football is today non-existent'.[39] In 1930 Rowe Harding, a Cambridge rugby Blue and Welsh international, described professional soccer as 'sordid grasping after easy money'.[40] In 1918 Pelham Warner thought that play in league cricket was 'keen enough' but lacked 'the proper cricket atmosphere. Perhaps it is too commercial, or too selfish; perhaps both.'[41] It was often claimed that amateurs, because they could play in a more adventurous style whereas professionals reduced risk-taking to produce reliable performances, added to the spectator appeal of county cricket.

The supposed connections between amateurism and sportsmanship are analysed further in Chapter 6.

As playing for the team instead of oneself was often taken as a hallmark of sportsmanship, team sports were often held in higher esteem than individual games. Lord Harris talked of the 'selfish game of golf'. In 1919 H. Hesketh Pearson, a travel writer and big game hunter, wanted cricket to remain compulsory at public schools because unlike tennis and golf, it had a game's ideal qualities: physical danger, collective discipline, and players playing for their team and not themselves.[42] So relatively little competitive tennis was played at private schools. Liverpool College, Merchant Taylor's, Crosby, Ruthin and Rydal, for example, never played tennis against other schools between the wars. Ruthin had no tennis until 1934 and then it was restricted to the masters and sixth form. In the 1920s Rydal had nine acres of playing fields but only two tennis courts.[43]

Playing sport was often held in higher regard than watching sport. It was more likely to promote sportsmanship and an acceptance that a game was only a game. The Rugby Union, for instance, usually argued that its game was essentially one for players rather than spectators and that the interests of players should take precedence over those of spectators. Appeals for funds by the National Playing Fields Association stressed that so many watched sport only because they had no opportunity to play. In 1920 a *Times* editorial argued that the 'huge crowds that roar themselves hoarse at football matches are largely composed of young men who would probably be playing themselves, instead of always watching others play, if they had grounds to play on'.[44] Spectators were urged to behave in a sportsmanlike manner, or were criticised for not doing so. Professional football was frequently condemned because it was watched by unsportsmanlike spectators. In 1925, Sir John Foster Fraser wrote that

> First class football today is not a sport; it is a professional game played for money ... professionalism means providing entertainment for spectators, whereas amateurism means sport for sport's sake ... I strongly deprecate the indications in some parts of the country for onlookers ... to jeer at, and generally to make uncomfortable the visiting team ... for any group at a football match to be loudly contemptuous about the play of a visiting team is, to say the least, a departure from what ought to be our standard of English sportsmanship.[45]

Apologists for more commercial sports argued that they were more exciting to watch. The novelty and thrills of speedway and greyhound racing were regularly stressed. When speedway was being established in England in 1928 an article in *The Times* described it as 'a highly exciting and spectacular sport'.[46] In his autobiography published in 1930, Sprouts Elder, the American speedway rider and one of speedway's biggest stars in England during the late 1920s and early 1930s, wrote that 'for excitement, it licks a bull-fight. Once you get the speedway habit you look upon bull-fighting as a kind of dairy farming' (Elder

1930: 14). Changes to the laws of rugby league were intended to create excitement and boost the game's spectacle.

More amateur sports avoided excitement. In 1925, for instance, a writer in
Golf Illustrated argued that none who played wanted it to 'pulsate with gladiato-
rial excitement, nor partake of the nature of a circus entertainment'.[47] Many
county cricket clubs, while desperately short of money, were reluctant to
change the nature of the game to increase its spectator appeal. Little attempt
was made to convert the County Championship into a more genuine league
competition. Counties only had to play the same number of matches annually
from 1929 to 1932. In 1932, the Advisory Committee, the body that administered county cricket, attempted to discourage 'freak' declarations, when
captains in matches where much time had been lost to rain agreed to declare
first innings closed in order to provide spectators with 'some amusement'. The
cricket correspondent for *The Times* argued that 'freak' declarations did 'much
to disturb the harmony of county cricket'.[48]

Encouraging excitement encouraged crowds, and there were fears about
soccer crowd misbehaviour and the possible importation of cricket barracking
from Australia. Early in the 'bodyline tour' Pelham Warner, the England manager, asked whether 'a dignified game' like cricket should be interrupted by
barracking. After the tour the MCC complained that barracking 'unfortunately has always been indulged in by spectators in Australia to a degree quite
unknown in this country. During the late tour, however, it would appear to
have exceeded all previous experience, and … become thoroughly objectionable'. The MCC felt that unless barracking were controlled, 'it is difficult to see
how the continuance of representative matches can serve the best interests of
the game'. A *Times* editorial called barracking an 'evil' that had 'never been
allowed to get out of hand in England'.[49]

Despite the great importance attached to sport, many insisted that it
needed to be kept in proportion. Games were 'only games'. In 1926 an editorial in the *Daily Telegraph* argued that insisting on 'the rigour of the game is
excellent, to require of Test Match players that they should be fit to go "all
out" till the last ball of the last over is reason and right. But English people will
be inclined to add that cricket, even a Test Match, is only a game, and there are
dangers in taking games too seriously.'[50] In 1933 Sir John Foster Fraser wrote
that we 'are still proud when we pull off a victory' but added that when
defeated 'we comfort ourselves with the assurance that it is the game and not
the win that is the chief thing'.[51] Taking sport too seriously, it was feared,
would undermine sportsmanship's moral authority. If sport became too serious, it could lose its play element and its capacity to promote comradeship and
cheerfulness. Dr R. Cove-Smith, a former England rugby union captain,
argued in 1933 that excessive competitiveness could 'kill spontaneity and
cramp the joy of games' and by cultivating ruthlessness and hostility could
undermine its capacity to foster co-operation and promote 'active and suitable
citizens'.[52] Soccer spectators were often condemned for being too committed

and partisan in their support of their teams. Much of the suspicion surrounding professionalism stemmed from fears that money prizes led to too much stress on the result. The conviction that games were only games helps to explain the limited degree of state support for sport and why sport was so rarely a matter of party political dispute.

Governments and sport

Government responses to sport also indicate its place in England's national life. Its esteem transcended party politics and it was rarely the subject of party political dispute. It may have been less important than issues such as taxation, unemployment and foreign policy, but party leaders generally agreed about sport. All parliamentary parties more or less accepted that the state's role in sport should be minimal. None took up the occasional calls for the establishment of a Ministry of Sport. Those on the far left of politics shared many of their attitudes to sport with those possessing wealth. The British Workers' Sport Federation, quickly taken over by the Communists, espoused amateurism in sport and regarded commercialised sport with suspicion, claiming that recreation was sport's prime purpose. In 1932 W.G. Raffe wrote in the *New Clarion*, whose sympathies tended to be with the Labour party, co-operativism and the trade union movement, that sport

> is a natural instinct which Socialists should seek to encourage ... But real sport means playing and not merely looking on ... It doesn't mean pot-hunting; it doesn't mean professionalism; it doesn't mean stupid betting on horses you never see. It means playing a real game yourself.[53]

Hardly any leading politicians criticised sport, though some condemned betting. Members of government wanted sport to be played more widely but for most of the inter-war period were not prepared to spend public funds on this. The promotion of sport was not a major priority for any parliamentary party. Few politicians thought that governments should provide support to enable British sports players to perform better in international competition, though in the second half of the 1930s some noted that state support in Hitler's Germany had contributed to German success at the 1936 Olympics. British governments were more concerned with sport and the promotion of health than with sport as a form of national prestige.

Governmental responses to the National Playing Fields Association are particularly revealing. From its launch in 1925, prominent politicians attended Association fund-raising events and spoke approvingly of its work, but before 1937 central governments gave it no money and did not finance the acquisition of playing fields by local authorities. The Association depended on raising money from the public – in 1927 the Carnegie Trust gave it £200,000 – and donations of land. Central government did allow local authorities to borrow money (often from the National Playing Field Association) for playing field purchase and preparation.

In the second half of the 1930s the National Government became more active in promoting school physical training and sport. Between 1935 and 1937 government grants financed 172 school playing fields and 117 elementary school gyms.[54] The Physical Training and Recreation Act of 1937 set up the National Fitness Council for England and Wales. By the summer of 1938 it had made grants of £5.5 million to local authorities and voluntary bodies for community centres and village halls with gymnasia or facilities for other forms of indoor physical recreation, swimming baths, playing fields, camping sites, youth hostels and equipment for sports and physical training. It also financed the training of physical training leaders. Its biggest single grant was £50,000 in 1939 for a YMCA community centre in Newcastle. Of the 46 grants given in Lancashire, nine were for £50 or less.[55] But more intervention did not attempt to replace the voluntary element with government-controlled schemes. Grants were made available for local authorities. They were not compelled to apply for them. It was stressed that there was still a role for charities to fund local sport provision. National Fitness Council grants were only a little above 0.5 per cent of total government expenditure.

This increased level of government support for sport and physical recreation owed much to fears about what seemed to be higher levels of fitness in totalitarian states, particularly Germany. In 1936, Neville Chamberlain, Chancellor of the Exchequer, spoke of having no intention of adopting totalitarianism but added that in 'physical development we surely may learn something from others'. Visitors to the Berlin Olympics, he mentioned, had noted 'the splendid condition of the German youth' and that while 'our methods are different from theirs, in accordance with our national character and traditions, I see no reason why we should not be equally successful in our results'.[56] A Board of Education pamphlet, published after a delegation had visited Germany, spoke with enthusiasm about physical training in Germany.[57] On Health Sunday in January 1938, the Bishop of London spoke of the 'marvellous results' and 'perfectly astounding … physical perfection' that had been rapidly accomplished in Germany 'by a system of outdoor camps, of compulsory exercises, and the successful inculcation of the belief that love of country comes first, before any personal enjoyment, and that patriotism comes first and "having a good time" comes last'.[58]

The need to promote better health was also prominent in the discourses surrounding national fitness. Encouraging fitness among young people was portrayed as progress against 'disease and early death', by ensuring for every child 'the chance of its rightful inheritance of good health'.[59] The increased level of government financial support may have been stimulated by fears that higher levels of physical fitness could give Nazi Germany a military advantage over Britain, but apologists for the scheme rarely mentioned this publicly. For supporters of national fitness, the threat of German physical achievements was ideological rather than military. Achieving levels of fitness equal to those of

Nazi Germany would undermine claims about the superiority of totalitarianism. Lord Aberdare, chairman of the National Advisory Council for Physical Training and Recreation, pointed out that schemes introduced in Britain, unlike those in totalitarian states, did not involve 'regimentation and compulsion'. These were 'alien to British tastes and traditions'. He felt that Britain could achieve the same 'impressive' standard of fitness as totalitarian regimes: 'by appealing to the interest and convincing the judgement of the individual, it would be an outstanding tribute to our free institutions'.[60] A *Times* editorial argued that it

> must be clear, even to those who most fiercely detest the totalitarian philosophy, that if democracy can combine political freedom with an equally high physical standard, this would be additional proof of the superiority of democracy and not the first step towards the imitation of political heresies'.[61]

Representations of sport

The mass media

The mass media reflected and helped to shape interest in sport between the wars. Their portrayal of sport expressed and fashioned the dominant images of sport and constructed what many took to be sporting reality. But the relationship of the media with sport was complex and subtle. Print, film and radio provided differing forms of information about sport and their representations of sport reflected differing assumptions about the nature of sport. Assessments of their impacts on sport can only be cautious as not all consumers of the mass media sought or derived the same messages from the media. Presentation rather than content may have been more influential in forming meanings attached to sport.

The press and sport

Newspapers were a major source of information about sport between the wars. Sales of daily morning newspapers increased by 80 per cent between 1920 and 1939. By 1938–39 the aggregate sales of daily newspapers averaged 10.48 million copies each day while those for Sunday newspapers were 13.59 million. By 1939 the *Daily Express*, selling nearly two and a half million copies each day, had the largest daily circulation. The *Daily Herald* was selling around two million copies each day while sales of the *Daily Telegraph* rose from 175,000 to 559,000 between 1930 and 1937.[1] Circulations of provincial morning newspapers fell slightly between the wars but in the early 1930s regional evening newspapers such as the *Birmingham Mail*, *Liverpool Echo*, *Manchester Evening News*, *Newcastle Evening Chronicle* and Plymouth's *Western Evening Herald* were taken by two-thirds of local households.[2] Saturday sports editions often had the highest daily sales for provincial evening newspapers. The expansion of newspaper sales was accompanied by a more extensive sport coverage, editors assuming that this would boost circulation. In 1927 *Radio Times* claimed that 'the Cup Final is worth millions to the evening papers'.[3] When the *Daily Mirror* was re-launched in 1933 to attract younger, more working-class readers, its sports coverage increased by a fifth. By 1937 its sports coverage was four times that of its 'serious' coverage of politics, society and the economy. The *Daily Mail*, however, expanded its sports coverage to over a third of its news content

Table 2.1 Specialist sporting press periodicals listed in *Willing's Newspaper Press Directory,*
1919–1940

Date	1918/9	1925/6	1932/3	1939/40
Number	117	197	197	135

Source: *Willing's Newspaper Press Directory 1919–1940.*
Note: Comparable figures in *Mitchell's Newspaper Press Directory*, the other leading directory for
periodicals, are 97, 119, 146 and 146. *Willing's* tended to update material more quickly, and
1939 wartime concerns may have led to a drop in periodicals.

but its sales declined in the 1930s (Bingham 2004: 218–19; *Royal Commission on the Press* 1949: 131, 250). The *News of the World* and the *People*, the best-selling Sunday newspapers, doubled their football coverage between the wars.

Table 2.1 shows the total daily, weekly and monthly specialist sport newspapers and magazines between the wars. Many concentrated on one sport. The racing press seem to have sold best. The London-based *Sporting Life* (founded 1859) sold 100,000 copies each day in 1926. Concerned almost entirely with sport and entertainment, it provided comprehensive racing results, details about the previous form of horses, reports from training areas plus news about theatres, cricket, rowing, tennis, athletics and golf. Many of its readers must have been working-class but its lists of stallions at stud and advertisements for cars, Martell brandy, Burberry clothes, expensive jewellery and credit bookmakers suggest a sizeable middle and upper-class readership. In 1924 *Sporting Life* took over the *Sportsman*, the other main London racing daily which had also covered other sports. Its circulation had been falling. In the north the *Sporting Chronicle* (founded 1871) was the leading racing daily. In 1924 it was acquired from its founder Sir Edward Hulton by the press barons Northcliffe and Beaverbrook. Regional racing dailies such as Newcastle's *Sporting Man*, Leeds' *Sporting Pink* or Nottingham's *Post Tissue* also met the demands of the illegal cash betting world.

The Manchester-based weekly *Athletic News* (founded 1875) concentrated on soccer and rugby in winter and athletics, cricket and cycling in summer. It rarely reported racing or professional boxing. It was selling 170,000 copies each week in 1919 but was soon hit by the greater coverage of sport in the national and local newspapers. It was absorbed by the *Sporting Chronicle* in 1931. The *Field* (founded 1853) was published weekly between the wars. This covered country sports and other sports which were predominantly amateur but rarely reported professional soccer or rugby league. Table 2.2 shows that many sports sustained specialist weekly or monthly newspapers or magazines. Soccer and rugby had the broadest coverage, though tennis and golf grew steadily, but we know little about the relative circulation of such periodicals.

Interest in country sports was sufficient to support *Illustrated Sporting and Dramatic News* (1874) subheaded 'for town and country', and *Horse and Hound* (1884) in addition to the *Field*. Pelham Warner, a former England captain,

Table 2.2 Numbers of specialist periodicals on selected sports 1919–1940

	1919	1926	1933	1940
Athletics	7	6	3	2
Country life and sport	13	16	14	12
Cricket	6	9	11	5
Cycling	7	2	2	7
Fishing	7	6	5	7
Soccer and rugby	11	49	38	28
Golf	5	5	6	7
Lawn tennis	1	1	4	5

Sources: *Mitchell's Newspaper Press Directory* and *Willing's Newspaper Press Directory 1919–1940.*

helped to launch the *Cricketer* in 1921. Very much in sympathy with cricket's established order, it appeared weekly during the cricket season and monthly in winter. It reported on first-class cricket, public-school cricket and the higher levels of amateur club cricket in the South. In the 1930s it gave very short accounts of northern league cricket. In the 1920s *Golf Illustrated* claimed to be the world's only weekly golf journal. Some new publications were short-lived. The weekly *Rugger* started in 1931 but closed in 1932.

Evaluations of how far the press influenced perceptions of sport can only be tentative. One can never be sure of how far newspapers followed, created or ignored the opinions of their readers and it is unlikely that all readers would have responded to a newspaper's sport coverage in the same fashion. Few studies seem to have been made of reader reactions to sport reporting. The proportion of sports coverage given to different sports differed between the various types of newspapers. Almost all dailies gave extensive coverage to racing, though the *Manchester Guardian* ignored it, and to cricket. The *Daily Worker* had no racing tips or results yet provided football pool forecasts. All covered soccer but those with the largest circulations, the *Daily Express*, *Daily Herald*, and *Daily Mail*, tended to concentrate on the Football League. *The Times* and *Daily Telegraph*, which were read in three-quarters of those families with incomes of over £500 according to Political and Economic Planning's 1938 *Report on the British Press*, paid more attention to rugby union, golf, tennis, hunting and public-school sport than popular newspapers. The press sponsorship of sport was largely confined to golf tournaments. Men's sport received far more attention than women's sport. Local daily and evening newspapers reported national as well as local sport but local weekly newspapers usually concentrated on sport in their locality. Except for boxing world championships newspapers reported sport overseas only when English competitors were taking part. The great bulk of sport reporting in all newspapers consisted of results and previews and reports of matches or races. Throughout the inter-war period newspapers remained the most detailed source for finding out what had just happened in sport and the depth of this coverage suggests that editors believed readers wanted this sort of sport news. Radio was able to provide results quicker but did not have so many match reports. Press previews of sport events no doubt heightened anticipation of them.

Changes in the style of reporting sport were gradual rather than dramatic between the wars. All newspapers included more photographs but the mass circulation press made most use of these. By 1939 most reports were shorter than in the early 1920s though they continued to be longer in the 'quality' press. The respected golf writer Bernard Darwin wrote in 1932 that compared with fifty years earlier sport journalists 'do not deal overmuch in statistics nor plough their way laboriously, without lights or shades, through the whole day's play. They try rather to give a general impression and to pick out some two or three crises of the match' (Darwin 1932: 208–9). By the end of the 1930s headlines had become slightly bigger. It is not difficult to find examples of sport journalists striving for literary effect but the cricket writer Neville Cardus, who wrote under the pseudonym 'Cricketer' in the *Manchester Guardian*, was perhaps the only sports journalist to become widely regarded as a literary artist. One can find reports lauding the skills of individual players but it is hard to be sure whether a greater emphasis on individuals in team sports became more common between the wars. It is also difficult to be certain of how far newspapers tried to sensationalise sport. Few attempts were made to exploit the private lives or peccadilloes of prominent players. The ghosted articles critical of the English test team captaincy by the cricketer Cecil Parkin in 1924 and 1925 were sensations at the time but did not lead to a flood of similar articles from other prominent sport players.

In general the press was a force for conservatism in sport. There was little investigative sport journalism and little call for administrative reform in sport. Press demands for the England cricket team to have a professional captain in the mid-1920s were prompted mainly by hopes that this might help England to defeat Australia. Less was heard of this in the 1930s. Newspapers celebrated and encouraged the playing of sport by women. In 1924, when there were no women's track and field events at the official Olympics, the *Daily Mirror*, the *News of the World* and the *Sporting Life* organised the international Women's Olympics in London. Amy Johnson's solo flight to Australia in 1930 was celebrated by the *Daily Herald* as 'the vindication of womanhood' and by the *Daily Mail* as 'the most marvellous feat of endurance recorded in the whole history of womanhood'.[4] When the press criticised sport it was often for breaches of sportsmanship by players or spectators. Defeats for England in international competition were not presented as national disasters but were often accompanied by comments that the English approach of keeping games as games was superior to the more serious methods of more successful foreign players. Britain's performance at the 1936 Olympics provoked some indignation in the press but none argued that the emphasis on sportsmanship in English sport should be abandoned. Having sport pages at the back of a newspaper, which was found only among newspapers that did not have a first page of small ads, may have reflected assumptions that sport was interesting, but not very important. Taking it too seriously could undermine its moral value.

Books and sport

The reading of books seems to have increased between the wars. Book sales grew even during the depression, rising from 7.2 million in 1928 to 26.8 million in 1939. In 1924 public libraries issued 85.7 million books but 247.4 million in 1939 (Stevenson 1984: 398–99). Sport had a substantial factual literature. Of the sport books acquired by the British Museum between 1931 and 1935, for example, 89 were on golf, though many were short club handbooks catering for a local market, followed by angling with 79 and cricket with 62.[5] Racing, betting, racehorse training and riding together had nearly as many. Many spectator sports had far fewer. Soccer, for example, had only sixteen books and rugby nine.[6] But such figures understated the volume of print which leading popular sports attracted. Each year newspapers and specialist works cashed in on demand with a variety of annuals, varying in size and cost, with the *Athletic News* football annual, the *News Chronicle*'s *Raceform*, *Chaseform* and *Racing Up-to-date* and the *Wisden* cricket annual leading the field. The soccer and cricket annuals of national papers like the *Express* or *News Chronicle* sold well, while annuals of regional newspapers such as Newcastle's *Northern Athlete* or Blackburn's *Sports Telegraph* competed for local support.

Sport does not seem to have been the major theme of any novel written for adults between the wars which received critical acclaim nor were any sport novels bestsellers equivalent to Surtees' hunting novels of the early Victorian period or the horseracing novels of Dick Francis from more recent decades. A lowbrow adolescent market for fictional sports stories was met by the Dundee firm of D.C. Thompson and Company. The weekly *Adventure* (started in 1921), *Rover* and *Wizard* (1922), *Skipper* (1930) and *Hotspur* (1933) all included sport, adventure, school and historical stories, in which male sporting heroes were clear-eyed, square-chinned, well-muscled and deep-chested, well-educated young men of integrity, incapable of dishonesty, engaged in an unending war against what appeared to be a far larger group of the dishonest, who were often wealthy and cunning. Stories in the distinctively pink-jacketed *Boys' Magazine* (1922) exemplified much about the inter-war approach to adolescent sport. The monocled detective Falcon Swift, for example, was a Cambridge triple Blue, skilled at boxing, soccer, sculling, fencing and hunting. His youthful assistant Chick Conway was a former street urchin who spent his spare time reading the *Sporting Chronicle*. Swift's adversaries in both sport and crime were exhibitionist master crooks whom he would defeat through a combination of sporting contests and cunning detection, thus allowing a variety of dramatic set-piece sporting contexts. Often, as in traditional sport, some sort of challenge might be introduced. The arch-crook of five continents, Claude Montana, for example, wrote directly to Swift, that after

> what I can proudly boast to be the most successful career in the history of crime, I have decided to take possession of the English Cup at Stamford Bridge Ground tomorrow … There promises to be a record crowd present and after all have paid admission I will call round and collect the gate money.
>
> (Turner 1957: 164)

The underlying message in much of this form of fiction was that all sports were potentially corrupt, and that evil could only be averted and contests won by playing the game in a manly way after heroically facing great danger. Comedy was also a strong feature, with poor English sportsmen and almost all foreigners being ridiculed. To make it more amusing, a common device was to give the hero an unlikely occupation, so there were boxing taxi-men or millionaires. Sport generally helped sales, but not of a paper on the slide. The *Marvel* (1893) changed its name to *Sport and Adventure* in 1922 and gave away pictures of football stars such as Charlie Buchan and Billy Meredith but to no avail.

For slightly older readers, the Aldine Publishing company issued cheap, short 'libraries' of pulp fiction, including horseracing, boxing and football. Romantic plots surfaced in a number of the books, usually with sensible, quietly attractive girls as in the case of Richard Worth's *A Footballer's Romance* (1926). Most relied on the standard adolescent mixture of sport, villainy and occasional xenophobic jingoism. In soccer, for example, the stories centred on 'the triumph of good over evil, honesty over deceit, in which genuine endeavour would always prevail over shady skulduggery' (Seddon 1999: 293). Heroes were always honest, brave, moral and hard-working, both in sporting terms and in terms of their main occupation, which was often working-class. Aldine football titles included *The Movie Winger* (1927), *The Actor-Footballer* (1928), *The Busman Centre-Forward* (1928) *The Filmland Forward* (1929) and *The Circus Saver* (1930). By contrast, Aldine's boxing novels, of which over eighty were published between *circa* 1924 and 1932, had a more clearly cross-class appeal with titles even including *The Boxing Squire*, *The Young Corinthian* and *The Fighting Parson* (all 1925), as well as more working-class ones.

Amalgamated Press's *Football and Sports Library*, brought out in the early 1920s and selling at 2d., and its later series, such as *Tales of Sport and Games* (from 1928) or the *Champion Library*, catered for a similar age group. Several of their leading characters had northern dialects, suggesting that their main market was located there. Even more significant was the early inclusion of some 'ladies football' fiction with mill girls as heroines, at a time when such games were attracting large crowds. These stories have been studied in detail by Alethea Melling (Melling 1998: 97–122). The heroines were brave and plucky with an attractive appearance calculated to appeal to males. Yet the fiction addresses gender roles, the dynamics of workplace hierarchies, and coercive male sexual demands. Although heroines were always feminine, other women players were celebrated for their size, strength, fitness and ability to play as a team, challenging patriarchal notions of female fragility. The stories reflected factory shop-floor culture, emphasising hard work, fairness and support for fellow-workers. Several challenged conventional capitalist ideologies and reflected strong antagonism to workplace authority structures. Strong stereotypes dominate the tales. The girls' dastardly middle-class factory bosses are often corrupt, solicitors are unscrupulous, and supervisors and overlookers are cowardly, cunning men who exploit the petty rules and regulations of the workplace for sexual harassment. All try to suppress women's football to further their own economic or sexual control, which the girls successfully resist, but the endings of such stories were often conventional, with the heroine falling in love with a caring, fairly wealthy middle-class man. Melling suggests that Amalgamated Press was more concerned to 'give the public what it wanted' than 'to adhere to the ethos of the dominant patriarchal structures'.

Feature films and sport

The cinema and sport were major leisure interests of inter-war England but sport did not figure prominently in feature, or fictional, films. One analysis suggests that only about 1.5 per cent of British films made between 1929 and 1939 could be described as 'sports' films (Gifford 1973). No feature film which revolved around sport achieved a critical acclaim between the wars similar to that of *This Sporting Life* or *Chariots of Fire* after the Second World War. As more women than men visited the cinema and as more men than women watched or played sport, film producers may have assumed that sport feature films would have little appeal to women. Many films were adaptations of novels or plays, and as sport was the essential theme in few of these, this may also explain why so few fictional sport films were made. Hollywood may have made few sport films because it could have been assumed that audiences overseas were not familiar with American sports other than boxing and horseracing. In 1938 Mass-Observation found that musical romance, drama and tragedy, history and crime were the most popular feature film formats in Bolton, but sport films may have been more popular had more been made (Richards and Sheridan 1987: 34).

While few fiction films were about sport, many featured sport in passing and betting on sport events was vital to the plot of even more. Horseracing was the sport that figured most often in feature films, perhaps because interest in it crossed class boundaries. The dominant image of racing in films was that it was generally 'all square' although trainers could be depicted as crooked, bookmakers dishonest and horses doped. Where racehorse ownership featured in films, the horse would usually win the big race in the final reels and so recoup fortunes that allowed the hero's merits to be recognised and the lovers to get back together. Upper-class settings, such as the country house party, were sometimes lampooned and their pretensions exposed, as in *Strictly Illegal* (1934), yet the upper classes, although often presented as 'toffs', were shown as usually 'straight' in their support of racing. The middle classes appear in a variety of roles. Amos Purdue was presented as an anti-betting 'crank' and Justice of the Peace in *The Sport of Kings* (1931). Given that most sporting films had comic elements, it was perhaps not surprising that vicars in these films behaved less than puritanically. In *Be Careful Mr Smith* (1935) a retired vicar buys a bookmaking business to escape his nagging wife; in *Dandy Dick* (1935) a country vicar bets everything on a racehorse; and in *The Double Event* a country vicar backs horses, while his daughter runs a bookmaker's business.

Racing films usually expressed approval of the social order and emphasised social cohesion. In *Strictly Illegal* (1934), a street bookie believes mistakenly that he has killed a policeman. On the run, he poses as a clergyman, is invited to be a country house guest, successfully maintains the socially exalted deception and prevents a jewel theft. In the musical comedy *The Lambeth Walk* Lupino Lane plays a cheery bookmaker's runner who learns that he is really a lord and is groomed to take over his inheritance. Such films suggested that with good luck the audience too could fit painlessly into a new and higher status.

The comedians Max Miller, Will Fyffe and George Formby, all stars of the variety halls, appeared in comic films featuring racing and betting. In *Come on George* (1939) Formby's character goes on the run after being falsely accused of theft. He calms an unmanageable racehorse while getting a ride in a horsebox and is hired as stable-boy/jockey to look after the horse and ride it in a big race. Despite losing his nerve at one point, he rides the horse to victory, while outwitting a gang of crooks. In *Trouble Brewing*, also released in 1939, Formby is paid in counterfeit money after winning a big bet, but eventually tracks down the gang and gets his cash, fighting an all-in wrestling champion en route. Other sports were key themes in Formby films. *No Limit* (1935) featured him riding in the Isle of Man motorcycle TT races. In *I See Ice* (1938) Formby played a sports photographer who had to referee an ice hockey match after the two teams had knocked out the official referee, which clearly drew on ice hockey's reputation as a rough sport. Formby's sporting comedies suggest that many of the working class, who would have made up the bulk of the audiences, did not feel that the moral discourses surrounding sports prevented them from being a source of laughter.

Films featuring boxing such as *Splinters in the Navy* (1931), *Blue Smoke* (1935) and *There Ain't No Justice* (1934) may have been intended to appeal to predominantly working-class audiences. Greyhound racing was the setting for *The Outcast* (1934). *All In* (1936) featured a racing romance and a wrestling stadium. *The Arsenal Stadium Mystery* (1939), based on the Leonard Gribble novel which had previously been a detective serial in the *Daily Express*, focused on the murder of an amateur forward in front of a large crowd at an Arsenal cup-tie. It was described as 'a lively and imaginative whodunit with a footballing background' (Low 1985: 214). It may be significant, however, as Dave Russell (1997: 108) suggests, that while Arsenal players appeared, the central characters were players in a public school old boys side, hinting that professional football was not appropriate 'at the heart of a cultural product designed for a cross-class audience'. Arsenal certainly had a gift for publicity. Arsenal matches and players featured in a majority of footballing films from the 1930s, including two films using the 1930 Cup Final, *The Great Game* (1930) and *Up for the Cup* (1931).

The cultural meanings underlying films which featured sport are complex and subtle. A unitary reading of them is impossible. They indicate unresolved dualities and concealed conflicts in the thinking of authors, producers and audiences. They had to be capable of being read in a variety of ways, so they had to validate the interests and concerns of women as well as men, middle as well as working-class audiences.[7] Many films mixed escapism, comedy, fantasy and wish-fulfilment, and emphasised tradition and social decorum. They were particularly popular with working-class audiences, reflecting in part a culture of hope and consolation. Some had familiar, realistic working-class characters, concerns and settings, although many were close to caricatures. Working-class heroes were often ordinary in appearance, but cheerfully optimistic characters who, like the audiences themselves, craved better luck. Unsurprisingly therefore, many such escapist films featured betting on horses, where a successful bet could mean happier times and circumstances, the provision of wealth and confidence that audiences could only dream about. Because of censorship, feature films did not show the complicity of policemen in illegal bookmaking. The British Board of Film Censors insisted that 'in this country we do not allow our police to be shown on the screen as ... accepting bribes from criminals'.[8]

Not all women in sporting films displayed a docile, decorative, female fragility. In *Racing Romance* over-ambitious Muriel is punished for breaking off her romance when her garage-owning fiancé buys a racehorse which lets her down by apparently coming second in the Oaks, only to find that it wins after an objection. Her fiancé subsequently marries the more conventionally pretty girl who had been the horse's previous owner. But women are certainly sometimes portrayed as competent, strong and independent outside the domestic sphere. In *Two on a Doorstep* (1936), a girl has a similar phone number to a bookmaker and begins to take some of the bets, setting up her own betting agency. She takes a big bet on a favourite and finds she owes more than she can pay, but recoups her fortunes by winning at a greyhound stadium. In the comic feature *Almost a Honeymoon* (1938), the girlfriend of the hero (played by Tommy Trinder) takes up all-in wrestling.

The relatively small number of fictional sport films means that they could not have had a profound impact on perceptions of sport. Films may have introduced some audiences to aspects of sport of which they had had little first-hand experience such as betting but as films were rarely critical of sport, they probably did not raise doubts about the widespread conception of sport as being intrinsically worthwhile. The comic element of sport films was affectionate humour rather than fierce satire.

Cinema newsreels and sport

Sport was a regular feature of cinema newsreels between the wars and provided the most visual form of sporting news, albeit in a popular magazine format, and often delayed several days or even weeks after an event (McKibbin 1998: Ch. 11). About a fifth of surviving newsreels cover sport. Newsreels allowed many to see, for the first time, distant and national events and stars they had only read about. In 1940 Mass-Observation reported that over 60 per cent of cinema viewers enjoyed newsreels but that fewer women than men liked sports items (Richards and Sheridan 1987: 392). Frequent exposure to newsreels must have influenced audience perceptions of sport. Watching sport on the silver screen gave people the illusion of being there and participating in some way.[9]

In the 1920s, before the advent of sound, *Pathe Gazette* dominated the sporting news, along with a number of smaller 'topical' companies. The coming of sound coincided with an increased number of newsreel companies. *Pathe Gazette* found itself in competition with *Gaumont Sound News* (established 1929), the smaller *British Pictorial Productions* and the two American-owned organisations *British Movietone News* (1929) and *British Paramount News* (1931). Each produced two one-reel issues a week, usually consisting of around half a dozen items that mixed current affairs, institutionalised events and disasters with one, two or even more sports items. Competition between companies was intense. Even when a sports organisation such as Aintree racecourse tried to profit by offering an exclusive contract to one firm, pirate cameramen from other firms tried to sneak in. In 1934, for example, *Movietone* and *Gaumont British* shared the Oval test match rights, but *Paramount* tried to get shots from a tower outside the ground. A large gas-filled balloon was raised to spoil the *Paramount* view and this distracted spectators from the game. When *Pathe* announced that they would show the 'only authentic and official pictures' of the 1933 Grand National they sent a staff of twenty-six to Aintree, some of whom were there to keep out opposition. For the Grand National of 1934 cameras were concealed in a bag of fruit, a chauffeur's luncheon basket, a bookie's satchel, on a coal barge at the canal turn and on a steam shovel in attempts to beat *Pathe*.[10] Sometimes sports promoters tried to keep all newsreel companies out entirely, to create a monopoly for their own film. The films of the 1936 and 1937 FA Cup Finals were produced by Wembley Stadium and filmed by the Featurettes company, which had earlier filmed boxing promotions. To maximise its profit Wembley Stadium sold these directly to cinemas. The Rugby Union invited tenders for still photographs and film rights of matches at Twickenham. In 1926 it accepted £85 for still photographs and £52 10s for films. By 1929 film rights had risen to £90, £5 more than those for still photographs. The Rugby Union asked £150 for film rights and £90 for still photographs for the 1931–32 season which perhaps reflects the impact of sound on newsreels.[11]

The range, though not the depth, of sports covered in newsreels was impressive. Newsreels, because of their need to appeal to all classes, introduced cinemagoers to a far wider diet of sporting activities and events than they could experience directly. Even if many were, as Rachael Low claims, 'safe, acceptable and familiar', others were probably unlikely to have been read about, especially by the working classes. Even in 1920, for example, *Pathe* showed a charity football match between actors and boxers, women footballers, and a London hospital cup match between Guys and Barts. In the 1920s coverage also included fox-hunting, polo, yachting's Americas Cup, Oxbridge sporting events such as the Boat Race or athletics, golf amateur and open championships, coursing's Waterloo Cup, the Isle of Man TT Races, county and test cricket, fights by top boxers like Carpentier and Wells, and horseracing from point-to-points to Ascot and Epsom. Many films showed the crowd as much as the event, giving an increased sense of vicarious participation to viewers.

Soccer was the sport covered most often in winter, despite the Football League's reluctance to approve filming because of worries about effects on match attendances. Though there was no outright ban, few league clubs co-operated with newsreels. An exception was Arsenal, who regularly exploited coverage, and seem to have benefited in attendance terms. The FA's approach was more positive and from January to May FA Cup ties involving leading clubs were regularly featured, although clubs could refuse to be filmed. Semi-finals and cup finals and the celebrations afterwards were always a popular feature. Horseracing was popular in summer, especially Epsom's spring and Derby meetings, and the Aintree Grand National, but cameras visited other English courses, such as Chester, Kempton and Newmarket, and key American races were also shown.

Boxing, tennis and golf also figured frequently in newsreels. In part these reflected the American parent company interests of some newsreel organisations. Professional boxing had a large following in the USA, and growing interest in England, and American heavyweights and British hopefuls were regularly featured. Golf newsreels had almost as much American material as British. There were relatively substantial pieces of film on women's golf. In 1936, for example, these included the American Ladies Professional Golf Championship, the Ladies Amateur Championship, the British Women's Open Championship, the English Women's Championship and girls' international golf at Stoke Poges. Women's successes at Wimbledon or Bournemouth, and in the Wightman Cup, were all featured, suggesting a recognition of increased female interest but perhaps also reflecting that cinema audiences usually contained more women than men. The more middle-class sports of amateur athletics and rowing came next in coverage. Cricket, though a 'national' game, was played only in the summer and not in the USA, and its subtleties were not easily visually conveyed, so it is perhaps unsurprising that it received significantly less coverage, although test matches were generally reported. Its coverage paralleled that of other predominantly middle and upper-class sports, such as polo, fishing, hunting and rugby.

Sports with a predominantly working-class image, like greyhound racing, speedway or professional pedestrianism, received more limited coverage. Perhaps the companies were anxious not to alienate what was a substantial middle-class cinema audience, attending the more expensive town-centre cinemas. One exception, strangely, was all-in wrestling, which was presented as a fun 'modern' American-style entertainment, filmed at Belle Vue, Manchester, or London venues, often with American performers and sometimes mixed with American footage. Occasionally female wrestlers were included.

American-owned companies imported American sports items into their newsreels, alongside the American feature films which were a staple part of the British market. This ensured that cinema-goers experienced a significantly increased Americanisation of their visual sporting experience from an early date, with much more limited coverage of events in Europe and the British colonies, though German sport featured more than one might expect. British companies followed suit. In December 1930, for example, *Universal News* included ice hockey from Germany as well as American walking, yachting, diving, cycling and horseracing. Through the 1930s American golf, horseracing, athletics and boxing were all quite regularly featured on British screens. In early June 1936, before the Berlin Olympics, *Gaumont British News* had already told audiences that the Columbus, Ohio, inter-state championship was

> in the nature of a trial for the coming Olympics … Jesse Owens of Ohio State set up a new world record for the 220 yards. Watch the style of Owens the negro as he flashes along in front of the field … at the next Olympics he'll take plenty of beating.[12]

Newsreel sports coverage provided cinemagoers with a sense of immediacy and of being part of a big crowd. While newsreels gave an impression of authenticity, they were carefully edited. Sound, such as music, crowd noises, punches or thudding hooves, was often recorded separately and intended to promote a particular interpretation. Commentators adopted a middle-class tone of voice and few regional accents were heard. The voices of some presenters, such as Alan Howland of *British Movietone News*, became well known. Comments were generally highly positive, jolly, hearty and often mildly humorous, with banter and weak puns, but relatively uncritical. Existing sporting structures were rarely criticised and investigative journalism non-existent. By and large the English were shown as winning, as internationally successful, helping to maintain the myth of national prestige, with England merged into a wider vision of 'Glorious Britain' or 'Triumphant Britain'. Successes abroad were trumpeted, audiences were told that Britain was 'justly proud' of their wins. When British competitors lost it was given a positive spin, in a patriotic rather than narrowly nationalistic way. When the yachtsman Sir Thomas Lipton lost yet again in the Americas Cup, viewers learnt that New Yorkers had given 'this fine old English gentleman a rousing send-off – For he endeared himself to all by his sportsmanlike acceptance of defeat ... They hated to see him go, and as many as possible shook him by the hand ... Better luck next time Sir'.[13] One can never be certain of how audiences responded to newsreels, but their content and presentation of sport hardly ever challenged perceptions of English sport being permeated with fair play.

Women's sport was represented through the male gaze and reflected assumptions that it was less significant than men's sport. Coverage was nevertheless significant. By the 1930s their participation in over twenty different sports was being shown annually, and about five per cent of sporting newsreels featured women. A description of a women's amateur athletic competition in 1930, for example, mixed heartiness, praise and encouragement with condescension.

> Half a dozen of them show their pace – and a jolly good pace too – in the hundred yards. Come on girls! Number two on the left does it. Twelve seconds for a hundred yards is pretty good time. The long jump – Oop – Over – a roll in the sand's her lot ... Number one now. Ah, a beauty. Seventeen feet five inches – a very, very fine effort ... Away they go on the half mile. Miss Humphries takes it easy in third place here – but soon shakes out her permanent wave and shows a clean pair of heels to the others – winning comfortably by half a dozen yards. Now I suppose it's a visit to the hairdressers for her.[14]

Newsreels increased knowledge of sports and sports players. Those with little interest in sport could always ignore the sports pages but at the cinema they could not avoid newsreel sport. While sport increased familiarity with sport, the brevity of newsreels may have meant little depth of awareness of a sport's finer points. By showing annual national sporting events such the FA Cup Final, the Boat Race, Wimbledon and leading horse races and also regional events such as the Grasmere Games or Shrove Tuesday folk football games, newsreels reinforced consciousness of a national sporting calendar and of a national sporting tradition. Filming royalty at sport events was part of the democratisation of monarchy.

Broadcasting and sport

Radio was a new form of mass communication in inter-war England and the BBC, with its monopoly of broadcasting, did not have to produce profits for shareholders. Only 36,000 radio licences were bought in 1922 but over two million were purchased in 1927 and over nine million in 1939.[15] By the late 1930s more people listened to the radio each day than visited the cinema. Initially the BBC's coverage of sport was limited. In 1923 the Sykes Committee had argued that broadcasting racing results would hit newspaper sales while the Newspaper Proprietors' Association had persuaded the government that the

BBC was a rival form of news reporting. So the BBC was not allowed to broadcast sports results and conflict between the BBC and the press over news reporting continued throughout the inter-war period (Nicholas 2000). In 1926 the BBC broadcast the Derby as an experiment but this was not considered a critical success. Later in the same year the Postmaster-General allowed the BBC to have outside broadcasts and after negotiations with news agencies and the press, it was decided that there would henceforth be considerable expansion of news broadcasting, including eyewitness descriptions of important events.

Broadcasting of important sporting occasions was initially portrayed as an American idea. In early January 1927 *Radio Times* described in detail how American football was broadcast in the USA, explaining that American newspapers often had their own radio stations and reported regularly on sport, creating 'more interest ... in the football and baseball pages than ever before'.[16] Almost certainly this was a press and public relations exercise, perhaps emanating from the office of Gerald Cock, the first Director of Outside Broadcasts. January 1927 saw the effective beginning of this new outside broadcast service, with a motor van carrying the complicated apparatus required for transmission. The first sport broadcast was the rugby international between England and Wales at Twickenham on 15 January, trumpeted as 'one of the most important events since the inception of broadcasting ... the beginning of a new era in wireless' and as evidence of the BBC's intention to cover sports as 'an integral part of the broadcast service'. Many letters were received from listeners, with the 'crowded hour of glorious life', and the 'wild glorious cheering from 40,000 throats' singled out for praise.[17] Over the next two weeks, soccer fans heard a league match between Arsenal and Sheffield United and a fourth round FA Cup tie between Corinthians and Newcastle United. Both used two commentators. Attempts to locate play for viewers involved a plan of the pitch divided into eight sectors. One commentator described the match while another called out the sector. Listeners heard 'Oh! Pretty work, very pretty (section 5) ... now up the field (7) ... a pretty (5,8) pass ... Come on, Mercer ... now then Mercer: hello! Noble's got it (1,2)'. Without the chart, little can have been conveyed beyond the cheers and groans of the home supporters, but *The Times* found that 'descriptions of swift passing movements, long clearances up field and shots at goal were totally vivid and impressive'.[18]

Further rugby internationals and FA Cup matches were broadcast in February 1927. March listeners heard the Grand National, the first coverage of racing. *Radio Times* provided a plan of the Aintree course which enabled listeners to follow the steeplechase from start to finish. The veteran *Sporting Life* journalist Meyrick Good, who usually 'read the race' for the king, provided the commentary, although he commentated in the open and close to the enclosures in order to use his binoculars to see the distant part of the course, which caused crowd noise to interfere with his remarks towards the finish. After the broadcast he claimed that those who have listened have been worked up to a high pitch of curiosity and want to see in cold print the evidence of their own ears corroborated and amplified ... the broadcasting of these great racing events is more of an asset to the newspapers than otherwise.[19]

The Boat Race presented a bigger technical challenge, with the commentary broadcast from a launch travelling over the course close behind the two crews. An aerial sent a signal to two receiving stations at Barnes. The FA Cup final, on 23 April, included sound of the vast crowd singing together before kick-off, claimed as 'the largest demonstration of Community Singing this country has ever beheld'.[20] Like crowd noise, this was an attempt to give armchair fans something of the communal atmosphere. *Radio Times* claimed that 10 million listened to these major sporting broadcasts.[21]

While early broadcasts were generally well received, they were not wholly successful. Keeping pace with fast-moving events proved difficult for novice commentators. Even so, BBC commentators, strong individuals, usually public school- or Oxbridge-educated and almost all men, were largely able to mediate the spectacle in the light of a wider cultural consensus. Their respect for tradition and authority, conservatism, and amateur sportsmanship, which much of the audience shared, played a key role in helping the BBC become a national authority in sporting terms. The BBC searched hard for talented, expert commentators for what was a novel form of communication. Initial criteria were 'journalistic instincts, a decent voice, a sound communicable knowledge of the subject, and the power to make listeners feel as though they were present at the event' (Briggs 1965: 60). The first boat race commentary had G.O. Nickalls, a former Oxford president and Oxford crew member from 1921 to 1923; J.C. Squire, who provided description, was a writer, journalist and editor of the *London Mercury*. Soccer commentaries soon used George Allison, later to become manager of Arsenal. In 1931 he saw his job as commenting 'in a way which conveys to the listener a mental photograph of what is taking place ... keeping a steely grip on one's natural enthusiasm, and reveal through the voice that excitement which is justified'.[22] Interviewed with him, Captain Wakelam, the first rugby commentator, who also covered soccer, cricket and tennis, stressed that there were different sorts of audience. Some needed to 'be told the finer and more intricate points' while some merely wished 'to be entertained'. John Reith, the BBC Director-General, wanted broadcasters to educate, inform and entertain and this balance between what media sociologist Gary Whannel (1992: 27) has called 'naturalism' and 'construction', or 'realism' and 'entertainment', appears to have been a constant challenge for broadcasters. Unlike newsreels, radio rarely tried to make sports a subject for humour. The reporting of sport by the BBC, an institution which under Reith's leadership acquired a reputation for upholding moral rectitude, reflected and probably added to perceptions of the respectability and social acceptability of sport.

Radio sports coverage by the late 1920s consisted largely of key individual events like those above plus flat racing classics and prestige events such as rugby and soccer internationals, the Boat Race, the Amateur Golf Championship and Wimbledon. Cricket test matches always had a special place, although not in the form of a running commentary, but with regular reports of play. Cricket's slower pace was not thought amenable to live coverage. Sport coverage expanded in the 1930s. By 1931 there were better transmitters, more regional sports programmes, such as 'Midland Sport', and more broadcasting of results. On 27 June 1932 the *Manchester Guardian* reported that the BBC had broadcast three and a quarter hours of running commentary, 'the first occasion a programme so ambitious has been undertaken'. By 1934 the BBC was regularly offering whole afternoons of organised sport, with rapid shifts from one sport to another. As coverage grew, leading newspaper sport journalists were hired to add specialist expertise alongside experienced commentators. The racing writer Quintin Gilby, for example, who had first provided description for the 1927 St Leger, was by 1937 describing the parade and course topography for major races at Epsom, Newmarket and Ascot (Gilbey 1970: 157). In the later 1930s more sports were covered, including clay pigeon shooting, darts, fencing, gliding, pigeon racing, racquets, speedway, baseball and table tennis, though greyhound racing had little live commentary. Regular foregrounding of a sport or team helped raise its profile. Arsenal, featured often in the early 1930s, became a glamorous, fashionable club, attracting the metropolitan middle classes through its successful efforts at self-promotion. By contrast, annual broadcasts of the Rugby League Challenge Cup Final at Wembley, a northern phenomenon, seems to have created little interest among middle-class rugby union followers in the South. The BBC provided little sports news in the 1920s so as not to interfere with sales of evening newspapers, but slowly expanded its Saturday evenings sports coverage in the 1930s. In 1937 it announced that 'sports experts have been added to the news staff, with the objective of making the sports service as efficient and as comprehensive as is possible in the time available' (Briggs 1965: 158).

BBC sport broadcasting was not without tension. No betting news was broadcast between the wars. Some sporting bodies feared that broadcasting would have a detrimental effect on match attendances and their demands to be paid for permitting broadcasts clashed with the BBC ideology of radio being a public service. The BBC pursued an intermittent cultural and economic battle with the FA and the Football League. When rights to the 1929 Cup Final were refused, eyewitness reports by relays of commentators proved unsuccessful. In early 1930 the FA withdrew all rights to broadcast cup-ties without a compensatory fee. The BBC offered £200 to a charity of the FA's choice, and Gerald Cock, the head of outside broadcasting, pointed out that the BBC was 'analogous to a newspaper' and that press reporters paid no fee. Cock complained that FA opposition stemmed from the League clubs, 'professionals whose whole interest apparently is commercial'. In order to appeal to the more conservative mindset of

FA officials, he adopted a more Corinthian, amateurist approach laced with public service rhetoric. He claimed that the 'blind, the invalid and the poor' could listen, and that broadcasts 'actually increase and spread interest in the sports described'. He also published the correspondence with the FA.[23] Much of the resulting post-bag unsurprisingly supported the BBC. This caused the FA to back down and allow the 1930 final to be broadcast.[24]

The FA, however, agreed thereafter only to the broadcasting of the Cup semi-finals and final and international matches. League clubs with poorer gates were particularly worried about potential negative effects of radio coverage, believing that it affected 'gate' money not only of the club being broadcast, but also at other important matches in the neighbourhood, and for smaller struggling clubs across the country. Evidence from crowd figures was inconclusive. Clubs opposed to broadcasting produced examples of diminished gates but other factors such as the intrinsic importance of the match, the proximity of other important matches, the local economic situation or weather conditions could also affect attendances. Initially decisions about allowing the broadcasting of League games were left to individual clubs, but in March 1931 a well-attended meeting of League clubs called on the League to prohibit all broadcasts. Soon afterwards the League banned all live broadcasts, modifying its view only slightly in 1937.

Sport aided the BBC's cultural role. Broadcasting sport helped the BBC to appear more democratic and less élitist. Along with broadcasts of civic occasions such as the trooping of the colour and religious festivals, coverage of major sport events helped the BBC to become what Paddy Scannell and David Cardiff have called '*perhaps* the central agent of the national culture as its calendrical role' which 'not only coordinates social life, but gives it a renewable content, anticipatory pleasures, a horizon of expectations' (Scannell and Cardiff 1991: 278–79). By 1939 a BBC sports broadcasting style had emerged, especially in its treatment of national sporting events, helping to explain the nation to itself. Sport broadcasts emphasised major sporting events as national rituals and contributed to a clearer sense of nationhood. Sport was presented as 'respectable'. Live reports provided more animation than press news and domesticated sport by bringing it into the home (Crisell 1997: 8). Broadcasts gave listeners a sense of being present at an event. Some women who had showed little interest in sport were thrilled by broadcast accounts of play, and became more interested in the newsreel and press reports of sporting drama. Radio fostered inclusivity for the blind and the infirm. A London listener wrote to the BBC that 'an invalid blind boy whom we visit told us that he was able by listening to the running commentary to get a better idea of the football matches than seeing brothers who went in person'. A Stockport man suffering long-term ill-health wrote that

> to one who has played the game and taken a great interest in sport, you can quite understand the great pleasure your minute description of the games

has given to me. May I just mention the Arsenal club and directors to thank them for allowing the broadcasting and I can tell them they have thousands of supporters and well-wishers in the north.[25]

Such letters suggest a limited nationwide broadening of Arsenal's fan base, pre-dating the better-recognised impact of television in eroding local loyalties. Radio also gave a voice to ordinary people in sports crowds. Their strident voices could sometimes be heard far above the commentary and the general crowd noise. A few were interviewed for vox-pop 'Man in the Street' features. A woman told one interviewer that 'a fight is more exciting on the wireless than when you are actually there'; a blacksmith 'liked a good fight commentary'; but a Leeds advertising clerk believed that while more boxing match commentaries would please him, 'some of the commentators on the fights you do broadcast are not good enough – not detailed and not technical enough'.[26]

The BBC started the world's first regular television service in 1936. Its first outside television broadcast was a golf demonstration in October 1936. In 1937 there was limited experimental sports coverage, including the Wimbledon tennis championships and FA Cup Final. By 1938 the BBC had grown more confident, extending its coverage to other national sporting events such as the Boat Race and the Derby. In 1937 the BBC also started *Sporting Magazine*, a monthly review of sporting matters. Yet as no more than 25,000 sets had been sold by August 1939 and as pictures could only be received in the south east, television can hardly be regarded as one of the mass media. Its power to transform the representation and economics of sport was still far in the future.

Representations of sport
Celebrity, stars and heroes

Sporting stars pursued their skills under a brighter media spotlight between the wars. Their 'talent', 'magic' and 'gifts' were increasingly stressed. The names of leading cricketers, jockeys and boxers were widely known. Newsreel coverage of sport in the 1930s increased their visual recognition, and other sports personalities, most especially from tennis and golf, began to rival them. In 1925 Sir Ernest Holderness, president of the English Golf Union, wrote that because golf was not a 'national game' in England as it was in Scotland, the winner of the Open Championship could pass unnoticed at Charing Cross Station whereas in Glasgow 'every passenger and porter will take an interest in him'.[1] By the later 1930s professional golfer Henry Cotton, who 'challenged American supremacy in the golf world and came out on top', had become regularly featured in the media, lauded as the 'famous Open Champion, probably the greatest golfer in the world'.[2]

Leading players in sports which attracted relatively few spectators or received only cursory London press or newsreel coverage tended to be known only to those with a special interest in them. No male or female hockey or badminton player, for example, seems to have been a household name between the wars. Amateur non-graduate rower Jack Beresford, the sportsmanlike, well-mannered winner of three Olympic gold medals, was little known outside rowing circles. Whilst some soccer teams achieved national recognition, only their leading players were widely known outside their town. Perhaps this was due to the stress by the establishment classes on cricket as England's national sport or to the lower status of professionalism. Great Britain's superb rugby league scrum-half, Jonty Parkin, who played for Wakefield Trinity from 1913 to 1930, was idolised there, but scarcely known outside Lancashire and Yorkshire.

The trappings of stardom were still restrained compared with that of modern sporting 'celebrities'.[3] They were generally on a larger scale than pre-1914, though no sports personality from the inter-war period became as celebrated as the Victorian cricketer W.G. Grace. While there are no objective methods for measuring celebrity, impressionistic evidence suggests that while the biggest names of inter-war sport were well known the royal family was more immediately recognisable, simply through continuous media coverage. Because more people paid to visit the cinema than to watch sport, leading film stars such as Charlie Chaplin, Rudolf Valentino or Gracie Fields were probably the next most widely recognised. Prime ministers, too, were perhaps more recognisable than many sport stars. But regular press exposure, appearances in newsreels and on cigarette cards, stardom in short films such as Steve Donoghue's *Riding for a King* (1925) or sporting cameos in longer feature films such as *The Arsenal Stadium Mystery* (1939) ensured that some became household names, enjoying wider celebrity than the writers, painters and sculptors who received the critical acclaim of the educated classes.

Who were the biggest stars of English sport between the wars?

Inter-war sports stars were not all English or even British. Leading foreign boxers such as Jack Dempsey, Georges Carpentier, Max Schmeling or Gene Tunney received as least as much coverage as their less successful English equivalents. Don Bradman, the most famous Australian of the twentieth century, whose first-class cricket career began in 1927, was famous in Britain too, heralded as the 'young Australian wonder batsman' in 1930, and interviewed on *Movietone*.[4]

Trawls though the sporting press, newsreels and sporting books provide some indication of the biggest sporting names in England between the wars. Steve Donoghue and Gordon Richards, both champion jockeys, were the best-known racing men. In the 1920s Jack Hobbs was the leading cricket star, the man small boys pretended to be, and by the late 1920s many regarded Wally Hammond as the second biggest name, though cricket *aficionados* had difficulty in deciding whether to place Herbert Sutcliffe ahead of Frank Woolley, Harold Larwood or Wilfred Rhodes. In the 1930s Fred Perry and Henry Cotton were well known. No professional English football player in England approached the sporting pre-eminence of Hobbs but Charlie Buchan, David Jack, Stanley Matthews and William Ralph 'Dixie' Dean were all famous. Dean was an especially favoured pin-up in the sporting press, and regularly featured in *Pathe* newsreels, such as the silent 'Give it to Dixie' in 1926, an interview with the *Sunday Express* sports editor Charles Eade in 1933, or the 1939 'Dixie Dean is in the news again' when he reached the FA of Ireland Cup Final with Sligo Rovers. The emphasis in rugby union on being a sport in which the game was more important than any individual perhaps explains why none of its players became a household name between the wars, although Prince Obolensky's miraculous try against the All Blacks was well remembered. The pilot Alan Cobham was well known, as were the drivers Henry Segrave and Malcolm Campbell. Women pilots received particular publicity. Amy Johnson, like American Amelia Earhart, featured regularly in the newsreels, meeting with the Australian cricketers in 1930, or driving in the Monte Carlo rally and visiting the National Women's Air Reserve at Romford in 1938. In part this perhaps stemmed from astonishment at women showing an aptitude for activities previously monopolised by men. When Winifred Brown beat 87 men to win the King's Cup Air Race round England in 1930 it received blanket newsreel and newspaper attention.

Sportswomen were less well known than sportsmen. This was unsurprising, since more men played and watched sport, and male sport was widely considered more important. In 1934 Fred Perry won the Men's Singles Championship at Wimbledon and Dorothy Round the Ladies' Singles Championship. This was the first time that both titles had been won by English players in the same year since before the war, and the press devoted more space to Perry, though this may have been because no Englishman had won the singles title since 1909. In the media, two leading foreign women tennis stars, Susanne Lenglen and Helen Wills Moody, received more sustained attention than English players such as Kitty Godfree, Dorothy Round, Kay Stammers or even Betty Nuthall, who won the American lawn tennis championship in 1930, a feat greeted enthusiastically with the headline 'Bravo Betty' by the English press. *British Movietone News* celebrated, saying 'with all our championships going to the USA it is all the more pleasing', and Nuthall was featured in the newsreels again as her Atlantic liner docked, but she never managed to win Wimbledon.[5] In golf and cricket, sports played by both sexes, no woman achieved equivalent fame to that of the main male players. Women who competed successfully against men received only fleeting fame, perhaps because they played sports that attracted little press interest. The Honourable Mrs Victoria Bruce won short-lived fame when she established the world record for driving the longest distance in 24 hours. Marjorie Foster, the markswoman who won the King's Prize at Bisley in 1930, against nearly 1,000 entrants from across the Empire, many with military backgrounds, received more press coverage than previous male winners, probably because it was so remarkable for a woman to succeed in a little-known male-dominated rifle sport.

In cricket the benefits awarded to county cricket professionals after ten or more years of first team appearances provide a rough guide to which professional players were held in the highest esteem, although reports of county cricketers' benefit income usually took up only one or two lines in the national press, suggesting limited wider interest. Usually benefits were higher at the better-supported counties, unless adversely affected by wet weather, though some insured against this. Seven cricketers received benefits of more than £2,500 between the wars. Yorkshireman Roy Kilner received the highest, £4,016, in 1925. His total was nearly £1,500 more than the far better-known Hammond received at Gloucestershire in 1934, and more than that of Herbert Sutcliffe, the Yorkshire player regarded as one of England's best-ever opening batsmen. Benefits also shed some light on who were the most popular players at a particular county. At Lancashire the average inter-war benefit was around £1,500. Charlie Hallows' £2,906 was the highest, more than the £2,458 of the more distinguished Ernest Tyldesley, but Hallows had performed the very rare feat of scoring 1,000 runs before the end of May in his benefit year. It is improbable that a player could have received a high benefit by his county's standards without being popular. In football transfer fees were a similar indication of star potential. Up to December 1925 the highest transfer fee paid was £6,500 by Newcastle United for Hughie Gallacher, but in October 1928 Arsenal paid the first five-figure fee, £10,340, for David Jack.

Racehorses and dogs could be stars too. Leading horses like Golden Miller or Papyrus did not match the fame of the leading jockeys, though one racehorse, Brown Jack, was given a 1934 biography (Lyle 1934). The greyhound Mick The Miller who won fifty-one races, including twenty-one major trophies, in England between 1929 and 1931, was more famous than any greyhound trainer or owner, regularly featuring in the press, having his retirement after his October St Leger win covered in the newsreels, and even starring in his own feature film, *Wild Boy*, in 1934 (Tanner 2003).

Sports players received more sporting fame than sport administrators, who were rarely well known. Most followers of first-class cricket would probably have heard of Lords Harris and Hawke, who were very much involved with the running of the Kent and Yorkshire clubs, and who were also powerful figures at the MCC, but their fame may have owed much to their being both aristocratic and former England captains. Professional cricket administrators such as William Findlay, secretary of the MCC from 1926 to 1936, and Frederick Toone, secretary of Yorkshire from 1903 to 1930 and manager of three MCC tours to Australia, were mentioned by the popular press only occasionally. Charles Clegg, president of the Football Association, and Frederick Wall, its secretary from 1895 to 1934, also received limited attention from the popular press. Being chairman of a Football League club might bring local renown but little national fame. Herbert Chapman, who masterminded Huddersfield Town's three league championships in the 1920s and then made Arsenal the leading English football club in the late 1920s and early 1930s, was the first football manager to become as well known as leading players, not least because he reputedly earned £1,500 a year. The secretary of the FA, ex-referee S.F. Rous, earned a salary rising to the same amount, but was far less well known (Johnston 1934: 23). In speedway the promoters and track managers Johnny Hoskins and Ronnie Greene attracted much attention because they were flamboyant personalities who generated publicity for the sport. Devotees of horseracing knew the leading racehorse trainers but in many sports coaches had a low profile, although in the rowing world Fairbairn, the Australian who coached London and Weybridge rowing clubs, was probably as well known as any oarsman. No referee or umpire between the wars achieved as much celebrity as Dickie Bird in recent years. No woman achieved general fame as a sports administrator or coach between the wars.

Only a few sports journalists were known to the sporting public, since many, and particularly racing journalists, wrote under pseudonyms. In the 1920s the main football writer for *Athletic News* was 'Tityrus' and its main

LIBRARY, UNIVERSITY OF CHESTER

cricket writer 'The Gentleman in Black'. Neville Cardus' cricket reports in the *Manchester Guardian* appeared under the by-line 'Cricketer'. Many sport reports were totally anonymous or were written by 'Our Cricket Correspondent' or 'Our Rugby Correspondent'. The sports cartoonist Tom Webster of the *Daily Mail* was the highest-paid cartoonist in the world in 1924 and Trevor Wignall, who had a daily column in the *Daily Express* in which he commented on a wide range of sporting topics, was paid 'a huge salary' which could mean that some sport journalists were thought to have reputations that helped to sell newspapers (Bingham 2004: 218). Cardus was perhaps the only sportswriter in England whose books brought him fame as a literary artist. Some sports radio broadcasters become famous between the wars. Captain Wakelam was perhaps the best known, thanks to rugby commentaries for the BBC and *British Movietone News*. Bernard Darwin was widely known as a golf journalist, radio broadcaster and author. No woman seems to have become widely known as a sports journalist. Marjorie Pollard wrote on women's cricket and hockey for the *Morning Post* but her reports were usually only one or two paragraphs.

Not all stars of English sport were English. Henry Segrave had an American father and had been born in Ireland but was very much regarded as an English sport star. Billy Meredith, one of the biggest names of pre-war English football, who played on into the early 1920s, was a Welsh international. Alex James, the scheming inside forward of Arsenal's successful side in the late 1920s and early 1930s, and Hughie Gallagher, the Newcastle and Chelsea centre forward, were both Scottish. Jim Sullivan at Wigan and Gus Risman at Salford, perhaps the two most famous rugby league players, came from Wales. In boxing, Jimmy Wilde, world flyweight champion from 1916 to 1923, came from Wales, as did leading British heavyweight contender Tommy Farr. Benny Lynch, world flyweight champion from 1935 to 1938, came from Glasgow. The American professional golfer Walter Hagen won the British Open Championship four times in the 1920s but was not always regarded with affection in English golf, not least because of his flamboyant display of wealth in the face of his exclusion from members' club rooms. When he retired in 1938 a *Golf Illustrated* editorial praised him for his 'inordinately shrewd' judgement and for being 'a great loser'. Pettiness in any form was 'foreign to his nature, and he was always big, whether playing the game of golf, the game of life, or in his dealings with his fellows'. It accepted that 'he attracted the crowd however he was playing', but felt that 'over here, he was not universally popular, for he was often outspoken'.[6]

Stars and spectator numbers

Events where the biggest names were competing were more likely to attract higher numbers of spectators, depending on the weather and the day of the week when an event was held. When Henry Cotton opened Chadwick Manor Golf Club in March 1938 *Gaumont British News* reported that 'there was a gathering of six or seven hundred people to watch, a surprising number, which testifies to Cotton's drawing power'.[7] When Fred Perry reached his third Wimbledon final in 1936, long queues waited through the previous night for tickets. In football some indication of the drawing power of stars was the number of spectators they attracted to away matches. Brian Tabner (1992: 145–47) has calculated for every season from 1888–89 to 1991–92 which three Football League clubs had the highest average number of spectators at their away matches. From 1929–30 to 1938–39, Arsenal was always the club with most spectators at its away matches, which reflected its reputation, its playing success with five league championships and two FA Cup final wins, and its top players such as Alex James and Eddie Hapgood.

In the late 1920s and 1930s the phenomenal batting power of Don Bradman made him the biggest star of Australian cricket. Days when he was expected to bat attracted raised attendance. The extent to which English cricket stars attracted similarly higher than average numbers of spectators is less clear, since English counties did not record the attendance of members, whose subscriptions gave them free admission to matches and also the right to be accompanied by a guest who was also admitted free, so full data are lacking. Anecdotal evidence suggests that Hobbs' appearance could add to spectator numbers. In 1934, his last season, when his captain allowed him to choose in which matches he played, George Duckworth, the Lancashire and England wicket-keeper, whose benefit match was against Surrey, pleaded with Hobbs to play in this match, presumably because he expected that this would increase crowd numbers.

At the highest levels of league cricket in the North and Midlands, clubs had long recognised that professionals with national or international reputations could boost gate receipts, even if an increase in gate receipts did not always cover their higher wages. The West Indian professional Learie Constantine had great spectator appeal. A big-hitting batsman, fast bowler and brilliant fielder, he played in an exciting style. *Pathe Gazette* once described him as 'the coloured catapult, [who] played superb cricket'.[8] In 1934 he took ten wickets in an innings for ten runs and scored 124 in just over an hour, and in 1937 made 192, a huge individual score for a league cricket match. The writer Don Haworth (1986: 29) recalled that when Constantine went to bat, the 'whole crowd rose in a buzz of excitement', and believed that Constantine appealed to spectators who wanted cricket played 'fast and violently', like football. In Nelson, where he was the Lancashire League club's professional from 1929 to 1937, it was said that Constantine generated excitement like 'a man walking a tightrope without a safety net' (Giuseppe 1974: 43). His spectator appeal was also related to his being a black man in a part of Lancashire where black people were rare. Between 1929 and 1933 Nelson's fixtures constituted only one-seventh of all Lancashire League matches but provided three-quarters of the League's total gate receipts.[9] Probably more than 75,000 paid to watch Nelson's home matches in 1929, over 65,000 in 1930 and over 50,000 in

1932, 1934 and 1935. In 1934 and 1935 Nelson had more paying spectators at its home matches than either the Leicestershire or Northamptonshire county clubs.

The construction of sporting celebrity

What qualities were needed to become stars? Despite claims that taking part was more important than winning, sporting success was essential, and international competition usually brought fame, even if not always heroic status or great affection. When he won the Wimbledon Men's Singles Championship for the first time, amateur Fred Perry thought that this was not welcomed by some of the All-England Club establishment because of his less privileged background but this could also have been because of his brash personality, and his ruthless will to win. He overheard Sir Samuel Hoare, the Conservative cabinet minister and president of the LTA, remark that he was 'not one of us' like his opponent in the final, the Australian Jack Crawford. In 1934, when professional Henry Cotton became the first British golfer to win the Open Championship for eleven years, he received further praise for refusing to go to America because he believed that 'victory in the British Open is too great an honour to be exploited abroad'. He wanted his victory to be seen as a British success, and felt that it was 'time we rid ourselves of this terrible inferiority complex in sport'.[10] Cotton, like Perry, provided an indication that some conventions of amateurism were beginning to be challenged.

Cricketers playing well in test matches against Australia always attracted respect and popularity, though when England won the Ashes on the 1932–33 tour captain Douglas Jardine's initial fame soon tarnished, as it became felt that England's bodyline tactics had not been entirely fair. Tony Mason (1990: 162) has shown that being selected for England made a football player a special hero in the town where he played, especially if this was an unfashionable club. No England footballer, however, seems to have became a national hero on the strength of one outstanding performance for the national side similar to Nat Lofthouse's game against Austria in 1952 or Geoff Hurst's hat-trick in the 1966 World Cup Final.

Olympic success rarely received great acclaim. Even during the Olympics newspapers gave more coverage to sports events in England. In 1936 the press did not celebrate at great length British gold medal winners, but lamented that there had been so few of them. The newsreels reported the New Zealander Jack Lovelock's world record in the 1,500 metres, but otherwise gave similarly limited coverage. Lovelock was not made a star. Reporting of Britain's winning of the ice hockey gold medal at the 1936 Winter Olympics was similarly low key. The most extensive coverage was probably provided by the *Daily Express*, which gave daily profiles of the players. As the ice hockey team consisted mainly of players born in Britain but raised in Canada, who had come to Britain solely to play ice hockey, this may have limited the celebration of their success. Three weeks after winning the Olympic title, one writer commented that

> the victors have been forgotten. For all anybody else knows England haven't got an ice hockey team at all … members of the team came dribbling back home in ones and twos and the pride of the ice hockey world arrived unheralded and unsung.[11]

Sport stars provided a strong focus for local identities. The achievements of famous sport stars could be a source of local pride and gratitude. The holding of civic receptions and tours through the main streets when a team or player won a national or regional competition, or succeeded in national or international competitions, which had started before the First World War, continued between the wars, and allowed local politicians to cash in on stars' popularity. After her King's Prize win Marjorie Foster was carried home to Frimley by the local fire engine and given a car with money raised by local subscription. Diana Fishwick, winner of the 1930 Women's Open Golf Tournament, rode in an open-top car with the Mayor to a civic reception in Broadstairs, with a brass band in attendance, to the applause of a large crowd. In 1938, when Stanley Matthews asked Stoke City for a transfer, 3,000 attended a public meeting, and a further thousand were outside, to call for an agreement between the club's directors and the player. A leading local industrialist declared that having three internationals in the Stoke team reflected credit on all of North Staffordshire (Mason 1990: 164). The funeral of Roy Kilner, a current Yorkshire and England cricketer when he died in 1928, demonstrated the appreciation that a locality felt for a man who had achieved regional and national acclaim. The presence of the local MP at the funeral and the heading of the funeral procession by Wombwell Town Band, the local St John's Ambulance Corps and the Wombwell Church Lads Brigade all indicated high esteem for Kilner. *The Times* suggested that 100,000 had lined the streets, one of the largest crowds ever gathered in the Barnsley district. The funeral was the leading front-page story of the *Barnsley Chronicle*.[12]

Playing in the right style, demonstrating skill, showing abilities that were far beyond those of the followers of a sport, were also important. Jack Hobbs was often praised for executing all the batting strokes with textbook precision.[13] In 1935 a contributor to the *National Review* praised the cricketer Frank Woolley for his 'particular quality of excitement and surprise', claiming that 'never, even when playing a game more patient than his nature, is he dull to watch … When he opens his shoulders for a drive, Jove thunders' (Warner 1935: 104, 785). Position, in a team sport, affected opportunities to reveal skills that could catch the eye of spectators. So backs in both rugby codes had more opportunities to sparkle than forwards. In football the skills of forwards were more easily noted than those of defenders. Tony Mason has argued that the national drawing power of Stanley Matthews, though more particularly in the years immediately after the Second World War, was related to his skill and relatively unimpressive physique. Matthews did not look bigger, stronger nor even more obviously physically gifted than many who turned up to watch. *You* could be him, with a bit of luck. You *might* have been, if things had turned out differently. He was the epitome of the ordinary bloke who became a star.

(Mason 1990: 175)

Some played to the gallery to gain popularity. The Lancashire and England bowler Cecil Parkin sometimes clowned to amuse cricket crowds. The Old Etonian cricket writer and publisher Sir Home Gordon called Constantine 'a shrewd chap, who felt that it paid to clown … he once broadly hinted as much' (1939: 105). The speedway rider Frank Varey tried to boost his spectator appeal by having his engines tuned so that they had a louder and higher pitch than those of other riders. In football some goalkeepers may have tried to make their saves seem more spectacular. Professional wrestlers played to the gallery all the time.

When success was unaccompanied by style, some commentators complained. In 1933 Neville Cardus grumbled about the '"old soldier", the professional who takes a hard, realistic view of his job'. Some professionals, he felt, were 'too realistic, too utilitarian' and put too much emphasis on 'staying there'.[14] Such qualities were probably much admired by some supporters in Yorkshire and Lancashire, the counties which won the county championship most often in the 1920s and 1930s. The Middlesex and England batsman Patsy Hendren pointed out that for a batsman 'high scores' were the way to the top in cricket. 'The scores', he argued, 'must be big enough to get people talking about you. Once the big scores begin to come the talk will follow. The newspapers will begin to give details of those innings which are being played.' He also argued, however, that 'spectacular shots … must be cut out of the repertoire because the risk is too great, so long as the necessity of making big scores which will compel attention remain' (Hendren 1934: 12–13).

Earnings of sports players were generally less than in America, and there was less media interest in them. American-owned *British Movietone News* reported Babe Ruth's signing to play baseball for £16,000 a year but there were no similar British newsreel stories. The press did, however, report the large sums paid to successful boxers and jockeys and the prize money available at professional golf tournaments. An English champion jockey earned most, not much less than £20,000 a year in total by 1935 (Huggins 2003: 162–63). In 1937 the *People* mentioned that Fred Perry had earned £234 a day during his first 52 days with the Elsworth Vines USA professional tennis circuit but the tone of its comment was one of amazement rather than approbation.[15] The respect for amateurism helps to account for the lack of emphasis on the earnings of sports players but the flaunting of wealth was often frowned on in inter-war England. Rugby union players who switched to rugby league where players were paid were ostracised in the rugby union world. Fred Perry was a tennis 'shamateur' for some years, supposedly representing Slazenger abroad, but when he turned professional in 1936, he not only forfeited his eligibility to play for the Wimbledon and other major championships and the Davis Cup, but had his membership of the All-England Club withdrawn. The sporting press was relatively mild in its comments, while *The Times* asked what player 'unless he were wealthy, would forgo the opportunity of making a fortune of the size put forward to stagger us (even allowing for exaggerations) if he had Perry's ability to earn it?' But it lamented that tennis had become 'so grim and strenuous in modern times' that 'never again are we likely to find men leaving their offices and going down to Wimbledon to win the championship'.[16] When the prominent young amateur golfer, middle-class Dulwich College-educated Henry Cotton, turned professional it was unusual, and while it helped to raise the status of the game, he was thought too much influenced by American attitudes.

The media, which helped construct sporting celebrity, were the major source through which sport followers learned about sporting deeds. The cinema made heavyweight Bombardier Wells a boxing celebrity despite his lack of international success. Adrian Bingham (2004: 222) has argued that editorial pressures in the 1920s for 'human interest' led to more emphasis on individual performances and the creation of heroes. Yet newspapers largely ignored the personal lives of players, concentrating almost entirely on their sporting exploits. Wives, girlfriends and families came more into the press spotlight in the 1930s, with the growth in women readers, and engagements and weddings of sports stars were then more regularly featured in newsreels. In 1934, very soon after he had won the Wimbledon Singles title, the *Daily Mail* carried two pictures of Fred Perry and his fiancée Mary Lawson, but this may also have owed something to Lawson being an actress. The *Lancashire Daily Post* ran a feature on 'Preston North End Wives' in spring 1937. In September 1937 *British Movietone News* announced a 'Tennis Champion's Wedding: Dorothy Round becomes Mrs Little', showing cheering crowds and women waving. By contrast, divorces and philandering received passing, if any, newspaper comment and rarely on the sports pages. When the former England cricketer Eddie Paynter was asked about Wally Hammond, his immediate response was to say that Hammond 'liked a shag' (Frost 1996: 172). The press ignored Hammond's womanising. Gambling debts and drink problems were likewise rarely reported.

To an extent the popular press attributed differing kinds of masculinity to male film and sport stars (Bingham 2004: 225). Male film stars were presented as 'handsome and sophisticated', winning 'male admiration and envy by exhibiting the sort of charm that won the hearts of beautiful women'. There was limited comment on the sexual attraction of male sport players in the press, though newsreels, like feature films, sometimes focused on appearance. The Corinthian football side were 'beautiful, bold and brilliant' in 1923.[17] A university Boat Race crew in 1926 were described as 'the handsomest crew since the war'.[18] Herbert Sutcliffe, with his glossy black hair and silk shirts, was urbane and debonair, supposedly the Clark Gable of cricket. One can also argue that the screen roles of film stars often emphasised similar qualities to those of sports stars: courage, physical prowess, toughness and observing the rules, while being individualists who put the interests of others before themselves.

Newspapers commented more often on the physical appearance of women sport players. Here 'feminine' qualities such as grace and elegance were the most stressed. The German ice-skating star Sonia Henie received newsreel praise for 'beauty and grace par excellence. Loveliness in line, litheness of movement in excelsis ... skating wizardry ... so perfect as to be unreal', and her younger English rival Cecilia Colledge got similar coverage.[19] Yet articles such as that by Lady Heath in 1928 headed 'Athletic Women ARE Beautiful' suggested a widespread belief that women sports players lacked physical attraction.[20] But like men, playing success was women's route to sports stardom. They were commended by the press for demonstrating that the physical capabilities of women were greater than had been assumed.

The press usually presented sport stars as admirable role models and heroes. Stars were expected to observe 'approved' forms of conventional conduct. In this respect the press may have been reflecting a widely held conviction though this could have strengthened support for such views. Funeral addresses and press comments on sport players who died at the peak of their powers suggest the qualities star players were expected to personify. Sportsmanship was mentioned most regularly. At Roy Kilner's funeral the former England cricket captains J.W.H.T. Douglas and F.T. Mann both stressed his sportsmanship. J.J. Booth, president of the Bradford Cricket League, described him as 'a bluff Yorkshireman, very honest and straightforward, a sportsman whom all admired'.[21] When Henry Segrave was killed in a motorboat crash in 1930 shortly after setting a world land speed record, the Prince of Wales and the Prime Minister were represented at the funeral, which was also attended by Sir Philip Sassoon, Countess Howe, Lord Louis Mountbatten and Sir George Armstrong. The ushers included three lords. A *Times* editorial praised Segrave's courage, determination, vitality and devotion to an end while an editorial in the *Daily Express* recalled his 'epic quality of adventure ... in his calm face but alert blue eyes there was the look of a man who knows no fear save that of failure'.[22] His obituary in the *Daily Telegraph* described how Segrave's records and Britain's winning of the Schneider Trophy had created 'a pardonable feeling of national exultation' while the *Daily Mail* emphasised that Segrave and those killed with him 'believed that it was important to raise British prestige and demonstrate the magnificent quality of British engineering'. It asked who could say that 'brave, alert young Englishmen' should avoid risking death in such enterprises.[23] At the funeral of famous Arsenal manager Herbert Chapman, which attracted a congregation of 800 and over 240 wreaths, the service stressed how he 'stood out for good sportsmanship on the field' (Studd 1998: 140).

Much respect was accorded to those who displayed great skill yet seemed to be modest and unremarkable in other ways. Stars were expected to be modest about their success and gracious towards opponents. In 1934 the English tennis star Bunny Austin, the first to dress in shorts and casual shirts, kicked his racket into the crowd at Wimbledon during his match with the American F. Shields. Austin claimed that showing 'some sign of irritation at a bad shot [was] surely no more than is to be expected'. Many disagreed. Geoffrey Simpson, whose daily 'Clubhouse Chair' column in the *Daily Mail* covered many sports, wrote that 'Self-control is just as important in lawn tennis as brilliant ball-control.' He argued that if 'a brilliant player behaves like a spoiled child, the public has a habit of remembering his manners more than his play'.[24] The *News of the World* praised Dorothy Round's 'dignity on the courts, her smiling appreciation of an opponent's skill, her charming air of resigned acceptance when she has blundered' and described them as 'an example to all athletes'. It described her as 'the best advertisement for English character and sportsmanship that lawn tennis can boast today ... the Sunday school teacher who has shown that the golden rules of good sportsmanship can be put into practice even at Wimbledon'.[25] Modesty was expected of post-match speeches too. At the dinner following the Wimbledon championship in 1934, Fred Perry said of Jack Crawford, whom he had defeated in the singles final, that when 'my time comes to be beaten, which will probably be next year, I hope I lose in the same charming manner as Jack did'. In her speech at this dinner, Dorothy Round said that she was 'proud, not in a boastful way, to have beaten Helen Jacobs because she is a good player, great fighter and a gallant sports woman'.[26] In 1936 Perry was shown by *Gaumont British News* at Lady Crosfield's garden party, making 'a modest little speech on his own victory'.[27] Even if their comments did not represent how Perry and Round felt, the fact that they made them, and their media coverage, are revealing about the qualities which those who achieved sporting success were expected to display. The emphasis in sport discourse on modesty perhaps explains why so few admitted that their sporting careers had been driven by a hunger for publicity.

The press hardly created any anti-heroes, sports players who acquired fame through their misdeeds or for violating established codes of sporting etiquette, though some became known for appearing to be victimised for standing up to the authorities in their sports. Harold Larwood refused to make a public apology for bowling bodyline during the Australian tour and was not selected for England again. Some felt the MCC had given him insufficient support, and when England played Australia at Nottingham there were cries from the crowd to reinstate him. Criticisms of the amateur England captain A.E.R. Gilligan by the eccentric England and Lancashire cricketer Cecil Parkin during 1924 ended his test career. He later argued that Gilligan should drop himself because of his poor form in Australia and be replaced as captain by the young amateur Percy Chapman under the guidance of professional 'Hobbs J.'. This led Lord Hawke, the president of Yorkshire, to cry, 'Pray God that no professional may ever captain England!', and say that if Parkin had been a Yorkshire player he would never have been allowed to set foot on a county ground again. The country was split. The English professionals touring Australia made a public protest about Hawke's comments, and plans to re-issue Hawke's memoirs had to be shelved.[28] But others clearly objected to Parkin's comments. His benefit in 1925 produced the relatively disappointing sum for a Lancashire player of £1,880, partly, perhaps, because his comments had caused some of the county's wealthy supporters not to contribute. The jockey Charlie Smirke, who was banned from racing for life after suspicions that he had ensured that his horse was left standing at the start, attracted some sympathy for appearing to be a victim of the Jockey Club, since the horse was known as a rogue. Smirke was allowed to race again some five years later, but only after it was intimated to the Jockey Club that the Prince of Wales believed that he been treated harshly.

The small number of sporting anti-heroes was also linked to the reluctance of the national press to provide details of infringements of sporting ethics and decorum. This was particularly the case with cricket. In 1924 Middlesex threatened not to play Yorkshire again following the misconduct on the field of play at Sheffield by Abe Waddington, the Yorkshire fast bowler, but no newspaper provided details of what Waddington had done. The *News of the World* commented that Lancashire and Nottinghamshire had also experienced 'incidents' at Sheffield, but these too were ignored by the press.

The prestige of sporting fame

There is much to suggest that among the political establishment and economic élite sporting fame was not greatly respected. Sports stars were unlikely to be knighted or receive other official honours. No professional footballer was mentioned in the New Year Honours List until 1957. Those from the world of sport who were knighted were usually administrators, although admittedly some were former players. Examples included William Findlay, secretary of the MCC, the test selector and journalist Pelham Warner, who had captained England before the First World War, the Yorkshire secretary Frederick Toone, who had been the manager of three MCC tours to Australia, Rowland Hill of the Rugby Union, the FA president Charles Clegg and Frederick Wall, secretary of the FA. The aviator Alan Cobham and the drivers Henry Segrave and Malcolm Campbell who set land speed records were knighted but this was partly because their records created world-wide publicity for British engineering. When Segrave returned to London after breaking the land speed record in America, he was received at Westminster Hall by Douglas Hacking, the Minister for Overseas Trade. In his speech Hacking emphasised that twenty-nine British manufacturers had made components for Segrave's Golden Arrow and that Segrave had demonstrated the 'excellence of British design, and British workmanship'. Hacking hoped that 'overseas buyers of motor-cars in every part of the world will take careful note of the pre-eminence and durability of British production'.[29] The knighthood for Cobham, who had taken part in air races and pioneered long distance flights, can also be seen as part of a campaign to boost British aeroplane production and to promote air travel, particularly as a means of imperial communication. In 1930, following Amy Johnson's solo flight to Australia, several newspapers regretted the absence of appropriate official honours for women who performed such feats (Bingham 2004: 75).

Obituaries of sport stars in the national press also suggest that sporting celebrity was not considered of great worth. *The Times* usually printed obituaries of sport stars on the sports pages rather than the normal obituary page. Its sport player obituaries were shorter than those of others far less well known to the general public. On 7 April 1928, for instance, Roy Kilner's obituary was half a column whereas that for Chauncey Depew, an American senator and railway magnate, ran to one and three quarter columns. In 1937 Walter Brearley, who played cricket for England before the First World War, had an obituary of half a column. That for the historian Spencer Wilkinson was three times longer. The England bowler B.J.T. Bosanquet who had invented the googly in the early twentieth century was exceptional in having a longer obituary than 12 others on the same day. Bobby Abel, perhaps the leading professional batsman of the late nineteenth century and early twentieth century, received no obituary in December 1936. The more popular *Express*, which printed fewer obituaries in general, had no obituary articles about Abel, Brearley or Bosanquet.

Sporting fame was not usually a springboard for a high profile career in another sphere though some sport players may have tired of the limelight. How many sport stars were invited to take up politics is not known. Some MPs were former Oxbridge cricket, rowing or rugby Blues though scarcely national sporting names. C.B. Fry, who had captained England at cricket before the First World War, played in an FA Cup Final and held the world long jump record, was defeated each time in the 1920s when he stood as a Liberal parliamentary candidate. F.S. Jackson was one of the best-known cricketers who went into politics. He had captained England against Australia in 1905 and was a Conservative MP from 1915 until 1926. He never became a cabinet minister but in 1922 was Financial Secretary to the War Office and in 1923 became Chairman of the Conservative Party. In 1927 he was made Governor of Bengal. How far Jackson's political career was related to his sporting fame cannot be calculated, but as the son of a lord, being educated at Harrow and Cambridge and being a director of Yorkshire Conservative Newspapers could have done more to further his political career. In 1931 the Olympic champion hurdler Lord Burghley became a Conservative MP but he was also the son of a peer. The Conservative peer Lord Aberdare's appointment as chairman of the National Fitness Council probably owed much to his playing cricket for Oxford and Middlesex and to being a champion racquets and real tennis player. In 1935 the Lancashire amateur cricket captain Peter Eckersley abandoned cricket when he was elected a Conservative MP. In 1937 the former rugby union international Wavell Wakefield was also returned as a Conservative MP. No professional cricketer, jockey, boxer or football player became an MP between the wars.

Sport stars made little effort to promote commercial products by capitalising on their fame. During their playing careers a few cricketers and football players were paid to advertise or endorse products, which provided a small-scale compensation for relatively short careers. 'Dixie' Dean, Everton's legendary centre forward, reputedly could earn up to £50 a session for doing so, and cup final teams regularly picked up endorsements. In the 1920s the cricketers Maurice Tate, Andy Sandham, Jack Hobbs and Patsy Hendren and the golf professional Archie Compston all advertised Sarony Virginia cigarettes, with Hobbs quoted as saying 'A Sarony after an innings or a spell of fielding is a pleasure indeed', even though in his autobiography he advised against smoking cigarettes.[30] He also advertised Waterman's pens. Girls were encouraged to 'have your bat autographed by Whysall the well-known county player'.[31] Some readers were more interested in books on how to play or improve their play, and this was the main area where sports players wrote (or had ghosted) publications. Hobbs, Risman and Denis Compton, for example, wrote for Foulsham's Sports' Library. Between the wars more than ten women tennis players wrote instructional books, while Marjorie Pollard's *Cricket for Women and Girls* traced the growth of cricket playing among women and tried to justify cricket as a game for women and girls. A handful of sport stars were employed in public relations. In 1938 the cricketer Wally Hammond was employed by the Firestone tyre company, but this may have been so that he would have an income that would enable him to play cricket as an amateur and be eligible to captain England. Former England cricket captains Lord Tennyson and Percy Chapman were employed in Percy Fender's wine business, perhaps in hope of boosting sales. The limited exploitation of sporting fame could also reflect the limited development of advertising and public relations and a lack of awareness about the commercial potential of sporting celebrity. Denis Compton in the late 1940s is thought to be the first sports player in England who hired an agent.

Sporting fame could be helpful to sports players who set up businesses but it is difficult to be sure about the extent of this, given that some lacked business acumen. Boxers, footballers and rugby players often became publicans in retirement, suggesting that breweries expected sporting fame would attract custom, although Billy Meredith, whose playing career for the two Manchester clubs stretched from the late 1890s to 1924, was a publican for fifteen years but was hard-up when he died in 1958 (Harding 1985: 207). The sports outfitting business that Cecil Parkin opened with Jack Mew, the Manchester United goalkeeper, in the 1920s did not last for long and was probably not a commercial success. Harold Larwood's venture into chicken farming in the late 1930s does not seem to have prospered. Very few sportswomen with national reputations tried to use their fame to launch business careers.

Definitions of amateurism restricted opportunities in some sports to exploit fame. In 1923 the Lawn Tennis Association decided that amateurs could be paid for writing about tennis but in 1928 it prohibited them from writing for the press about tournaments in which they were playing, though they could write about them at other times. Shortly afterwards the Rugby Union declared that players writing about matches was contrary to the spirit of rugby football and hoped the practice would stop.[32] In 1935 the LTA was prepared to support a proposal that the International Federation permit amateurs to be paid for appearing in coaching films. In the same year the wife of Bunny Austin wrote that her husband had never been paid by a racket manufacturer or an athletics outfitter.[33] In 1938 *Golf Illustrated* described Henry Cotton as having 'great business acumen'. In the same year it carried a whole page advertisement of Cotton endorsing Spalding wooden clubs. A comment in this magazine that amateur golfers received 'great publicity' but 'should never allow their names to be associated with anything which is tantamount to an advertising enterprise', may imply that some amateurs were paid by advertisers.[34] Scarcely any instances have been found of amateur cricketers advertising cricket equipment.

Hiring stars who were still playing to write for newspapers suggests that editors hoped this would boost circulation. But the numbers who wrote for the press were never very great, and most stars who wrote for newspapers during their playing careers did so for only a short time. The amateurs Percy Fender and Rockley Wilson were paid by newspapers when they toured Australia in 1920–21. In 1929 the fast bowler Harold Larwood had a weekly column in the *Sunday Chronicle*. In 1933, just after the bodyline tour, he was expecting £500 from the *Sunday Dispatch* for the serialisation rights of a book that was being ghosted for him (Larwood and Perkins 1965: 183). Hedley Verity, a member of the bodyline touring party, sent back reports for the *Yorkshire Evening News*. Former England player Jack Hobbs reported on the bodyline tour for the *Star*. Amy Johnson was hired as the flight correspondent of the *Daily Mail*. A few, such as cricketer Pelham Warner and footballer Charlie Buchan, became professional sport journalists after their playing careers. Not all who did this had been very big stars. The greatest achievement of Joe Binns, for instance, an athletics reporter for the *News of the World*, was the AAA mile championship in 1902. Very few sport players who became sport journalists moved into other areas of journalism.

Few sport stars were able to extend their fame to writing books about sport while they were playing. Very few sport players' autobiographies were printed between the wars. Three ghosted autobiographies of Jack Hobbs were published and books containing much autobiographical material were written by at least five other inter-war Test players and also by Learie Constantine and Lords Harris and Hawke, although neither Wilfred Rhodes nor Wally Hammond produced autobiographies. No professional football or rugby league players wrote autobiographies between the wars, though when Stanley Matthews' *Feet First* appeared in 1948, he mentioned that he had considered writing his autobiography in the 1930s. Two autobiographies by the jockey Steve Donoghue were published between the wars – *Just My Story* in 1923 and *Donoghue Up!* in 1938 – but the autobiography of Gordon Richards, an equally renowned inter-war jockey, was not published until 1955. Sprouts Elder and Frank Varey, two speedway riders, published their autobiographies in the 1930s. None of the Australians who raced regularly in England, or Jack Parker, often regarded as the leading English rider in the 1930s, did so. Fred Perry wrote his autobiography *My Story*, in 1934. Most autobiographies and biographies of sport players concentrated on playing exploits and contained little that was critical about how sport was organised, the ethos of sport or other players, although Constantine (1933: 170–73) was critical, but in very circumspect terms, of the West Indies always being captained by a white player. Joyce Wethered, who won the women's Open Golf Championship four times in the 1920s and the English Ladies Championship five times, was one of the very tiny number of sportswomen who wrote an autobiography and part of this consisted of advice on how to improve one's play (Wethered 1933). Autobiographies by two American Wimbledon champions, Helen Jacobs and Helen Moody, had English sales, but neither Kitty Godfree nor Dorothy Round, both Englishwomen who won inter-war Wimbledons, wrote one. Next to no details about the sales of sports autobiographies are available but no doubt more would have been issued had publishers believed that there was a great demand for them.

The effects of stars on sport

The publicity given to women sports players may well have encouraged other women to take up sport. The *Daily News* was convinced that girls would want to emulate in many fields what Amy Johnson had achieved in flying.[35] When in the mid 1930s British tennis, and men's tennis in particular, became more internationally competitive, the number of tennis clubs in England was rising but this may not have meant that stars such as Fred Perry and Bunny Austin were encouraging more to play. In the 1920s, when British tennis had less international success, the numbers who played were also rising. No doubt many boys played sport because they fantasised about becoming sport stars and for the poorer sections of the working class sport offered more prospects of celebrity than most other activities, but many adults who played must have known that they would never become well-known players. The praise heaped on stars who played in a sporting manner suggests a widespread assumption that recreational players could be influenced by the big names. Opponents of bodyline feared that it would be copied in club and school cricket. How quickly recreational players took up changes in sporting attire publicised by leading players is unclear, but endorsements of equipment by leading players suggests that they could affect recreational players.

Richard Holt and Tony Mangan (1996: 3) have pointed out that in the USA sport stars were celebrated as a validation of the American dream that its democratic society meant that with dedication one could go from rags to riches. In inter-war England the values surrounding sport caused unease about stars. The England cricket captain Douglas Jardine wrote that

> few will be found to admit that the hero-worship, almost amounting to idolatry to which, for example, Bradman was subject, is desirable for the

game's good, or fair to the individual ... this habit of extolling one man must naturally lead to the lack of appreciating others.

(Jardine n.d.: 60)

In 1930 the sport journalist Trevor Wignall wrote that footballers and boxers were often 'tin gods' but doubted whether any of them had 'ever reached the lofty pedestals on which the dirt-track monarchs so jauntily sit'. Originally speedway riders had been 'rather conscious of their place in the scheme of things' but they now comported themselves 'with dignity, or else with boredom or an air of aloofness'.[36] Sport discourses often extolled team sports but criticised individual sports because they could lead to selfish individualism. Such views were heard across the political spectrum but were paradoxically given special emphasis by the wealthier classes, who advocated individualism in economic affairs. Without spectators and followers there could be no stars, but playing, even to a low standard, was deemed more worthy than watching. Exalting stars could result in watching taking priority over playing. For the better off, sport was a means of promoting morality, or at least this was a view which many felt obliged to express. Yet to be capable of promoting moral values, sport had to be a game, a form of having fun. Taking sports too seriously, it was imagined, undermined their capacity to encourage selflessness, honesty, camaraderie and courage, while fostering cheating and selfishness. As attaching too great an importance to sporting success could weaken the moral capacity of sport, its stars had to be revered as much for their sportsmanship as much as for their sporting prowess. The stars had to demonstrate that what they did well was not so very significant.

Traditions and innovations

Conservatism characterised much of English sport between the wars. Of the new sports which were launched, only greyhound racing, motor racing and speedway attracted large followings. Governing structures that had been established before 1914, such as the highly conservative Jockey Club, continued with little change after 1918 and few calls were made for them to be reformed. Professional boxing was one exception to this. Before the First World War the National Sporting Club in London, a private club that had begun promoting fights in 1891, had been effectively the supreme authority for professional boxing in Britain. In 1919 the British Boxing Board of Control was established but this still had close links with the National Sporting Club. In 1929 the BBBC was reformed when the National Sporting Club closed. No sport between the wars experienced a breakaway on the scale of the split that occurred in rugby in 1895 which had led to the establishment of the Northern Rugby Football Union. In 1922 the Northern Union became the Rugby Football League but this was merely a change of title and an acceptance of how the sport was known in Australia. In soccer, the Amateur Football Association, a one-time rival to the FA, with its strength in London, the universities and the southern counties, had been formed in 1907 for amateur players, but it affiliated to the FA as the national governing body in 1914, while continuing its organisational functions. It changed its name to the Amateur Football Alliance to reflect this in 1934, after being granted representation on the International Selection Committee. In cricket, a sport with no structure linking the various levels of the game, there were few calls for it to have a more unified organisation. The MCC's control of the laws of cricket and its status as the ultimate authority for first-class cricket went unchallenged. Speedway was introduced to England as a commercial venture in 1928 but its promoters were content, even eager, to allow the Auto-Cycle Union, which controlled all other forms of motorcycle sport in England, to be the supreme authority for speedway in England. The social backgrounds of those who administered sports that were well established before 1914 remained broadly similar between the wars.

Some traditional sporting activities still survived in the English regions. Cumbria, for example, was one of a number of more rural areas where cock-fighting was still sustained, albeit in attenuated and clandestine form, with farmers, a dentist, a haulage contractor, a grocer, a painter and decorator amongst those arrested at Orton in 1938, one claiming he got as excited at a cockfight as he did at a football match. Here cocks still represented the pride and status of the owner or his village.[1]

Continuity was valued. Long-standing events such as the FA Cup Final, the Derby or the Boat Race had acquired a symbolic function, seen clearly in newsreel reports, which constructed them comfortingly as part of their annual calendar. Local traditions were sufficiently valued nationally to ensure that each year one or more of the Shrove Tuesday or Easter traditional town football matches at Alnwick, Ashbourne, Chester-le-Street or Workington would be screened by newsreels. Newmarket's Town Plate, a horse race open to all townsfolk, which had been run for 274 years in 1939, made a regular newsreel appearance, even when local women jockeys began to win. Press and newsreels also regularly called upon the spirit of Victorian cricketer W.G. Grace in their reports, summoning up his iconic image even for portrayals of women's cricket, which a 1922 *Pathe* silent newsreel described as 'Dr Grace plays cricket in petticoats at Ashford'. In 1929 *Pathe* asked rhetorically 'What would Dr Grace have said?' In 1937, at a women's test match, the commentator condescendingly remarked that 'the ladies put up an excellent show, even if they didn't look like W.G. Grace', hinting at both change and continuity in the same sentence.[2]

Another newsreel described Alnwick's annual football match, where 'the whole town' supposedly joined in, as 'an old Northumberland custom, and long may it reign'.[3] Such sports celebrated the community and its ability to display itself and its traditions. At Workington, annual, highly physical Easter football matches between the rival communities of 'Uppies' (from the upper part of town, often colliers) and 'Downies' (often sailors and ironworkers), were played right across the town, its harbour and river. With no limit on numbers, they took place despite long accounts of wanton damage, gratuitous violence, and even the death of a young steelworks labourer during the game in 1932. The police joined in the game in 1921, to help keep the ball away from property, while various mayors and members of the corporation watched or participated. The town was attached to its game, and was happy to display the toughness of its men to the large numbers of excursionists who came to watch and spend money. The sports at Grasmere, which included Cumberland and Westmorland wrestling, hound trails and guide fell-racing, were simultaneously a way of furthering traditional regional culture, protecting it against 'modern' sporting influences, displaying it to summer tourists visiting the Lakes, and an opportunity for the 'county' nobility and social élite to display their social dominance (Lomas 2002). The sports were reported in *The Times* and newsreels, ensuring comforting national awareness of the event, while Cumberland and Westmorland wrestling became once more a popular feature of Cumbria's regional sports, galas and fetes at this time.

The inter-war period saw a similar revival of Cornish wrestling in the South-west, with a Cornish Wrestling Association set up at Bodmin in 1923. A tournament at St Columb in 1926 attracted an estimated crowd of 17,000 (Johns 1995: 10). Revivalism even reached Brighton, which reintroduced the old game of stoolball in 1918. It was underpinned initially by a largely middle-class sense of local patriotism and an idealised 'love of a simple village pastime'. Some players even wore specially made Sussex rustic smocks. It spread through Kent and Sussex, and by the mid 1930s there may have been 1000 stoolball clubs in England (Lowerson 1995: 269–70). In a period of rapid social and economic change, the traditional features of sport provided some with security as well as pleasure. They provided a focus for local identity and celebrated its status.

Established sports created few major new competitions between the wars. In flat and National Hunt racing all the most prestigious meetings and races dated from before the First World War. No new competitions were introduced into professional soccer, although the Football League took over the Southern League and made it its Third Division for the 1920–21 season. In the following season the League admitted twenty-two clubs from the North of England and split the Third Division into Northern and Southern sections. County cricket introduced no new competitions although new methods of establishing the order of clubs in the County Championship were introduced in 1920, 1924, 1927, 1929, 1931, 1933 and 1938. In 1921 Glamorgan was admitted to the county championship. Rugby union's County Championship had started in 1889. All of rugby league's domestic inter-war competitions were in place before 1914. Golf's Open Championship, Amateur Championship, Match Play Tournament and British Ladies Amateur Championship had all started before 1914. The Ladies Doubles and Mixed Doubles Championships, Wimbledon's last major championships to be introduced, began in 1913. A tennis county championship was started in 1925 but in 1928 *Tennis Illustrated* complained that it was not 'a genuinely national competition'.[4] The expansion of international sports competitions is discussed in Chapter 7.

Paradoxically, interest in the past of particular sports was limited despite the strength of conservatism. Attention, as at all times in sport, was on the here and now. Current matches, or those about to be played, attracted most interest. Inter-war academic historians, looking back at nineteenth-century England, dismissed sport in a few lines, even though it can be argued that the creation of so many modern sports was among Victorian Britain's great cultural achievements. R.C.K. Ensor's *England 1870–1914*, the fourteenth volume of the Oxford History of England, was published in 1936 and had more than 550 pages of text. Three of its fifteen chapters were entitled 'Mental and Social Aspects'. These discussed social and cultural developments but only four pages were devoted to sport though this was more than the space given to the music hall and cinema.

Hobsbawm and Ranger (1983) have suggested that as tradition was a source of prestige and respect in nineteenth-century Britain, traditions were invented to reinforce authority. Much of the ritual surrounding monarchy, for example, though often appearing old, was created in the Victorian period. Few sports between the wars tried to invent traditions, although the belief that Webb-Ellis started rugby football by picking up a football at Rugby School in 1823 and the attempts to trace back the origins of cricket, boxing, athletics and other sports, often dubiously, to the distant past came close to this. In soccer, the Southern amateur Isthmian, Athenian, Spartan, Olympian and Nemean leagues deliberately adopted high-status classical Greek nomenclature. A few histories of sport were published but these tended to concentrate on great players and famous contests. Most sports had no publication equivalent to the annual *Wisden Cricketers' Almanack* which had a long section of cricketing records.[5] The pavilions of county cricket grounds displayed paintings and photographs of former players and teams but we have found no evidence that any sport established a museum before 1939. The annual handbook of the Club Cricket Conference included the formation dates for all its affiliated clubs, which suggests that this was thought important in club cricket, but the number of club histories written to mark the 50th, 100th or 150th anniversary of cricket clubs was nothing like that of recent years. The MCC celebrated its 175th anniversary in 1937 and the FA played a match against a FIFA (Fédération Internationale de Football Association) eleven as part of its 75th jubilee celebrations in 1938 but Football League clubs made little fuss about their 50th anniversaries. Sports had individuals who collected match and career statistics but no sport seems to have had a society of statisticians.

Some sports were represented as expressions of modernity. Mechanised sports expanded between the wars and were linked with notions of the machine and speed as harbingers of social advancement. Motorcar and aeroplane racing had started before 1914 but expanded between the wars. The King's Cup, the major domestic air race, 750 miles around England for a trophy presented to the Royal Aero Club by George V, started in 1922. The first British motorcar Grand Prix was held at Brooklands in 1926, and car racing became a new craze. The setting of speed and distance records was celebrated as evidence of scientific progress. A.J. Webbe, a *Daily Herald* sports journalist described speedway as 'a great modern movement, brand new and full of the vibrant enthusiasm of youth … It symbolises a general idea of getting on with things in a prompt, simpler and businesslike manner'.[6] The various mechanised sports were often seen as united in their support for the concept of the machine as progress. For instance, Lady Bailey, famous for her solo flights over Africa, Sir Henry Segrave, holder of the world motorcar speed record, and Malcolm Campbell were invited to speedway meetings and expressed their approval of speedway. The speedway press drew attention to speedway riders learning to fly. Yet even in the mechanised sports, tradition was strong. Governing bodies such as the Royal Automobile Club and the Royal Aero Club were controlled by the wealthy and public-school educated. Because of the costs, those who owned or raced aeroplanes, motorcars or powerboats belonged to the wealthy classes. Of the mechanised sports only speedway and other forms of motorcy-cle sport had a working-class ambience.

New sports

No sport that was played or watched widely in Edwardian England suffered a drastic decline, though billiards waned as a spectator sport as the massive scores stemming from the development of the multiple cannon made matches less interesting. Most attempts to create a following for sports which had been scarcely played or watched before 1914 failed. In 1933 the financial support of John Moores, who controlled Littlewoods football pools, led to the setting up of a national Baseball Association (Smyth 1993: 252). Moores seems to have wanted a summer sport for coupon betting. Lancashire became an early centre, and by 1935 baseball teams with paid players had been formed in Bolton, Ashton, Manchester, Blackpool, Rochdale, Oldham, Eccles and Liverpool. In 1936 they were playing as the North of England Baseball League. Four of them had a second team in the Second Division of the North of England which also had five other teams, though it is not clear whether all of these were profes-sional. In 1936 a Yorkshire League with teams from Leeds, Bradford, Sheffield, Hull, Dewsbury, Wakefield and Scarborough was started but by 1939 the North of England Baseball League consisted of only three teams from Lancashire and four from Yorkshire.[7] Fragmentary evidence suggests that baseball attracted more spectators in Yorkshire than Lancashire. In 1935, 1,500 watched Ashton defeat Bolton Scarlets in the National Baseball Knock-out Cup.[8] At Belle Vue in Manchester gate receipts for the 1934 season came to nearly £174. Had the admission charge been 6d, the total number of spectators would not have reached 14,000.[9] In Yorkshire games often attracted 5,000 and sometimes 10,000 spectators. In 1936 eight professional baseball teams were established in London. There were also east and west London amateur baseball leagues.[10] Most professonial matches in Lancashire were held at greyhound stadiums. By 1939 a national amateur championship was being held. National newspapers usually ignored baseball, but some local papers, such as the *Rochdale Observer*, which appeared twice each week, devoted as much as a column to baseball. A display cabinet at Rochdale Local Studies Centre claims that all but one of the first team players for the Rochdale Greys, one of the Lancashire clubs still playing in 1939, were Americans but because of Ministry of Labour regulations they were probably Canadians. In 1936 the first team of the Hackney Wick club in London were all professionals from Canada. The West Ham team had also imported three Canadians.[11]

Efforts to extend rugby league as a spectator sport in England outside Lancashire and Yorkshire flopped. Clubs were launched at Pontypridd, Carlisle, Acton and Willesden, Streatham and Mitcham, and Newcastle. All collapsed primarily through failing to attract sufficient paying spectators. Only Newcastle played for two full seasons. Wigan Highfield first played in the Rugby League in

1922–23. It moved to London in 1933. After one season it moved to Liverpool, becoming called Liverpool Stanley, and continued playing there until 1968. Castleford, situated close to other rugby league towns in Yorkshire, was admitted to the Rugby League in 1926 and survived.

Greyhound racing and speedway, both introduced to England between the wars, attracted sufficient followings for them to survive. Greyhound and whippet racing had a long history in England but the modern version of the sport, with the electric hare and electrically operated traps, was introduced from America in 1926 and tried first at Belle Vue in Manchester. It grew rapidly. By December 1927, eighteen tracks had been opened in Britain. By 1933 there were over 220, many running three days a week. Within ten years greyhound racing, with 38 million paying spectators, was rivalling soccer in its numbers. In London alone in 1932, over 9 million watched greyhound racing at tracks licensed by the National Greyhound Racing Club (NGRC). *The Times* estimated that there were more than 230 tracks in Britain by 1935, with the majority in England. Almost every town had a track, and London County Council had eleven.[12] Big cities usually had more than one track. Manchester had Belle Vue and White City and neighbouring Salford the Albion Stadium. How many tracks were purpose-built is not clear. Some existing stadiums took up greyhound racing. Wembley introduced greyhound racing in 1927. Greyhound racing was started at Stamford Bridge, the ground of Chelsea FC, in 1932. West Ham Stadium, which it was claimed could accommodate 100,000 spectators, held greyhound racing from its opening in 1928 but it is not clear whether it was built originally for dog racing. Manchester's Belle Vue track was built on a venue previously used for earlier forms of dog racing. Manchester's White City track, like its London namesake, had initially been built as an athletics track. Salford's Albion Stadium was a purpose-built greyhound track.

Track standards and control varied. From its creation in January 1928 the NGRC regulated around fifty élite tracks in the large urban areas, often boasting far more modern, comfortable and up-to-date facilities, including bars, restaurants, dancing facilities and club rooms, than leading racecourses such as Goodwood, Ascot or Newmarket.[13] This may have made them attractive to women. In 1927 and 1928 it was thought that 40 per cent of greyhound racing spectators were women (Cronin 2002: 109). In 1938 London's White City was perceived as the 'last word' in comfort, capacity and organisation.[14] The British Greyhound Tracks Control Society was created in 1932 for some twenty middling tracks, mainly in the North and Midlands, that were unable to satisfy NGRS requirements. They included Bolton, Blackpool, Leeds, Newcastle and Hackney Wick in London. Scattered across the country were also large numbers of unlicensed 'flapping' or 'gaff' tracks, often with poor reputations. These expressed values and meanings more overtly focused on betting, and drew predominantly working-class spectators and owners, keen to demonstrate their cunning, knowledge and understanding.

The licensed tracks always tried to ensure that bookmakers were not involved in management of stadiums or ownership of dogs. This was difficult for the smaller unlicensed tracks, less well run, situated in less well-populated areas. In 1933, while without facilities for tote betting because it was thought to be illegal on dog-tracks, and again totally reliant on bookmakers, they struggled for custom; bad weather and poor economic conditions also adversely affected attendance. Bookmakers were increasingly financially involved in their organisation. In January 1934 leading policemen across Britain responded to a Home Office enquiry with fairly general praise for licensed tracks, and the honest way they were run. Birmingham's three tracks were 'conducted in a straightforward and honest manner'. The police had 'no knowledge of any irregularities' at White City in Manchester. The West Riding NGRC-regulated tracks were 'above suspicion' and had a fairly good attendance. They were far less complimentary about the unlicensed tracks, where crowds were lower and more working-class. St Helens' track attendances varied from 1,000 to 3,000 through the week, Hyde Park Sheffield averaged about 700, but Leicester's Syston track attracted 'about seventy-five' and Yeovil only 'fifty'. Bookmakers often controlled both the tracks and the dogs running on them and a variety of tricks were reported, including unfair grading (handicapping), substitution, manipulation of hare speeds, and ways of slowing dogs down through cutting a dew claw, tight muzzling, Vaseline in an eye, administering dope or putting them into the start backwards.[15]

Speedway was launched in England as a commercialised spectator sport in 1928. The establishment of speedway in England was dependent on the expertise of Australian promoters and riders, but just before their arrival, a vast crowd, variously estimated at between 15,000 and 30,000 had attended a day's racing organised at High Beech in Essex, which is usually taken to mark the start of speedway in England. As a spectator sport, speedway experienced mushroom growth in the late 1920s. In 1928 the Auto-Cycle Union licensed speedway meetings at thirty-four tracks and at over sixty in 1929. In 1929 two professional leagues were started with a total of 27 tracks. This growth did not last. By 1932 only ten tracks were left from the two leagues and these merged to form the National League. By 1935 the National League had only seven tracks and of these, only Belle Vue in Manchester was outside London. After this there was a partial recovery. By 1939 the National League had two divisions. The First Division had seven tracks but the nine of the Second Division included the Belle Vue reserve team. Belle Vue was the only venue that took part in speedway for every season from the start of league racing to the outbreak of the Second World War. Speedway's biggest events could draw very large crowds. In 1938, 93,000 attended the World Championship Final at Wembley (Williams 1999b: 5–6). Speedway did not develop a broad base of amateur competition, though grass track racing may have been sufficiently akin to speedway for those wishing to pursue the sport on a recreational basis.

Though new sports, greyhound racing and speedway had conservative aspects. The National Greyhound Racing Club compared its position in the sport with that of the Jockey Club in horse racing. The leading greyhound races were given the names of the most prestigious horse races such as the Greyhound Derby, Oaks and Grand National, all held at London's White City in 1927 and the Greyhound St Leger introduced at Wembley in 1928. When international speedway matches began to be held between England and Australian teams, cricket terminology was employed. They were called 'Test' matches and contests for the speedway 'Ashes'. This adoption of the practices of other sports suggests a widespread acceptance that established sports practice was how sport ought to be organised.

Greyhound racing's popularity depended on betting. Firm evidence about the social background of greyhound racing spectators is rare, but the élite tracks, with their large car parks, attracted a mixture of social classes, with substantial middle-class involvement. Investors and officials were almost entirely middle-class. *The Times* and *Telegraph* both gave results and future runners for the leading meetings, where top price seats cost between five and ten shillings. Wimbledon, for example, was 'patronised by some of the best people in the land, including a number of peers of the realm and other distinguished people'.[16] Brighton's clientele was largely 'holiday making visitors, people in search of health and a residential population consisting largely of retired businessmen'.[17] One can argue that the expansion of greyhound racing demonstrates the centrality of gambling in working-class popular culture. In 1927 a *Times* editorial, while acknowledging 'the fearful delights of betting', emphasised

> the thrill of those marvellously swift dashes around the arena, brief as they are, for the dogs themselves as well as for the spectators. The entertainment is cheap, it is easily got at, and it is provided in the evening hours when the day's work is over. There is, too, a strange intoxication in the sight and sound of the shouting masses of spectators packed in the comparatively small space of the stands.[18]

Without the availability of greyhound tracks to be used as stadiums, speedway may not have survived or even been able to establish itself. No major speedway stadium was built solely for the sport, though it is often claimed, wrongly, that Belle Vue was a purpose-built speedway stadium.[19] Nine of the National League's ten tracks in 1933 also held greyhound racing. A representative of the National Greyhound Racing Association was on the board of International Speedways, the consortium that had brought promoters and riders from Australia to establish speedway in England in 1928.

Ice hockey had been played as an amateur recreational sport in England before the First World War and became established as a commercialised spectator sport in the mid-1930s. It was very much dependent on Canadian expertise. British-American Tours imported Canadian amateur players whose expenses, reportedly of £12 per week, were so generous that they were in effect professionals.[20] While accepting the overall control of the British Ice Hockey Association, it loaned the Association the funds to bring over Canadian players and provided it with rent-free office accommodation for two years. The owners of the Wembley Pool and the Harringay and Earls Court exhibition centres recognised that ice hockey could be an additional source of income. Arthur Elvin, the proprietor of Wembley, was reported to have said that the Wembley Pool, which opened in 1934, was built particularly for ice hockey (Bowman 1937: 38). In 1935 the National Ice Hockey League had seven teams. Two played at Wembley and the others, except for Brighton Tigers, were also based in London. In 1936 two teams from Paris joined the National League but in November 1936, when financial difficulties forced them to disband, they were replaced in the League by teams based at rinks in Manchester and Southampton. Throughout the 1930s ice hockey as a spectator sport remained dominated by London, partly because rinks outside London had limited seating for spectators. During the 1938–39 season only Brighton Tigers of the seven National League teams was not based in London. In February 1939 Streatham was expelled from the League for playing suspended players. Only Wembley and Harringay could accommodate more than 10,000 spectators. The first women's ice hockey match was played in 1930 soon after the formation of the All-England Women's Ice Hockey Association.[21] Women's ice hockey did not develop a commercialised variant between the wars.

Continuities in the playing and watching of sport

The social class of those playing and watching sports does not seem to have changed vastly between the wars. Sports which were socially exclusive before 1914 remained so although an Artisan Golfers' Association was formed in 1921, and by 1939 there were about 30 public golf courses. The Amateur Rowing Association only finally dropped a clause, suggestive of class prejudice, which excluded all manual workers from being defined as amateurs, in February 1937. There was no equivalent in other sports to the earlier working-class adoption of association football, nor of any sport with a predominantly working-class following broadening the class basis of its appeal, although the rise of greyhound racing and to a lesser extent speedway extended the range of sports with a working-class following. Pigeon-racing unions still retained a following in mining and weaving regions. Social distinctions in sport owed much to clubability and people wishing to spend leisure time with their own kind, or those with whom they worked. In working-class areas the facilities for organised sports and games provided by the numerous miners' institutes and Working Men's Club and Institute Union attracted far more of their funding than other pressing social concerns. Larger works and businesses, especially in more buoyant sectors of the economy, made increased provision for sport too, fostering *esprit de corps*, improving workforce health and fitness, and raising productivity. Those who controlled sport rarely called for a stronger working-class presence. Even though soccer was played and watched overwhelmingly by the working class, the Football Association continued to be dominated by those from public schools.

In county cricket it was largely taken for granted that the *haute bourgeoisie* should dominate club committees. Having costly subscriptions and electing members helped to retain the social tone of golf, tennis and cricket clubs. Even those on the political left complained rarely about the social privilege in sport, probably because they felt that other forms of social and economic inequality needed to be challenged first. Because the upper and middle classes exercised leadership in other areas of life, this may have strengthened assumptions that they should control sport. Interviews have shown that colliery joint committees, which administered sport facilities financed through the Miners' Welfare Fund and on which management and men were represented, were often dominated by bosses because bosses were used to taking decisions and giving orders.

The numbers of women who played sports between the wars rose though not on a dramatic scale. A few women had played cricket before the First World War, but cricket was probably the only men's team sport that women took up in any numbers between the wars and even this was on a restricted scale. The formation of the Women's Cricket Association in 1926 encouraged cricket playing by women on an organised basis but by the late 1930s the number of women cricketers was still only around 6,000. Immediately after the First World War, soccer playing among women expanded, but its popularity levelled off or faded by the 1930s though some teams survived. Women's bowls was still rare, though tournaments were becoming more common around 1930, and after the seaside town of Hastings instituted the first annual women's bowls competition in 1931, shortly followed by the establishment of the English Women's Bowling Association, it was seen as a 'new fashion'.[24] As we have seen, some women competed with great success against men. The Honourable Mrs Victoria Bruce set a world record for the longest distance driven in 24 hours and was the first to fly a light aircraft around the world. Amy Johnson took part in the annual King's Cup Air Race and completed a solo flight to Australia in 1930, the same year that Marjorie Foster became the first woman to win Bisley's King's Prize. Between the wars men did not take up sports which before 1914 had been played exclusively by women. Attempts were made to promote stoolball, a women's game, as a sport for ex-servicemen who had lost arms or legs in the war (Lowerson 1996: 411).

Male sport continued to be regarded as more prestigious than women's sport. Most press coverage was of men's sport. Sport stars were usually men. There were no major competitions for mixed teams in hockey or athletics. A handful of women in England were golf and tennis professionals but they were paid primarily to teach the game. A few women, such as Marjorie Pollard, who reported on women's cricket and hockey, became journalists. Amy Johnson was the air correspondent for the *Daily Mail*. Many women who played sport accepted the values that men ascribed to sport. Grants awarded by the National Fitness Council between 1937 and 1939 show that while sport and physical recreation were considered desirable for women and girls, sport was still thought more of a male preserve. Lancashire received forty-six grants. Some were for facilities such as swimming baths which both sexes could use. Twenty-three grants were made to organisations catering specifically for men and boys and only five for women and girls.[25]

Commercialisation and sport

Suspicion of commercialisation was another conservative feature of sport between the wars. Greyhound racing, speedway and ice hockey had been started as commercialised ventures, and part of the initial opposition to greyhound racing was on the grounds that it was an 'alien' (i.e. American) form of entertainment, not a sport, just 'a gigantic commercial enterprise to exploit the gambling spirit'.[26] Professional boxing, and 'all-in' or 'catch' wrestling, if it is regarded as a sport, were entirely commercialised. No governing body from what could be regarded as the major sports in England that had prohibited professionalism before 1914 legalised it between the wars. There was a professional tennis circuit, based on America, played by some of the world's leading players, but those who took part in this were not allowed to compete at Wimbledon. Respect for amateurism was one reason why so many sports in England tried to keep commercialism at arm's length.

The establishment of limited liability companies did not always indicate a more commercial attitude. This varied between sports. No county cricket club was a limited liability company, although the grounds of some counties, such as Hampshire and Warwickshire, were owned by limited liability companies. In Lancashire, where league cricket was especially strong, probably only Burnley CC of the Lancashire League was a limited liability company. The directory of the Club Cricket Conference does not indicate that any of its affiliated clubs was a limited company in 1939. Golf had been in the vanguard of limited liability companies even in the 1880s and 1890s, when some larger rugby union clubs such as Leeds or Blackheath also became incorporated, but this was often only to spread the large set-up costs. Profit was not the aim. The majority of greyhound stadiums and Jockey Club-controlled racecourses were owned by limited companies. All but one Football League club, and several rugby league clubs were limited liability companies.

Yet few clubs seem to have been intent on profit maximisation. A detailed study of racing has shown that racing companies were not profit maximisers. They put the needs and comfort of racing insiders above those of the general public and had little willingness to adopt more commercial approaches. Few thoroughbred breeders made profits consistently (Huggins 2003). The Football Association did not allow football club companies to pay dividends of more than 10 per cent and although much more research needs to be conducted into their finances, most seem to have paid dividends of less than this. Very few calls were made for the restriction to be lifted. Indeed, as Fishwick (1989: 26–47) points out, few directors were motivated by financial considerations, and at most clubs money made in boom times went into strengthening the team, not into dividends. The decision of the Division Three side South Shields to relocate to Redheugh Park, Gateshead, to counter poor attendances at the end of the 1929–30 season, was the sole American-style franchise shift. The Football League did not regard football pools as an opportunity to raise revenue and in 1935 refused an offer of £100,000 from the Pools Promoters Association to use its fixture list (Clegg 1993: 66). Rugby league clubs struggled to pay any dividend between the wars. Association football and rugby league companies retained the word 'club', with its undertones of voluntarist recreation, in their titles. Directors rarely stated that their aim was to boost profits. Many English sporting governing bodies owned their own sports grounds. The Jockey Club, for example, owned the race and training grounds at Newmarket, while the Rugby Football Union purchased the land at Twickenham, and neither was strongly profit oriented.

While the governing bodies of many sports resisted commercialisation, much business depended on the playing and watching of sport, though it is not possible to measure the extent of this. The five-yearly censuses of production show that the manufacture of sports equipment increased in Britain between the wars, but the relevant data was collected only from firms employing more than ten persons and no census was published for the second half of the 1930s. The value of leather and canvas sports goods production, which included gloves for cricket, fives and boxing, cricket pads, cricket balls, footballs and bags for tennis, golf and hockey, rose from £109,000 in 1924 to £625,000 by 1935. In 1935 the value of sports goods produced by woodworking concerns, which included rackets, presses, cricket bats and stumps, golf clubs, croquet and hockey sticks, bowls and tennis posts, exceeded £1.5 million, but formed only a tiny fraction of the total output of £84 million for wood and cork manufacturing concerns.[27] Between the wars Britain was a net exporter of sports goods. Between 1921 and 1925 exports of cricket, hockey, lacrosse, croquet, tennis and polo materials were roughly five times higher than imports. Between 1930 and 1933, the value of the export of these goods fell because of the world-wide economic depression, but exports still exceeded imports. Exports fell from £156,000 in 1930 to £78,000 in 1933 while imports dropped from £63,000 to £57,000.[28] The total value of sports clothing manufacturing is not clear as official statistics do not separate this from other forms of clothes manufacturing. Most gambling expenditure was dependent on sport, and gambling expenditure grew almost fourfold over the period. Statistics about the sales, and consequently about the profits, of sports books, are notoriously difficult to find. Sports news probably improved newspaper sales but this cannot be calculated with precision. Travel to sports venues boosted the revenues of transport concerns. The erection of stadiums, pavilions and clubhouses would have stimulated the building sector. Some businessmen may have made deals at golf clubs. County cricket clubs had bars, and pubs close to football grounds probably did more business on match days. Shooting gave employment to gunsmiths, beaters, animal breeders and keepers. Motorcar and motorcycle sport were partly encouraged by manufacturers who hoped to boost sales.

The highest levels of some sports in America, such as athletics and tennis, remained amateur but baseball, often taken as a symbol of American democracy and a celebration of the American way of life, was highly commercialised. In the 1980s Corelli Barnett and Martin Wiener argued that English culture, and especially that of the public schools, had contributed to Britain's relative economic decline in the twentieth century by fostering disdain for industry and by exalting literary values, and had discouraged risk-taking entrepreneurship and aggressive, wealth-accumulating, economic individualism, qualities which, they argued, had stimulated Britain's economic and industrial supremacy in the first half of the nineteenth century. By no means all cultural historians agree with this interpretation and it is likely that many from the public schools who went into such gentlemanly forms of capitalism as stock broking acted as profit maximisers (Barnett 1986; Wiener 1981)[29]. None the less, given the importance they attached to sport, their exaltation of amateurism and reluctance to allow sports that permitted professionalism to become out-and-out commercial concerns, seem to support the contention that English culture was not dominated by commercial values to the same extent as that of America.

For many sports reluctance to embrace commercialism may have been making a virtue of necessity. Gate receipts were the major source of income for most sports but many sports that attracted paying spectators had insufficient to become more commercialised. No leading horseracing course closed through failing to attract spectators, but modernisation of courses was limited. Very little research has been conducted into the finances of Football League clubs between the wars, but many lower division clubs struggled. Stalybridge Celtic had been reportedly keen to avoid promotion to Division 2 in January 1923 because it would be 'far too expensive considering the support the club could get', while several remunerative local derbies would be lost. By the end of the season financial problems led to its resignation from the league.[30] Wigan Borough resigned from Division 3 in October 1931 with bankruptcy looming. As it was not the worst-supported club when it left the League, probably other clubs were struggling to survive. Thames FC withdrew an application for re-election in 1932 due to lack of funds. The limitation on the wages of Football League players may have made it easier for some clubs to survive but having no wage restrictions might have forced clubs to adopt a more commercialised outlook. Most county cricket clubs had a hard time making ends meet and by the late 1930s county cricket was facing a financial crisis. Most of the Rugby League clubs also struggled financially, but all of those from Lancashire and Yorkshire that were playing in 1919–20 survived to 1938–39. Gate receipts at Wimbledon could probably have supported a professional tennis tournament. Spectator numbers may have been sufficient to support some cash prizes in athletics. The governing bodies of most sports seem to have been unaware of the potential of sponsorship by commercial bodies but their suspicion of commercialisation in sport probably discouraged them from even thinking about this.

Change and continuity in styles of playing

Styles of playing sport never remain unchanged but the developments in most sports between the wars were gradual rather than revolutionary. In cricket no new batting strokes similar to the leg glance pioneered by Ranjitsinhji in the 1890s were introduced. There was much criticism that batsmen were playing more defensively and adopting the 'one-eyed stance' which reduced risk-taking. The preparation of wickets in county cricket was often thought to give too big an advantage to batsmen. The adoption by England on the Australian tour of 1932–33 of bodyline bowling, where fast bowlers directed short-pitched balls at the batsman's body to a cordon of leg-side fielders, was widely seen as a major innovation in bowling techniques. Some, however, pointed out that similar tactics had been employed by the Australian fast bowlers McDonald and Gregory in the 1921 Test series against England and Fred Root, an England fast bowler, had experimented with leg theory, which concentrated on the batsman's body and legs, in the 1920s. Although bodyline had helped England to win the 1932–33 Test series in Australia by neutralising in particular the batting of Bradman, it did not become widespread in first-class cricket. England used it in the Test matches against the West Indies in 1933 and on the tour of India in 1933–34 but as Australia refused to play against England unless it were abandoned, it was not used in the 1934 England v. Australia test matches or in subsequent Test series in the 1930s. In November 1933, a joint meeting of the County Cricket Advisory Committee and the Board of Control decided that 'any form of bowling which is obviously a direct attack by the bowler on the batsman would be an offence against the spirit of the game' and had 'complete confidence' that captains would not countenance such bowling. Soon afterwards the county captains agreed not to use such bowling.[31] In the 1934 season three counties used bodyline, including Nottinghamshire whose bowlers Larwood and Voce had been England's main bodyline bowlers on the 1932-33 tour of Australia. After the 1934 season Arthur Carr was sacked as the Nottinghamshire captain for persisting with this form of bowling.[32] By 1935 bodyline had virtually disappeared from first-class cricket, though very similar forms of fast bowling were seen after the Second World War. In 1935 the LBW law was amended so that batsmen could be out to balls pitching outside the off stump. This change had been canvassed for many years but its introduction in 1935 may have been intended to discourage bodyline bowling by giving an advantage to bowlers whose line of attack was on or outside the off stump.

The revision of the offside rule in 1925 changed the style of play in soccer. Before then three players had to be between a player and the opponents' goal for him to be onside. From 1925 a player could be onside if two opponents were between him and the opposition goal. The reason for this change was that professional clubs had perfected the tactic of having defenders move up the field to catch opposing forwards offside. This had been used before the First World War but had been taken to new heights in the early 1920s by McCracken and Hudspeth of Newcastle United. The spread of this tactic reduced the spectator appeal of football by confining play to the middle forty yards of pitches and by making goals harder to score. The new rule at first made goal scoring easier: 1,192 goals had been scored in the First Division of the Football League in the 1924–25 season and in 1925–26 1,703 goals were scored. The new offside rule soon led to a new tactical formation, often called the 'third back game', to strengthen defences. The centre half became a more defensive position, in effect a third full back playing between the other two full backs. One or two of the inside forwards began to occupy a deeper position to take over the creative role that centre halves had previously provided. Newcastle may have been the originators of the third back, although southerners usually credited Arsenal. This new formation was quickly taken up in professional football with the result that the game became more defensive (Soar and Tyler 1983: 39–40). In the 1938–39 season the number of gaols scored in the First Division had dropped to just over 1,400. How far this tactical formation spread in recreational football is not clear.

Many sports made minor changes to rules but few introduced more fundamental changes that changed styles of play. Cricket made wickets an inch taller and an inch wider in the 1920s and reduced the size of the ball to give bowlers more of an advantage, but the 1935 LBW law probably had more long-term significance by making it more hazardous for batsmen to use their pads as a defence against off-spin bowling. The changes made to rugby union were mainly technical and do not seem to have had such an impact on the nature of playing styles as the prohibition on kicking directly into touch from outside a side's 25 introduced in 1968 or the more recent lifting of players in line-outs. Rugby league, a sport which has often changed rules to increase its spectator appeal, reduced teams to thirteen players, abolished direct kicking into touch and line-outs and introduced the 'play the ball' move before the First World War. No rule changes between the wars were on a scale similar to these or to the 1966 four-tackle rule. No major changes were made in the 1920s and 1930s to the rules of tennis, golf, hockey, rowing and athletics.

Explanations for the conservatism of sport between the wars

There is no single reason why sport in England between the wars was characterised by conservatism rather than innovation. No doubt very many were satisfied with the existing nature of sport. Probably enthusiasts for most sports had become interested in them in childhood and this had led them to assume that the existing modes of playing, organising and watching sports were the most suitable and appropriate, perhaps even natural, means of doing so. In many respects the 1920s and 1930s were a time of uncertainty and threat. Long-established British industries faced more intense international competition. Britain was not a world leader in many of the new lighter industries. Agriculture, which still employed more than any single industry, found it difficult to produce food cheaper than imported food. The world depression following the Wall Street crash of 1929 provoked deeper pessimism about the performance of the British economy. Unemployment was high in 1921, 1926 and particularly the first half of the 1930s. Although the Labour Party pledged to work through Parliament and not to seize power by force, many were still alarmed by its rise as a political force. Such fears were compounded by militant trade unionism in the early 1920s and the general strike of 1926. The creation of the Irish Free State and the rise of the Congress Party in India challenged Britain's imperial role. The communist regime in Russia and the rise of Nazi Germany in the 1930s were further causes of unease. Many did not welcome the American influence over popular culture stemming from Hollywood films, music and clothes fashions. Though women's emancipation made only limited progress between the wars, it may have been sufficient to disconcert many men and some women. The relatively unchanging nature of so much sport may well have provided reassurance in what appeared to be an alarming world, but proving this is difficult.

The First World War may also have encouraged conservatism in sport, though this also is not provable. The horrors of the War caused many to regard the pre-war years as a time of security and innocence, of calm and reason that was destroyed by the war. Such views, of course, idealised Edwardian England and overlooked the social and political conflicts surrounding House of Lords reform, Irish Home Rule, women's suffrage agitation and industrial disputes. The record attendances for many sports in the immediate post-war years were no doubt in part a form of emotional release after the privations of wartime, but may have owed something to a nostalgic desire to return to part of the world from before the war.

Sport was not the only aspect of English society and culture that changed relatively little. The eclipse of the Liberals by Labour and the formation of the Labour Governments of 1924 and 1929 were major political changes but Labour did not win a decisive majority at any inter-war general election. Support for communism and fascism at general elections was negligible. The leading Conservatives were in government for much of the inter-war years. The absence of support for republicanism also reflected conservatism. The school leaving age was raised to thirteen in 1918 but the Fisher Education Act was never implemented fully and no education reform in the 1920s or 1930s rivalled the Butler Act of 1944. Free trade was abandoned for imperial preference, but much of economic policy continued to be dominated by a desire to reduce government spending and no government tried to stimulate economic growth by adopting Keynesian manipulation of the money supply. No industry was nationalised. Writing in England was influenced by modernism but no English painter had an international reputation as a modern artist to match Picasso, Matisse, Ernst or Klee. English architecture produced no movement with a reputation equivalent to that of the *Bauhaus*. Cinema and radio, new forms of mass communication, rarely espoused radical political and social values. The conservatism of sport resonated with the spirit of the times.

Gaining meaning from sport
Sport and pleasure

In 1936, the newly launched magazine *Sport and Pleasure* claimed that the English

> have more of the day which we are relatively free to enjoy as best we can. This increase of leisure hours has led, naturally enough to a greater interest being taken in sport and the editor … hopes to provide articles of topical and general interest that will appeal to the many interested in sport and pleasure, who have, unfortunately, not enough leisure to enjoy a full perusal of our well-known sporting contemporaries.[1]

His hope was vain, with the magazine failing to establish itself, but the links between sport and pleasure were nevertheless important.[2] The roots of sport's attraction were variously defined as 'pleasure', 'enjoyment' or 'amusement' between the wars. Those who played, watched, read about and conversed about sport did so because they enjoyed it.

Sport, release and festivity

For the better off, the first years after the war brought novelty, fashionable frivolity and escapist excitements, and 'the pursuit of pleasure' became the 'popular approach' (Birley 1995: 131). Most forms of entertainment expanded. In 1923 *The Times* welcomed this, and found it exhilarating to see people behaving as if 'amusement was a legitimate human function once again'.[3]

In part this was release from the horrors of the First World War, but it was also related to a greater commodification of leisure and modest rises in real wages for most of those in work. Sport provided temporary escape from the routine of the workplace, domestic responsibilities, the restraints of convention or feelings of exhaustion, dreariness and alienation. As one worker put it, 'much of the lust for outdoor games … is due to pent up feelings of monotony and boredom' (Barratt Brown 1934: 184). The novelist J.B. Priestley, for example, in *The Good Companions* (1929: 5–6) exploited the idea of such escape to show how football in fictional Bruddersford turned you into a member of a new community, all brothers together for an hour and a half, for not only had you escaped from the clanking machinery of this lesser life, from work, wages, rent, doles, sick-pay, insurance-cards, nagging wives, ailing children, bad bosses, idle workmen, but you had escaped with most of your mates and your neighbours, with half the town.

Regarding sport as a release from the humdrum of the daily round has much in common with Roland Barthes' notion of pleasure as *jouissance*, often translated as similar to the bliss or ecstasy that accompanies the releasing of sexual energy. The release and escape of sport can also be linked to Mikhail Bakhtin's writings on how carnivals and festivals uphold the established social order by channelling social tensions into harmless forms through the temporary suspension of normal behaviour and the reversal of social roles.

Advocates of new sports in particular emphasised their high level of excitement and argued that this enabled them to satisfy the demands of modern society. The speedway journalist Tom Stenner attributed the 'amazing popularity' of speedway not to this 'age of speed' but to its meeting

> the modern need as does no other sport or entertainment. In these days of rush or turmoil, in the fierce struggle for existence that obtains today, in this keyed-up age of pent emotion, we need an outlet. We need something alive, something vital to hurl us away from everyday troubles.

During a race spectators 'leap from their seats … in a frenzy of excitement … And when the race is done they sink back to their seats again with sighing satisfaction and a warm glow of thankfulness for that fleeting glimpse of an emotional paradise.'[4] H.D. Teddington, an ice hockey journalist, recommended that

> if you want to key yourself up, watch an ice hockey match, one hour's play will keep you on tip-toe from beginning to end, no dull moments, no uninteresting minutes, but a whole time period of exciting, clean healthy sport … the air is electric, you catch the feeling, you want to get at it. Speed! Speed!! Speed!!![5]

By the inter-war period the FA Cup Final, the Grand National or Derby, the Boat Race and test matches had become national occasions from which spectators derived a variety of pleasures. Sociologist John Hargreaves (1986) has suggested that they were becoming the 'new sacred' as church attendances fell. They were eagerly anticipated parts of the sporting calendar, combining festivity, celebration and ritualistic display, their fame denoted by crowd size, national attention in the result and growing interest from women. The focus on such events by the press, their coverage in newsreels and by radio, allowed those not present to experience them vicariously. The pleasure for those at an event was probably enhanced by the knowledge that far more were awaiting the result and account of the event at home.

Excitement for spectators was enhanced long before the occasion itself by anticipation, imagination, hope and expectation. Sports were packaged and socially organised by the local press and community, exploiting feelings of conscious competition and allowing fans to savour daydreams of success. In football, for example, previous 'injustices' such as questionable penalties, unfortunate defeats or lucky goals would all be mentioned in local coverage. Major events were looked forward to for weeks before, and prefigured in the media. The anticipation of this future pleasure, a psychic economy driven by the potential of painful defeat, added to the intensity of feeling. Sport was pleasurable partly because fans viewed the finish of the race or the final whistle ambivalently, with relief or regret at the result, delight at their team's success yet sad that the game was finally over.

For major events, preparations for getting there were part of the fun for fans, with conspicuous display, social interaction, wealth and tradition determining the varieties of transport employed. For example, racegoers wishing to attend the Derby could go to Epsom by train, taxi, private motorcars, motor buses or charabancs. Railway companies laid on 'specials' from across the country, some offering food and Pullman coach standards of comfort. Travel companies organised special trips. Thomas Cook and Sons, for example, advertised entrance, dinner on the course and travel in a Daimler Landaulette for three guineas. Some car owners ensured a comfortable journey and a good pitch by coming down the night before to park and sleep over. The best views could be found in Epsom's magnificent modern grandstand, which accommodated 20,000 with separate bars, restaurants, cloakrooms, passenger lifts, and over 200 private boxes. Even in the early 1920s over two hundred buses would apply for parking facilities on Epsom Heath. The heath was also a magnet for public house charabancs, carrying their cases of beer and sometimes parcels of food. A few of the older and wealthier clung to tradition, still travelling to meetings by four-in-hand coaches in the first years after the war. The sporting grandee, the Earl of Lonsdale, for example, created regular impact at Epsom or Ascot by arriving in a horse-drawn wagonette, decorated in his yellow livery, with exactly matched chestnuts, flanked by liveried grooms and postillions. For the most modern, private planes were being used to bring a few wealthy racegoers by the late 1920s.

Travel was also an important part of the Cup Final experience, a heightened and more colourful version of the fan culture found on many of the away trips organised by supporters' clubs. Jeffrey Hill (1996: 85–112; 1999: 1–21) has demonstrated how the Final became a narrative and icon of England, and for most fans, a Final was a once-in-a-lifetime opportunity, reinforcing London's role and the national prestige of Wembley. The trip to London offered them a long train journey, a sightseeing trip, a packed ride to the stadium, a chance to enjoy a brief moment in the limelight and to see the presentation of the sacred cup to their captain. There was enjoyment of colour and pageantry too. Fans displayed their team colours on scarves, rosettes, hats, umbrellas or headgear, carried their balloons, slogans, streamers and mascots, sang their club 'theme song' and demonstrated their support and loyalty on the national stage. There was even a short-lived fashion for wearing berets in club colours. In 1927 Arsenal fans grouped themselves together at Wembley to create a bank of red and black while Cardiff City fans had blue and white.[6] They waved symbols, such as leeks or hammers. For fans such as those of Preston North End travelling down to the 1937 FA Cup Final 'it was an opportunity to drink, dress up, enjoy and bond with others, known and unknown', with Preston Station full of 'noise, brightness and colour', and trains accompanied by alcohol. On the train down 'fans indulged in community singing ... they rang bells, sounded horns and waved rattles, all adding to the general din'. There was even a car covered in the team colours, while a man wore a white smock bearing the words 'Play Up Preston' (Naylor 2004: 11–15).

The Rugby League Cup Final moved to Wembley in 1929 and differed from the FA Cup Final in that the two finalists' communities made up a far larger proportion of the crowd. This was mainly because the game lacked a strong base in London and lower demand meant its finals were not all-ticket. But there was still sufficient interest to attract spectators beyond the two clubs' fan base. In 1936, for example, for a final between Leeds and Warrington, about 25,000 made the trip from Leeds, including (depending on reports) somewhere between 1,500 and 2,000 boys from Leeds schools, with their teachers. There were 12,000 from Warrington. Of the thirty-five special trains organised by the London, Midland and Scottish Railway Company, twenty-four came from Warrington and Leeds. But some trains, from Cumberland or Wales, clearly catered for fans elsewhere.[7] Many came similarly long distances by car and bus for rugby union internationals at Twickenham, forcing the RFU to build a seven-acre west car park in 1923, and soon add a smaller east car park (1925) and larger north park (1930).

Travelling to matches at the home ground of the club one supported was also part of the pleasure of watching sport. This could include talking about the match as one walked or took a tram or bus, or visited a pub before or after a match. For soccer and rugby league, many spectators stood in the same part of the ground each week, which suggests that habits of ritualised behaviour figured in spectating pleasure.

At the event, spectators took different pleasures in watching sport. Having the visual skills and knowledge, the 'sporting gaze' or ability to 'read' the play, was central to enjoyment. Sport provides clear parallels to the 'medical gaze' analysed by Foucault, or John Urry's 'tourist gaze' (1990). The 'sporting gaze' was a collective gaze, a view constructed and shared with large numbers of others. Sport was watched in special places away from one's normal residence or one's work, and many sports stadiums became larger and added more facilities during this period. Gambling locations like the racecourse or greyhound stadium were also places for display, where punters could play different roles, sounding expert, being apparently calculating and aloof, or ebullient and gregarious. As in the pub, they

could talk knowledgeably about the form of dogs or horses, infer they had special insider knowledge or claim to have a system. Although the Boat Race
provided a rare exception, it was professional sport, with its mass character, urban
spectacle and more orchestrated thrills and excitement, which was most able to
adapt to class, gender and generational shifts in sporting tastes. The commercial
attractions of inflicting physical pain, violence and suffering saw professional boxing increase its popularity. Professional wrestling also became an increasingly
popular form of urban entertainment, a commercialised, contrived pseudo-event,
with its well-staged narrative of heroes and villains. Crowds became very
involved in its spectatorship, gesturing and shouting abuse or encouragement,
and loved watching the skill, strength, fitness and resilience of two men apparently disputing physical mastery, with 'thrills' being the most frequent motive for
attendance (Harrison and Madge 1986: 116–17).

Being amongst the crowd was itself pleasurable. Spectators might not be able
to influence the game directly, but exhortation, adjuration, gesture, and other
expressions of feeling all acted as hoped-for forms of sympathetic magic, or
relieved tension. The more spectators wanted a side to win, the more fear of
defeat became aesthetically appropriated as part of the pleasure of the match.
The ecstasy of winning brought fans temporarily together. During the 1932
FA Cup Final, trade unionists, employers, miners and managers erupted when
Newcastle United scored the winning goal, and 'men who had never met
before shook hands. Byker and Jesmond, Scotswood and Gosforth had forgotten all social barriers'.[8] In soccer and rugby league, in particular, crowds were
very involved, identifying with the teams, worrying about the result, savouring
the passion and drama of the action. They were not distanced like the more
decorous middle classes at tennis or polo. At the same time, as Russell points
out, newspapers and newsreel footage normally conveyed a lively atmosphere
with soccer supporters variously exchanging 'chaff', 'clips' or other retorts with
the opposition, and behaviour was generally represented as 'encapsulating the
humour, restraint and balance which were key elements of the English self-
image' (Russell 1997: 120). Crowds were exuberant and energetic, creating a
shared community of fans and participants. At the very least such occasions
offered opportunities for the mobilisation of popular enjoyment and provided
relatively unconstrained social fraternisation.

Most events attracted more male than female spectators. Watching sport
was often an expression of masculinity and perhaps a strategy whereby men
could ensure that they did not feel marginalised in male society. For some men
sport may have been an escape from the more refined forms of behaviour they
were expected to display in the presence of women. It is possible, though supporting evidence is hard to find, that being in sports crowds helped men to
recapture the male bonding of service life experienced in the First World War.
Knowledge about how many women watched sport or whether their numbers varied between sports is sketchy but it is often assumed that watching
sport became more popular among women between the wars. Comments that

watching sport was incompatible with notions of respectable feminine conduct do not occur frequently in sport discourses. While sexual mores were becoming more relaxed in the 1920s and 1930s, by the standards of today English society was still very prudish. Many of both sexes may have taken a voyeuristic delight in watching the partially clad bodies of sports players. Photographs of female athletes, swimmers and tennis players can be seen as attempts to give pin-ups respectability. Comments in the *Daily Express* about the physical attractions of the Great Britain ice hockey team in 1936 suggest some female interest in the sexual appeal of male sport stars.[9]

The carnivalesque aspects of sports crowds meant that stadiums or courses were often liminal zones, an opportunity for the suspension or reversal of normal behaviour. The anonymity of the crowd offered escape from the patterns and rhythms of workdays and freedom from the collective scrutiny of street, church and work. There was often an atmosphere of playful permissiveness. At racecourses, for example, moral and economic constraints on eating, drinking, spending and betting were relaxed, giving way to indulgence and excess. Stallholders, booth-keepers, bookmakers, gypsies and tipsters all actively encouraged sporting consumption and attempted to catch the sporting gaze, encouraging spectators to part with their cash. There was intensity of feeling, of disappointment at the failure of one's horse or ecstasy at its success. Alcohol was sold at many sport venues. All county cricket grounds sold drink. Clubs in the Lancashire Cricket League also sold alcoholic drink but only one in the Bolton League had a drinks licence. At Epsom, all classes were able to enjoy themselves, with the *Daily Telegraph* noting how

> chips in a bag and winkles on a pin are cheek by jowl with the charabanc loads from nearly every village in the home counties, whose freightage extended not only to cases but casks of beer. There were too, more dainty feeders, whose napery was spotless and whose cutlery scintillated in the sunshine.[10]

At soccer matches it was not uncommon to see men drunk, and photographs show that carrier bags were often used to take beer bottles into the ground for liquid refreshment. But alcohol might not lead to bad behaviour. The official report on the crowd troubles at the Wembley Cup Final of 1923 did not mention drink. In the 1930s Mass-Observation found the bar at Bolton Wanderers' ground crowded at half-time but did not report drunkenness or drink-related spectator misbehaviour (Collins and Vamplew 2002: 81). Fears that drink might cause violence, however, could explain why pubs near the Liverpool and Everton grounds were not allowed to open during and after matches (ibid.: 74, 78).

Part of the pleasure of sport for spectators was the later post-match inquest or celebration. Mass-Observation (1987: 186–87) noted that discussion of sport was a feature of 13 per cent of pub conversations, with betting involving a further 16 per cent. The *London Survey*, which merged sport and betting, had an even higher figure, 37 per cent. When Preston's Mutch stepped up and scored what proved to be the winning penalty kick at the 1938 Cup Final, radios were left blaring in empty rooms, while Preston's streets filled. The *Lancashire Daily Post* described how people 'rushed into the streets to shake hands with their neighbours and tell each other how happy they were ... front doors in street after street, opened all at once, to release excited, laughing folk'.[11] This provides a highly illuminating example of the consumption of football through solo or group consumption, prefiguring later responses to television.

Spectators, convention and rituals

While sports events were opportunities for pleasures associated with the relaxation of everyday constraints, much of their enjoyment also derived from observing forms of conventional and ritualised forms of behaviour. On the field of play working-class players could defeat their social betters, but social status among spectators was rarely challenged at sport events. Sport arenas helped to make social distinctions obvious. They were socially zoned with separate areas segregated by price and with tacit expectations of different behaviour. Observing those from other social classes added to the pleasures of watching sport.

Some sports were opportunities to see royalty. George V was deeply involved in racehorse breeding and ownership and enjoyed the social side of racing, strolling with friends on the lawns at Epsom, staying in the Jockey Club's Royal Suite at Newmarket or at the Duke of Richmond's home for Goodwood, and arranging a house party at Windsor Castle for 'Royal Ascot'. Royalty's sporting involvements were deliberately given a more popular twist, which was picked up and consistently projected in the national press and newsreels.[12] Where relevant, the presence of the King was always among the dominant images shown. The ceremonial side of royalty's presence at sport events enhanced the crowd's pleasure. The symbolic raising of the Royal Standard over Epsom grandstand, for example, would be greeted immediately by murmurs of 'the King, the King' (Huggins 2003: 130). The popular public, colourful and glamorous processions to Epsom course were a visible display of the monarchy's cultural centrality, its wealth and position. At Ascot there was a long tradition of the King and Queen driving in semi-state from Windsor Castle. They would then enter the Royal Box, and later chat with dozens of friends summoned up by pages from the Royal Enclosure below. In 1928, for example,

> just after one o'clock all necks were craned and eyes raised to the far distance of the golden gates, whence emerged the royal procession of seven four-horse open landaus, with postillions and outriders bobbing up and down like corks of scarlet on a sea of emerald green. There is no ceremonial rite in the whole social year to compete in majesty with this semi-state occasion, and the roars of patriotic fervour that greeted the leading landau, drawn by four superb greys, and containing the King and Queen, the

Prince of Wales and the Duke of York, increased in volume to such an extent that to listeners in the paddock it sounded like a competition ... handkerchiefs and hats were waved enthusiastically as the leading carriage made its final wide, majestic sweep before turning in through the long lane of privileged subjects who lined the royal enclosure.[13]

According to Jeffrey Hill (1999: 9), royalty's attendance at sporting events with a strong working and lower-middle-class following represented a further step in a continuous adaptation of its position as a national family, both articulating itself to the people, and affirming an official presence in the people's sporting activities.

Landed aristocrats could also be seen at sporting functions, demonstrating their wealth, prestige, authority and hierarchy. At the Lake District's Grasmere Sports, for example, Lord Lonsdale would motor over from Lowther Hall with his party in a fleet of yellow Rolls Royces. He had his own private stand and marquee erected each year, and acted as starter and judge. By the 1930s he was affably signing autographs and posing for pictures. Royal Ascot, often seen as the zenith of the London 'season', attracted pages of coverage each year in the columns in *The Times*, the *Daily Telegraph* and the popular press, presenting it as 'The World's Greatest Dress Parade' with a big stress on the 'pageant of fashion', details of hem-lines, hairstyles, shoes, stockings and other fashion points, and descriptions of the most fashionable women.[14] Much less emphasised was that it was also the epitome of élite male fashion. When Selfridges opened its Orchard Street extension in 1922, it advertised its new menswear department with a display aimed specially at Ascot (Laird 1976: 192–94).

The theatricality of major sporting events made them more of an occasion as they became increasingly ritualised and managed. The Cup Final, for example, developed its programme of ancillary activities in the 1920s. These began earlier in the afternoon, and were designed to entertain and involve the spectators before the match, and thus stagger arrivals. Music was a popular feature of many such national sporting events, and was often provided by military bands, visually and aurally merging militarism, music and sport. It was first provided at Wembley in 1925, after it was offered by the marching bands of the RAF and the Irish Guards, and various service bands played each year thereafter. Royal Ascot had not two but three military bands for several years in the 1930s. At Twickenham many of the bands that played came from the nearby Royal Military School of Music. Soccer fans still sang on the terraces, but in the 1920s organised community singing became extremely popular. It was a feature of rugby matches at Cardiff Arms Park from 1924, and slowly became more widespread in England. Such singing was, for example, the opening feature of the first BBC soccer broadcast, of the Arsenal versus Sheffield United game on Saturday 22 January, 1927, with standards such as 'Pack Up your Troubles' and 'Tipperary'. In February the *Football and Sports Favourite* published a series of football-focused chorus songs, with pictures of crowds singing on its cover, telling readers to 'say it with music, another thirty rousing choruses in this – Everybody's singing now.

Another batch of popular parodies in next week's football favourite. Take your copy wherever you go and sing'.[15] Parodies included 'Keep the Forwards Scoring' sung to Novello's 'Keep the Home Fires Burning'.

Later that year 'Abide with Me' was introduced into Wembley's community singing programme when Cardiff City played Arsenal, perhaps as an aid to crowd control. The *Radio Times* commented that 'to hear this vast crowd singing together before the kick-off, the largest demonstration of Community Singing this country has ever beheld, will not be the least interesting part of this afternoon's broadcast'.[16] Newspapers later praised the crowd's performance. The *Field*, for example, applauded

> the wholehearted rendering of the National Anthem, and the singing by the crowd of Abide With Me … a noble hymn which has given comfort to millions of people … it is very certain that the hymn could not have been sung more reverently or with a greater fervour if the scene had been the interior of a great cathedral … every man and girl among them knew the words of the song from beginning to end.[17]

The crowd removed their hats for the singing in an expression of reverence, and the *Daily Dispatch* noted that 'every man in the packed stadium stood with bared head and joined with fervour in the song'.[18] Hill suggests that for some, it must have triggered memories of personal loss and grief, and that it became a deeply emotional, effective expression of remembrance, creating a sense of national unity through participation in sacred song, which thus obscured the class and regional tensions of the game (Hill 1999: 14–15).

Celebrations of sporting success in national competitions were opportunities to indulge in what had become traditional and ritualised practices before 1914, such as civic receptions and the winning team touring the town with the trophy.[19] Blackburn Rovers' FA Cup win in 1928 attracted an estimated 100,000 people to welcome them home, despite dismal weather, rapturously celebrating their success with bands, streamers, flags, speeches and parades, coloured trappings and fancy dress. Among those who congratulated them were the Bishop of Blackburn and the Lord Mayor. Similar celebrations took place in rugby league, where, for example, Hull's success against Huddersfield in 1936 led to a civic reception. The team was joined at Ferriby station by the Lord and Lady Mayoress. There was a coach procession led by mounted police, through dense crowds of people, to the Guildhall, where the team appeared on the balcony and displayed the Cup, to a deafening burst of cheering. The Lord Mayor said it was 'a proud day for Hull and for Yorkshire. A good team is of great help to the city … it has done as much as if we had spent a thousand pounds in advertising'.[20] When Hunslet won the Rugby League trophy the team's charabanc was followed from pub to pub round the main streets by 'crowds of lads prepared to risk staying out hours after their bedtime for the excitement of seeing their local champions' (Hoggart 1958: 108–10).

Winning the Football League championship did not provoke celebrations on a similar scale. No crowds packed the streets to celebrate when a team won the County Championship though success at the highest levels of league cricket could have this effect. Rugby union had no league or cup competitions for its clubs and therefore no similar celebrations. Success against Australia in Test cricket stimulated displays of enthusiasm. When England regained the Ashes at the Oval in 1926 cheering spectators rushed onto the pitch. When members of the side which won the bodyline series returned home, crowds welcomed them and civic receptions were organised. On Eddie Paynter's arrival in his small town of Clayton-le-Moors in Lancashire the President of the District Council presented him with an illuminated address and gold watch plus a cheque for over £113 which had been collected from a shilling fund organised by a local newspaper.[21] Celebrations of sporting success helped to emphasise local identities and can be related to Geertz's contentions that rituals are narratives through which people tell themselves who they are.

Sport and the pleasures of gambling

Some who never watched sport bet on it, although regional differences, religious belief, personality and temperament, together with the nature of a sport and its facilities for betting all affected the extent of betting. Interest in gambling crossed class boundaries and betting attracted a substantial middle-class following. But we know less than we should about what betting meant to punters. The 1932 Royal Commission on Lotteries and Betting took no direct evidence from punters or those who filled in football pools. Most research on inter-war betting shows that for the working classes it was often a response to a life where income was irregular through lay-offs, accidents at work, or illness, and that gamblers followed fairly set routines, which minimised the likelihood of reckless betting (Huggins 2003: 66–99). As Ross McKibbin points out, saving was difficult, but betting with small stakes, on a weekly basis, sometimes provided a small windfall to improve lives for a short time while offering physical and psychological excitement and a topic for conversation at work or in the pub (McKibbin 1998: 375–76). The theme of escape surfaced here too. Many claimed in 1936 that doing the pools was exciting and relief from monotonous work (Hilton 1936: 23). Likewise, betting even for the worker who never saw a race, added 'a bit of colour and the spice of excitement to the monotony of his life', according to a 1927 analysis of turf life (Fairfax-Blakeborough 1927: 24).

For regular gamblers, much betting was careful and calculated, offering intellectual satisfactions through the exercise of judgement based on careful reading of the sporting press, studying form and other factors. A few were plungers, hoping for the remote possibility of a big strike, wanting the jackpot pools win or betting a combination double or treble on dog or horseracing. Reliance on luck, superstition or just plumping for a horse was most common among those who bet less often, and usually on the major races. *The Times* referred to them as 'pin pointers', explaining that 'a large section of the population still prefers to call the whole mysterious mechanism of the universe to its aid ... It is this romantic streak in human nature'.[22] Most bet only what they could afford, half-expecting to lose, but playing for the thrill and hope of profit, staking enough to make the events exciting. For those in poverty, however, it could have an adverse effect, although here again we know little about those who were addicted, though modern research suggests their numbers were tiny.[23]

The pleasures of playing sport

The great majority of those who played sport must have done so because they enjoyed it. Except for those forced to play at school, participating in sport was voluntary, a means of having fun. Apologists for sport, and organisations such as the National Playing Fields Association, often stressed that many who enjoyed playing were denied opportunities to do so by the shortage of facilities. Playing brought a range of satisfactions not unique to the inter-war period – release from the everyday routine, the joy of exercising the body, the edge of competition with the pleasure of victory but the dejection of playing badly or losing, the sociability of playing with and against others, receiving admiration and possibly consolation for lack of status and achievement in other areas of life. For some there was also pleasure in the human body itself. This could be the sensual pleasure of exercise and physical contact, of being gazed upon or watching the bodies of others. Such pleasures could be noted in organisations as diverse as the popular Women's League of Health and Beauty or the male body-building cult. Sportsmen and women had long displayed their bodies in fairgrounds, pubs, circuses and music halls, and one of the attractions for both participants and spectators of sports like boxing or wrestling was the opportunities offered for such display.

For the very talented there was the attraction of applause, prestige, perhaps fame and glory and for a tiny number being paid to play and the prospect of higher living standards. To former leading rugby union player Howard Marshall, rugby meant

> the heave and strain of the scrimmage; the smell of sweat and embrocation in the dressing room; the joy of achievement, the thunder of battle; the train journeys, the surging of Welsh crowds; Princes Street on Calcutta Cup day; great players and great games ... loyalties and friendships and memories.
>
> (Marshall 1936: 115)

Discourses surrounding sport emphasised that even for those playing at the highest level, sport had to be fun, a diversion. In 1938 Lord Burghley, the Olympic champion and Conservative MP, advised 'never forget that the prime object of sport is recreation in the proper sense of the word' (Rudd 1938: v).

The emphasis on keeping games as games meant that they had not to be taken too seriously, a view that was often especially strong among the wealthy and which was sometimes recognised as having a deleterious effect on English performance in international competition. Coaching and practice were often seen as inimical to keeping sport as fun. An American found that at Oxford and Cambridge in the mid-1920s practice for soccer and rugby was 'unorganized and certainly unscientific ... Nothing could be more casual' and that coaches were 'rather instructors, advisers, and critics than what Americans regard as coaches' (Savage 1926: 87–88). In 1923 a tennis correspondent in *The Times* thought that English players had no 'zest for imitation' of the intensive practice from an early age that had made Tilden and Lenglen champions.[24] In 1925 Mrs J.E. McNair wrote in *Golf Illustrated* that in Britain 'women golfers seem to have a rooted objection to practising'.[25] Coaching was limited even in professional sport. The journalist and former footballer Ivan Sharpe thought that British professional soccer players resented coaching and that young players were expected to become better players 'by mere association with the seniors'. Football coaching was taken more seriously abroad (Sharpe 1952: 77).

Sport and sociability

Historians have pointed out that playing and watching sport were opportunities for camaraderie and companionship, providing a form of social bonding, emotional satisfaction and group intimacy. Neil Tranter (1998: 54) has linked the sociability of sport to men's increasingly limited role in family and household affairs. By the inter-war period a major element of sports clubs was conviviality. In the 1920s more clubs were devoted to organised sport than any other activity, and increasingly imposing clubhouses became powerful symbols of the sporting landscape. Clubs were impressive both in numbers and in vitality, offering younger members a move away from parents, family and domesticity. In all but the more select, workers and the lower-middle classes probably formed the nucleus, although the popularity of different sports varied from town to town. In Liverpool, a survey in 1930 found that there were about 1,000 football, 500 tennis, 400 cricket, 200 bowling, 200 hockey, and 100 cycling clubs used by the working classes. In York Seebohm Rowntree's late 1930s survey suggested that there were 1,568 cricketers, 1,530 bowls players, 1,395 footballers, and about 1,000 tennis players in voluntary clubs alone (Jones 1986: 67).

Clubs reduced the costs of sport through shared facilities and the provision of club premises. Membership numbers varied between sports and from area to area. In bowls, for example, during the 1930s, Suffolk's County Bowling Association clubs varied in membership from 30 to 145 members, with no particular pattern predominating, while in Bedfordshire almost all had between 20 and 60 members, with more than two-thirds having fewer than 40.[26] By the mid-1930s the average number of members per tennis club was 30 though in the 1920s the larger clubs affiliated to the LTA had between 50 and 100 members. Some clubs collapsed between the wars. In Bolton and its surroundings the number of cricket clubs grew from 19 to 83 between 1920 and 1939 but over the same period 18 disbanded.

Clubs took time to recover after the membership losses of the war years. Many middle-class clubs extended their membership and more middle-class sports became increasingly socially acceptable pastimes for young ladies. In hunting, for example, during the early 1920s, women formed a large proportion of hunt members, and according to Derek Birley (1995: 147) were a majority in some hunt clubs. Likewise, in the early 1920s tennis clubs were often dominated by a female membership. On Tyneside and Wearside, for example, in 1921, men formed a majority of the members at only a fifth of tennis clubs, although lower subscriptions for women may have been a factor (Patterson 1921). Tennis clubs differed in their social exclusivity. On Tyneside, Brandling had the highest status, with an entrance fee and high subscription open only to 'gentlemen'. It supplied the majority of county players who could afford to travel to competitions on weekdays and stay overnight. By contrast Delavel Hall Tennis Club, despite its title, played on the local cricket pitch when it was not in use and subscriptions were only five shillings.

Tennis clubs functioned as potential or actual social centres where middle-class youngsters could meet the opposite sex. One contemporary, F. Gordon Lowe, claimed that 'tennis has a great social side: men and women can play it with equal pleasure' (1924: 16). Players often merely desired to enjoy the physical and social pleasure of the game alongside those of a similar standard. Tennis supposedly gave a man

> that enjoyable companionship with men he admires coupled with the physical and mental exercise and relaxation so necessary for a businessman to sustain him if he desires to be at his best. The good fellowship of the tennis court is a tonic to a man harassed by business cares.
>
> (Tilden 1933: 2, 256)

Similar ideological justifications, linking sport to the world of business, were often put forward for more middle-class sports. Prospective bowls players, for example, were told:

> if you are worried by cares of business a game of bowls will make you forget; if you want to make friends with your fellow man a game of bowls does the trick. You will benefit in health and your mental outlook will improve.
>
> (Hartley 1935: xiii)

Tennis, golf, rugby union, bowls and squash clubs were cultural institutions which continued, as they had before the First World War, to forge middle- or lower-middle-class identities. Middle-class identity was shaped through consumption and cultural institutions as much as by income or relationship to the means of production. A club had the power to define who belonged, and who didn't, and so helped to maintain local middle-class power and authority. Some clubs were formed to ensure social exclusivity, others because members were excluded from élite clubs. Membership signalled fine degrees of status or playing style, in select, private domains, with club positions providing a hierarchy through which members could move. Appeals for new members by county cricket clubs were invariably directed to 'gentlemen' which could have been intended to discourage applications for membership from working men. Sometimes it was argued that becoming the member of a county club was a duty for a gentleman. Confirmation of one's social status was a pleasure associated with socially exclusive clubs.

In 1925 the editor of *Golf Illustrated* complained about 'very many golf clubs who do nothing to promote the social side of the game'. 'More than any other game', he wrote, golf was 'constituted to promote good-fellowship between the parties who are contending for victory. It is the only game that lends itself to communion in the intervals between the strokes'. He regretted that too little use had been made of the 'imposing club-houses' and the tendency of golfers to 'lose their old characteristic of a fraternity, and to form small cliques – dozens of such cliques … the result is to create so many exclusive little sets, each with its own pleasures'. He advocated that clubhouses could be used in the evenings 'to serve the same purpose as the clubs in Pall Mall and Piccadilly'. He praised clubs which had cards evenings during the week and held dances. In another editorial he wrote about club committees having an attitude of 'Olympic detachment' and ignoring artisan players. Yet while wanting clubs to encourage artisan players which could create a 'more friendly spirit between the classes' and perhaps unearth young players who might eventually represent Great Britain, he still wanted to preserve the social exclusiveness of clubs. 'Certain stipulations' would be needed to protect the interests of club members. Instead of allowing more artisans to become club members, he advocated occasional matches against artisan teams and the provision of more municipal courses.[27]

Regulations, blackballing and other devices supported the class, race and gender prejudices of the membership at sport clubs. All-male élite clubs, such as the MCC, the Jockey Club, or the National Sporting Club, created a masculine sanctuary, generating cultural capital, affirming social aspirations, preserving social identity and building up useful contacts. In golf, Jews were often excluded. Not all clubs welcomed women and some limited women's play. In the 1920s the golfing journalist Mrs R.J. McNair knew of one club which displayed a large notice in the ladies' room stating that on the tee women had always to give way to men, but she fancied that it was 'a survival of the bad old days and … is not strictly enforced now'.[28]

In cricket, the MCC Pavilion and Ground Regulations still kept out women from the pavilion during games in 1939. They conceded that ladies accompanied by a Member may view the Long Room after the close of play on any match day on which Members have the right to introduce a friend. Ladies under no circumstances are permitted to view the interior of the pavilion above the ground floor or enter the bar.

Bowling clubs likewise resisted women's membership, with their presence on the green in the 1920s often regarded as an intrusion, though some men welcomed women's presence, arguing that 'women added a quiet dignity to the games and thereby added to the mutual pleasure of the sexes' (Hartley 1935: 44). The leading middle-class private clubs were unyielding, especially in the South, where Brighton, Bournemouth and Bromley strongly opposed women's involvement. Many northern bowls clubs were associated with pubs and working-men's clubs, institutions in which women had few organisational roles. They voted down any applications from women to use their greens. In Bolton, women did not play on pub greens even in the later 1930s. Although significant numbers of women began to enter a minority of bowling clubs, they had most success in municipal greens and public parks. In cricket clubs in particular, and sometimes in other sports, women were more often involved only in preparing and serving teas, or in attending dances or concerts to raise funds.

Some women preferred their own sports clubs. Most women who played hockey, lacrosse, netball or cricket did so for all female clubs. The Women's Cricket Association, set up in 1926, forbade its affiliated clubs from including men in their teams or playing against men's teams. Marjorie Pollard thought that men and women could play individual games together but not team games. She had found mixed hockey 'a farce and a failure' and believed that mixed cricket would be 'as dismal a waste of time'. For Pollard, playing in a team of women was a great pleasure. 'The team game spirit', she wrote,

> which is, after all, only a desire to be with a bunch of other folk and all doing a job to a common end – is very strong and almost irresistible ... Looking back on years of team games – and I have had a varied and not unexciting games life – I find that the actual games themselves, who won or lost, or whether there were personal triumphs or disasters, are not the things that remain in the memory. It is the going to matches, the hospitality, the friendships made, the fun and comfort of being one of many playing together, getting tired together, achieving together.
>
> (1934: 14, 16–17)

Alongside clubs with a more middle-class membership came increased numbers of more working-class and lower-middle-class clubs. Many of these were attached to other institutions and exploited and helped to reinforce their sociability. Many such clubs had been grafted onto churches, chapels and the adult sections of Sunday schools in the 1890s and Edwardian period. Church clubs were especially strong at the lowest levels of recreational sport, and particularly in football and cricket, in the North and midlands. Localised data from the North suggests that the numbers of such clubs peaked in the early 1920s but declined sharply in the second half of the 1930s as grounds were lost to house-building. Many towns in the textile districts of Lancashire and Yorkshire had Sunday school cricket and football leagues. In 1922, 107 of 129 cricket teams from Burnley and its surroundings and 69 of 136 football teams were connected with churches or Sunday schools. By 1939 54 out of 101 cricket teams and 23 out of 51 football teams were connected with churches and Sunday schools.

The number of workplace sporting clubs helped emphasise and extend the workplace's role in social contact. Such clubs increased partly because employers promoted them as a way of off-setting emergent trade unionism. The trajectory of their growth steepened from 1918 to 1920, although detailed research on the Lancashire cotton industry suggests that involvement was still heavily dependent on the size and structure of firms and market conditions. An inquiry in 1935 found that of 88 selected firms, 75 had their own sports grounds (Elvin 1938 quoted in Jones 1986: 68). Lower-middle-class employees often formed 'sections' for more social sports like tennis, providing opportunities for rank-and-file employees on their committees to exercise skills of administration, financial management and leadership. By providing facilities for indoor games such as billiards, darts and snooker, Liberal, Conservative, Labour and Reform Clubs added to their role as centres for sociability and recreation, while trade unions and co-operative societies often had their own sports clubs. From 1930 the National Workers' Sports Association, founded under the auspices of the Labour Party and the Trade Union Congress, promoted a range of sporting activities.

Clubs in many sports organised social events that added to their sociability. Many sport leagues and clubs held annual presentation evenings, which could also involve a concert, for the awarding of trophies. Some were held in pubs. Clubs with members from the wealthy classes often held annual dinners but the style and scale of these could vary. Blackheath Rugby Club required dinner jackets to be worn at its annual dinner held in the Victoria Hotel in Northumberland Street, London but Lytham St Annes Motor Boat Club, founded in part as an attraction for visitors, only offered a hot pot supper in 1932. The annual dinners and smoking evenings at cricket clubs were likewise often all-male affairs although research indicates that they rarely led to indecorous behaviour (Williams 2003: 94). Such homo-social activities were a key part of congenial companionship for many, often incorporating time-honoured rituals like speeches, songs, cheers, or toasts, and helping to assert a club's importance, team spirit and uniqueness. The format of such celebrations varied with the standing of the club.

Fundraising events by sport clubs were often important occasions in the calendar of local entertainment. In the North many clubs playing at the highest levels of league cricket held annual sports days or galas which included a range of amusements. At Egerton near Bolton the cricket club's carnival was the high-point of the village's social calendar. Being chosen as its rose queen was a great honour for a girl.[29] In 1936 Bradshaw cricket club gala had stalls for coconut shies, breaking pipes, a shooting gallery, darts, a Chinese laundry, a tall hat competition, American bowls, rolling pennies, skittles, fishing in bottles, a balloon and one selling sweets. There was also a tennis tournament, golf, a balloon race, dancing to a jazz band, the Joy Boys concert party and Professor Taylor's punch and judy show. Entertainment was designed to appeal to both sexes and to adults and children. Sports clubs also held bazaars to raise funds. These too in the North could be important local events. Many clubs organised smaller fundraising events such as weekly whist drives. Between 1934 and 1939 Little Hulton cricket club, situated between Bolton and Salford, held jumble sales, an annual bazaar, an annual garden party, New Year and Shrove Tuesday dances, raffles and draws on the Derby and the Lincoln. In 1935 it ordered 10 lbs of roast beef, 7 lbs of pressed meat, 10 white loaves, 4 small brown loaves, 3 lbs of butter, 2 dozen tea cakes, 12 dozen sweet cakes, 3 dozen whist pies and 6 quarts of milk for the catering at its bazaar.[30] This suggests that many were expected to visit it.

Social events attracted members. Many sports clubs held dances. Hunt balls could be important events in the social calendar of the regional élite. Clubs playing in Sunday school leagues, often the lowest level of recreational cricket, organised events such as flannel dances at which men were expected to wear cricket whites. In 1928 when Players Athletic, the cigarette firm's soccer side, hired the Nottingham Palais de Dance in November 1928, the secretary later received a bill for expenses incurred in refitting two fire extinguishers, replacing two step ladders, repairing three screens and two tables, and replacing eleven broken chairs (Phillips 2003: 36). But such occurrences were probably unusual, especially as they could have reduced the appeal of dances for women. The social activities of sports clubs whose playing members were male can be interpreted as a tactic to neutralise the opposition of women to their menfolk's involvement with sport though oral evidence does not show that this is how they were thought of it in the 1930s. They were often regarded as pleasurable ways of fundraising and a means through which members could keep in contact outside the playing season. Northampton Tennis Club believed that

> the popularity and success of the club is not all due to tennis only, though this has been the main feature, but the social side is keenly looked after … various social events that have helped to foster and maintain the club in its present enviable position.[31]

Much more research needs to be conducted into the social activities of sport clubs for women.

There were special opportunities for sociability on holiday. Resort and county tourist guidebooks and newspaper advertisements for the seaside resorts all regularly referred to their sporting facilities. Lytham St Annes had 'a magnificent swimming pool. All sports, including five golf courses'. Newquay trumpeted its 'GOLF-TENNIS-SAILING' alongside its 'unspoiled natural beauty'. The 1939 *Come to Sussex Guide*, for example, included general chapters on cricket, golf, hunting, yachting, swimming, bowling, croquet and angling, while individual chapters on towns, written by their clerks to the council, always mentioned relevant sporting facilities. Sports boosted resorts. Annual cricket festivals at Scarborough and Canterbury were reintroduced after the First World War. At Canterbury there were house parties in the neighbourhood, special performances at the theatre and bands at the cricket ground. Resort tournaments for bowls or tennis attracted competitors from across the country to enjoy a holiday and compete. Some, like Eastbourne's tennis tournament, had begun before 1914, but increasing numbers of seaside corporations began to introduce them or provide financial support in the 1920s. Southsea's open bowling tournament began in 1929, attracting 550 entries by 1936 for prizes and trophies worth some £250. On the north-east coast Redcar's annual single-handed and pairs bowling tournaments attracted over 200 entries from as far afield as Eastbourne and Carlisle in 1936. Many resorts encouraged fishing festivals, often in September to help extend the season.

Travel increased sporting pleasures in other ways too. Some amateur sports clubs had long recognised that tours during holiday weeks offered a heady mix of sporting pleasure and escape. Leading amateur and professional soccer clubs were often even able to find expenses-paid fixtures abroad. Notts County, Hartlepool United, Durham City, Crook Town, Civil Service and Ilford were amongst British clubs visiting Spain in the summer of 1922. As club tours became more common generally in the 1930s, English seaside resorts, such as Weston-super-Mare, became major beneficiaries. Blackheath Rugby Club, for instance, introduced an annual Easter tour in 1928. In 1930, its *Rugby Annual* reported that

> the Easter tour was again a great success and much enjoyed by all, and is of the utmost value in bringing players together and gaining cohesion for the team ... Headquarters were again at the Grand Central Hotel ... golf as usual took a prominent place and once again we have to thank the Weston Golf Club for their kind hospitality.[32]

The Suffolk Bowling Association organised its first week's tour to Weston-super-Mare in 1937, with a different fixture each day, attracting support by explaining that 'the experience of others has proved it to be most enjoyable'.[33]

Larger hotels increasingly provided sporting facilities such as tennis for wealthy patrons. Squash, for example, was originally a public-school game, with other courts found mainly in West End social clubs and country houses. It spread first into clubs devoted to other ball sports, and then into leading hotels. By 1938 nearly sixty hotels had courts, as did some of the leading cruise liners (Arlott 1975: 986).

Sport, drink and pubs

Sport also drew on and enhanced the sociability of pubs, but less so than previously. Hardly any women's tennis, rounders, netball, hockey or cricket teams had formal links with pubs. Men's cricket and football teams were rarely named after pubs and leagues of pub teams playing either sport were rare, although pubs were often used for meetings and for changing. In Barnsley a league of football teams based on working men's clubs, which can be regarded as another variety of pub, was formed in 1922 but disbanded after one season. A licensed houses cricket league was started at Halifax in 1922 but this too was short-lived. Burnley had a club and institute cricket league in the late 1930s. None of over 1,360 clubs affiliated to the Club Cricket Conference in 1939 seems to have been a pub team. In 1923 a guide for publicans advised making rooms available where football and cricket teams could change and committee meetings could be held (Capper 1923 quoted in Collins and Vamplew 2002: 30–31). Players of football and cricket clubs may have met informally in pubs but no evidence has been found about the extent of this. In the South of England, cricket clubs held annual social evenings and smoking concerts in pubs.

Other sports had much stronger links with pubs. The formation of the National Darts Association by a group of publicans in 1924 saw darts grow in popularity as a pub sport with highly organised brewers' darts clubs and leagues, playing on the more popular and larger 'southern' board with its additional treble inner ring. Meetings to organise bowling matches, pigeon racing and angling competitions were often held in pubs. Pigeon racing, with its co-operative culture, especially in mining communities, had clubs named after public houses, but experienced some decline in the North during the Depression (Mass-Observation 1987: 290–91). Annual angling competitions were often organised by local breweries, with large silver cups as incentives, and outings arranged by pub teams. Prize presentations, of cups and certificates of merit were usually informal yet sociable affairs, often followed by music and singing. Illegal pre-paid bets on horse races could often be placed in pubs. Talking about sport was an important part of pub conviviality. Churches, chapels and Sunday schools may have had so many football and cricket clubs because it was hoped that these could be counter attractions to public houses.

Alcoholic drink, in John Burnett's phrase, 'liquid pleasure', sustained and complemented much sport, and not just the post-match heavy drinking of many rugby clubs, where the increased installation of bars from the 1920s further cemented after-match sociability (Burnett 1999; Collins and Vamplew 2002: 75). County cricket grounds had better opening hours than the heavily regulated inter-war pubs. Bars at rugby union and golf clubhouses were well frequented, and profits subsidised membership fees. In 1929 a representative of the National Golf Clubs Protection Association did not believe many golfers would play if clubs could not sell alcohol.[34] Tony Collins and Wray Vamplew have argued that installing bars from the 1920s 'helped to cement the strong role that sociability played in rugby union' (Collins and Vamplew 2002: 75). In soccer supporters' clubs grew in numbers and these often possessed their own bar. A similar development took place in greyhound racing, where members' clubs, with dance floor and bar, were common at leading stadiums.

The notion that sports were only sports, that they were essentially a means of having fun, was crucial to the significance that was attached to sport in England between the wars. Beliefs that sport was an expression of morality, that it could promote qualities such as selflessness, courage, companionship, respect for those from different backgrounds, cheerfulness, observing rules but also the spirit that underlay rules, were all thought to be in danger if sport were taken too seriously. If the desire to win got out of hand, sports would no longer be fun and sportsmanship, with all its ethical benefits, would be undermined. The paradox of English attitudes to sport was that what was most important about sport required sports to be regarded as of little importance.

Gaining meaning from sport
Sportsmanship and decorum

In 1931 Cecil Moore and his wife were the plaintiffs in a libel case where the defendants were the president (the headmaster of Tonbridge School), the vice-presidents and committee of the Tonbridge Tennis Club. The club had written to Moore and his wife stating that if they played as a pair other clubs would refuse to play against them, that Mrs Moore had claimed points which she had not won, that three clubs had accused her of cheating and that Moore had weakly supported her. Moore was teaching at Tonbridge School. He had been a Balliol scholar and was a former Indian civil servant. In 1911 he had reached the last 16 of the Wimbledon championship. Moore dropped his action when the club officials accepted that Mrs Moore had not cheated.[1] In England between the wars notions of what constituted correct behaviour were crucial to the moral and social significance attached to sport.

Assumptions about what was fit and proper included beliefs about the spirit in which sport should be played, the observance of etiquette and good manners, which had been sanctioned by tradition, and concern about correct forms of sporting attire. The decorum of sport was thought to be as important for spectators as for players. Not all sports, of course, had the same traditions or etiquette but apologists from all sports stressed the need for sportsmanship. Much of the emphasis on the decorum of sport was linked to convictions that maintaining the correct traditions of sport would promote this. The need for sporting decorum was common in upper- and middle-class discourse but many from the working class also expressed their commitment to good manners and sportsmanship. Such commitment can be interpreted as part of a wider insistence in England about correctness that was reflected in assumptions about other cultural forms – received pronunciation of English, correct styles of clothing, the cult of the gentleman and a reverence for long-established institutions and customs. For the economically privileged the notion of correct forms of playing and watching sport, and the conviction that they were the natural guardians of such traditions, would seem, in the light of Bourdieu's concept of *habitus*, to be cultural practices through which they confirmed their social status and sense of social identity.

The nature of sportsmanship

Respect for the game and other people lay at the heart of sportsmanship. Observing sportsmanship was to demonstrate the good manners of putting others before oneself. Novice golfers, for example, were instructed not only to play the game in a keen, fair and kindly spirit, but also to 'observe a wide spirit of courtesy and generosity to an opponent, a proper and sympathetic respect for the wishes of their partner in a foursome, and show a kindly disposition to their caddy's faithful service' (Campbell 1927: 27). In its booklet issued to all British competitors just before the 1924 Olympics, the Council of the British Olympic Association defined a sportsman as one who

> Plays the game for the game's sake
> Plays for his side, and not for himself
> Is a good winner and a good loser, i.e. is modest in victory and generous in defeat
> Accepts all decisions in a proper spirit
> Is chivalrous towards an opponent
> Is unselfish and always ready to help others become proficient
> As a Spectator, applauds good players on both sides
> Never interferes with Referees or Judges, no matter what their decision.[2]

Many would probably have added to this list that doing one's utmost to win without resorting to any form of sharp practice was an essential ingredient of sportsmanship. In 1925 a *Times* editorial argued that

> wanting to win is of the essence of the game ... The real and only justification for wanting to win is that it leads to trying to win. It is the trying that counts, whatever the result ... total blindness to the possibility of ultimate and final failure is a mark of something unconquerable in man.[3]

Sportsmanship also meant that games should be played in ways which exhibited self-control, courtesy, unselfishness and perseverance. In victory, quiet, unassuming pride but not gloating was acceptable. Defeat had to be met cheerfully, with dignity and without complaint. When the Reverend H. Ewbank, a 'sporting vicar' in Sheffield, addressed sports players at a special service, he asked them to 'play the game without taking any undue advantage, even if it were within the rules' and to 'take a beating without bitterness, and if you win, be modest'.[4] It was well known in racing, as the Aga Khan pointed out in a York Gimcrack speech in 1933, that some owners never raised a racing objection with the stewards, 'thinking it unsportsmanlike to win a race by so doing'.[5] Tennis players were expected to show good court manners at all times and play in the right spirit. Sportsmanship and court deportment were closely allied: 'every umpire's and linesman's decision, whether right or wrong, must be taken without a murmur ... Playing to the gallery is ... an unforgivable sin' (Lowe 1924: 115–16).

Taking part was supposedly more important than winning. In 1935 *Amateur Sport and Athletics*, the official magazine of the Amateur Athletic Association, argued that the 'great truths' of sport were 'not to fight but to take part. The important thing in life is not the triumph but the struggle. The essential thing is not to have conquered but to have fought well'.[6] Excessive training and preparation were sometimes seen as unsporting because they revealed too eager a desire for victory and undervalued playing games for their own sake. In 1926 an American observer thought that Oxford and Cambridge oarsmen had 'a vague feeling' that the intensive preparation of American university rowing was unsportsmanlike. He also found that Oxbridge rugby players thought it unsporting to practise tackling against dummies (Savage 1926: 37, 127). Wanting to keep the desire to win within reasonable bounds, it was contended, encouraged adventurous, all-out play for victory even at the risk of defeat. This was preferable to playing in a utilitarian style that eschewed risks and placed the stress on avoiding defeat. Blackheath rugby union club in its 1925-26 *Annual* saw itself as setting out to

> play a fine sporting game, opening up the play well and playing to win, never resorting to that curse of rugby football, playing solely to avoid defeat at all costs and resorting to kick and rush, touch line and obstructive practices.[7]

During the early 1920s some believed that the tennis drop shot was 'bad form'. When the American Bill Tilden used this stroke at Wimbledon in 1924 against a British player there were complaints and 'fuss' from some of the spectators because it was 'not sporting' (Lowe 1924: 16).

Sportsmanship was often assumed to be an especially English quality and a source of great national pride. In his *Character and Sportsmanship* (1927) Sir Theodore Cook, editor of the *Field*, who had been captain of football and boats at Radley, a Cambridge rowing Blue and captain of the England fencing team, argued that 'the instincts of sportsmanship and fair play' were among 'the most deep-seated instincts of the English race'. Fair play 'was bred in our bones and courses through our blood' (pp. vii, xiv, 286). In 1925, following a series of international sporting defeats, the golf journalist Mrs J. E. McNair wrote that it was 'of far greater importance … to maintain our reputation for being a nation of sportsmen and sportswomen … who play their games in the right spirit, and it is a reputation of which we should feel proud'.[8] M.D. Lyon, a Cambridge cricket Blue and Somerset amateur, saw the English approach as the 'exact antithesis' to the American football coach, whose view was said to be 'win somehow, I don't mind how, but win you must' (1933: 514). Chapter 7 discusses how such beliefs influenced attitudes in England to sport overseas and how far it was thought that other nations could aspire to English standards of sportsmanship.

In part the exaltation of sportsmanship was inherited from the Victorian period. Tony Mangan (2001) has shown how the rise of sport in the Victorian and Edwardian public schools was accompanied by an emphasis on fair play as a form of character building. Many of the senior administrators of English sport had been educated before the First World War and had ingested the teachings about sportsmanship and decorum. The selflessness of sportsmanship was thought to express Christian virtues and gentlemanly values. The moral qualities absorbed from playing sport were believed to be transferable to other areas and were seen to guarantee that those from the public schools could be trusted to exercise political and social leadership in Britain and in the colonies for the benefit of others rather than for themselves. The enormous numbers of public schoolboys killed in the First World War was interpreted by many as a vindication of the selflessness of the public-school games cult and probably further reinforced belief in the importance of sportsmanship, though some argued that in the modern world the public schools would have to concentrate more on intellectual development.

Sport narratives stressed that that the wealthy and the well-educated were 'natural' defenders of sportsmanship, the ones who best exemplified its moral qualities. The word 'gentleman' was often linked with sportsmanship. As Jack Fairfax-Blakeborough, the racing journalist, put it, 'the gentleman must be a sportsman in the true, fullest and best sense of the word, or he wouldn't be a gentleman'. He associated sportsmanship on the turf with 'men of unblemished character as sportsmen and gentlemen', whose 'exemplary conduct', 'straight and above board', represented 'all that is best, truest and most honourable in the world of sport' (1927: 22). In 1938 W.R. Inge, Dean of St Pauls, claimed St Paul as a 'sportsman' and God 'the greatest ... gentleman' of all (Inge 1938: 6). Some feared that a larger working-class presence in a game could undermine its sportsmanship. In rugby union D.R. Gent in 1933 was one of many who deprecated attempts to make rugby 'the game of the masses rather than the classes', because lust for victory might lead players to adopt 'methods foreign to the true intention of rugby'. His concern was that 'the style of play' and 'the spirit of the game' would be forgotten. The 'first consideration' he believed for those

> who love it must be to do it justice; never to impoverish it by thinking always and only of emerging the winner. Rugby Union leaders everywhere are not a little concerned at the growing tendency to assess values on the basis of wins and losses.

He felt nervous that an 'unhealthy desire' to win the match was becoming discernible (Gent 1933: 8,201).

Reverence among the wealthy for sportsmanship was very much intertwined with support for amateurism. Social distinction and snobbery were part of this. Banning professionalism ensured a strong representation in a sport of those with wealthy backgrounds. Having amateur captains in sports which permitted professionalism helped to ensure that such sports were played in accordance with the values of the economically and socially privileged. The most frequent justification for amateurism and amateur authority was that amateurs would ensure the survival of sportsmanship. Major Guy Campbell, in his eulogy on the spirit of golf, linked it with how sport was played by amateurs in other ball sports, arguing that

> golf is a game, and played in the right spirit – the spirit in which Kent play cricket, Rugby school play football, and the Corinthians play Association – it is one of the greatest games. Introduce business methods into it, and it only serves to show how easily it can be ruined.
>
> (Campbell 1927: 114)

By 'business methods' he meant putting off, or distracting an opponent. Amateurs, because their livelihoods were not dependent on playing sport, could afford to play in a sporting manner. Professionals, it was implied rather than stated baldly, would be more tempted to cheat or to play in an unadventurous but reliable style which emphasised not losing, in order to guarantee continued selection and regular earnings. At the same time those who defended amateurism in cricket and golf often accepted that professionals in these sports did play like sportsmen.

Those from the wealthier classes often regarded amateur sports, or sports with a strong amateur presence, as more infused with sportsmanship than professional sport. FA president Charles Clegg claimed that when the coming of professionalism became inevitable, he saw that 'it was the duty of amateurs who wished to preserve a great pastime for the people to undertake the control of paid play and keep the sport on the right lines' and that he had devoted himself to this (Sharpe 1952: 154). One reason why the FA and Football League were so strongly opposed to the football pools was their belief that betting would drive out sportsmanship. George Lawrence, the Sheffield United director, argued that 'as soon as betting comes into football the sport of it goes ... and the sporting side of it must be preserved at all costs'.[9] Professional soccer was often condemned for lacking sportsmanship. Bishop Welldon argued that

> Association football will never be an entirely noble sport, so long as players are paid to desert one club for another, and, still more, so long as they are, or may be, bribed to lose matches in which it is their duty to spend their utmost effort for victory.[10]

In 1937 a *Times* leader claimed:

> reading of newspaper reports on Mondays is profoundly disquieting to all who love Association football as a game of skill. Again and again that unpleasant word 'incident' has a way of cropping up, reports of matches resound with stories of free kicks, and crowds seem altogether too vocal and biased in their opinions on the conduct of the referee ... the unforgivable sin in any game is the cold blooded and intentional foul, and it is

unfortunately true that the modern game of professional football is all too full of it.

(quoted in Walvin 1975: 129)

Respect for sportsmanship was not restricted to the wealthy. It is not difficult to find expressions of support for sportsmanship from professional sportsmen with working-class backgrounds. The professional cricketer Jack Hobbs was often regarded as the personification of cricket's tradition of fair play. Much of the discourse of sportsmanship stressed that playing sport could encourage all classes to accept such virtues. Professional sportsmen hardly ever admitted to committing deliberate fouls to win a match which suggests extensive popular support for fair play. Some footballers were known as very hard men but they were not made sporting heroes between the wars.

The extent of sportsmanship

One cannot be certain how far all levels of sport in England were played in a sportsmanlike manner, or whether observance of sportsmanship was growing or declining. Those who believed that amateurs were essential for the survival of fair play worried about economic changes making it harder for amateurs to play at the highest levels. By its very nature successful sharp practice was often hard to detect. Comments by the editor of *Wisden's Rugby Union Almanack* for 1925–26 about obstruction, tackling men without the ball and 'certain actions in the line-out' by the New Zealand team against England and about the Rugby Football Union reprimands of England players both in this match and the England–Scotland game were phrased in a style which suggests that such play had not previously been typical of international rugby.[11] In 1930 Trevor Wignall of the *Daily Express* claimed that foul play was becoming more common in first-class sport. He had seen incidents in soccer that 'were impossible to excuse ... because sportsmanship, as it should be understood, is not too frequently observed'. He thought that boxing was 'very nearly ringed' by fouls and that the Oxford and Cambridge rugby match had been

> not free from episodes that were distasteful, and it is hardly to be wondered at that people are saying that methods of play have crept in that may one day strip us of our most valuable and most highly-to-be-desired asset – our reputation for fair play. Fouls are detestable in any pastime, but we do see far too many of them these days.[12]

Certainly fouling was not unknown in professional soccer, and may have been increasing. In a Tranmere reserve game, Dixie Dean lost a testicle after a deliberately high tackle aimed at curbing his pace. Frank Barson, the Aston Villa and England player, was warned by the referee *before* the FA Cup Final about his play.[13] English professional soccer had emerged in the North-west and

Midlands, where climate and muddy pitches put a premium on workrate, physicality and power, and limited opportunities to demonstrate technique. So it was unsurprising that in these areas, and increasingly beyond, there was a continued cross-class pleasure in hard, rough play.

But concerns about sportsmanship were not often expressed by the press which, given the respect for sportsmanship, could mean that it was not widely believed that fair play was in decline. No major domestic sporting event held in England was widely reported as being won through a deliberate foul. Greyhound races were fixed at working-class 'flapper' tracks but leading tracks like the White City were generally free of such allegations.

For some even the adoption of new equipment violated sportsmanship. When rowing trainer Steve Fairbairn introduced swivel rowlocks instead of the fixed pin, he was attacked for breaking the 'ideals' and 'unwritten codes' of rowing. Eric Halladay (1990: 130–31) argues that the 'old guard' among the amateur élite who controlled rowing felt threatened by such challenges to orthodoxy and saw them as heresy and betrayal, calling into question the time-honoured code. The swivel rowlock, however, was soon taken up by rowers and doubts about its fairness disappeared. Once American golfers legalised steel shafts, they were quickly adopted by amateurs in England when it was found that they made driving easier than hickory shafts. Professionals complained about steel replacing hickory shafts but this may have been because they feared losing the income they currently received from repairs.

It was often argued that sportsmanship involved observing the spirit rather than the letter of a sport's rules. In the *Cricketer Annual* for 1922-23 Bishop Welldon wrote that insisting 'upon the letter and not the spirit of the rules in a game or to distort the letter of the rules for personal advantage' was 'not cricket'.[14] In 1932 a writer in the *Field* complained about 'a tendency to disregard the accepted interpretation of the rules and spirit of play … spreading among some of our popular games'.[15] But not all agreed about what was the spirit of a sport. In 1928 the editor of *Tennis Illustrated* conceded that most people considered special training and preparation as 'rather too close approximations to the ideals and methods of professionalism' but he condemned such views as 'foolish and out of date'.[16] Jack Hobbs argued that it would 'let the umpire down' if a batsman said in an umpire's presence that he had been given not out when he should have been given out. Hobbs added 'with a twinkle' that next time the umpire might give the batsman out (Swanton 1985: 70). In the match between Victoria and the MCC in 1929, the Victoria captain allowed Duckworth, who was not playing in the match, to keep wicket when Ames, the MCC wicketkeeper, was injured. This was contrary to the laws of cricket but Chapman, the MCC captain, described it as 'a great sporting action'.[17] On the same tour England's slow, cautious batting to build a match-winning total was condemned in *Athletic News* as 'lacking the sportsman's gesture and spirit'.[18] Major Guy Campbell complained that in golf more rules had become necessary because of a general disregard for its unwritten rules and etiquette, which had increased as the number of players had grown. He felt in 1927 that players had begin to place more emphasis on the score, winning trophies or hitting the ball better than on 'a scrupulous spirit of sportsmanship'. This had in turn had created more rules so fewer studied them closely (Campbell 1927: 99–100).

Even in first-class cricket, often lauded as the game with the highest standard of sportsmanship, sharp practice was found. Bowlers often illicitly lifted the seam. Sometimes counties played those without the necessary residential qualification. The fairness of bodyline bowling provoked more debate in cricket, and in English sport generally, than any other issue between the wars. Bodyline involved fast bowlers delivering short-pitched balls on or just outside the leg stump with a ring of legside fielders. This increased the possibility of batsmen being caught by legside fielders but there was also a high likelihood of batsmen being hit by the ball which led some to see bodyline as physical intimidation. England employed bodyline against Australia on the 1932–33 tour and won the series by four matches to one. The method was very much the decision of the England captain Douglas Jardine, an amateur educated at Winchester and Oxford, but who was determined to regain the Ashes. He saw bodyline as a means of neutralising the Australian batting and that of Don Bradman in particular. Australian players, officials, press and spectators regarded bodyline as unsporting and a violation of cricket's traditions of fair play. On 18 January 1933 in a telegram to the MCC the Australian Board of Control condemned bodyline as a 'menace to the best interests of the game' and 'unsportsmanlike' and likely to upset the friendly relations between England and Australia. In a return cable the MCC Committee deprecated the accusation of unsportsmanlike play. It expressed its full confidence in the captain, team and managers. If the Australian Board wished to cancel the rest of the tour, the Committee would accept this but with 'the greatest reluctance'. The tour continued after the Australian Board conceded that the sportsmanship of the England team was not being questioned.[19]

Reactions to bodyline in English cricket were divided. Significantly the amateur fast bowler Gubby Allen, a member of the touring side, thought it unsporting and refused to bowl it. Pelham Warner, the tour manager, also disliked it but made no public comments during the tour. Former England amateur captains such as Lord Hawke and Sir Stanley Jackson made no public objections to bodyline. Others pointed out that it had been used by the Australian fast bowlers McDonald and Gregory against England in 1920–21 and 1921. Some of the England tourists such as George Duckworth defended bodyline at first but within a year or two condemned it. The English cricket establishment soon disowned it too. In November 1933 the MCC condemned bowling that involved a direct attack on batsmen and county captains agreed not to use it. In part this was because it of a growing feeling that bodyline was perhaps not in keeping with cricket's tradition of sportsmanship but a more important factor may have been a fear that Australia would not tour England in

1934 unless it was outlawed. As county clubs needed their share of test match profits to survive, a cancellation of the 1934 tour would have been disastrous for county cricket.

Paying amateurs could be regarded as cheating and unsporting, though we do not know the full extent of shamateurism. The North American ice hockey players who came to England in the 1930s were supposedly amateurs but were widely reported to be receiving expenses of £12 each week which would have been far above what it cost them to play. In 1938 *Golf Illustrated*'s reminder that being paid by advertisers was a violation of amateur status suggests that amateurs had been doing this.[20] Some amateur cricketers were given well-paid jobs by supporters of county teams to enable them to play as amateurs. Others certainly received excessive expenses. Arthur Carr, an amateur captain of Nottinghamshire and England, believed that some received £500 per year in expenses, roughly equal to what the leading professionals were paid (Carr 1935: 70). In 1931 *Tennis Illustrated* thought that the expenses paid to those playing in international tournaments created 'a class of amateur perilously near to a professional, even though he be a man with a private income'.[21] *Football Pictorial* in 1935 wrote of the 'problem' of shamateurism in football and of the authorities' reluctance to investigate without 'proof of malpractices'.[22]

Allegations of cheating surfaced more often in speedway than in most other sports. Until the invention of a starting gate with tapes in 1933, races often had to be re-run because riders tried to jump the start. The only effective method of ending the practice of riders in the last place deliberately falling off their machines in order to have the race re-run was to ban fallen riders from a re-run race (Hoskins 1977: 161). The speedway manager Johnny Hoskins claimed that foul riding, including jabbing opponents in the ribs when going round bends, shoulder charging along the straights and deliberate stalling to baulk another rider had caused a 'terrible crop' of injuries in 1935. He believed that 'many riders view with alarm the advent of younger men, and, fearful of losing their jobs, they employ all the tricks I have mentioned to terrify the struggling junior'.[23] The Auto-Cycle Union drew the attention of its stewards to 'numerous cases' of foul riding in 1939.[24]

More research will have to be undertaken before we can be certain of the extent of sportsmanship in recreational sport. Examining all levels of cricket in Bolton has led to the conclusion that 'complaints ... were sufficiently rare never to have challenged the belief that playing cricket was an expression of fair play and sportsmanship' (Williams 2003: 78–85). The Reverend Kenneth Hunt, a former English international, praised the Boots Athletic response to a disallowed goal against Oxford City in the FA Amateur Cup in January 1920:

> I should like to say how very impressed we were with the sporting way in which your fellows took the decision. I heard no complaint ... May I, in virtue of my experience, and without appearing to preach, urge your men

to maintain that attitude? Then, whether in defeat or victory, they will always be admired and respected.

(Phillips 2003: 34)

Yet the fact that Hunt made these comments could have meant that such sporting conduct was unusual. Not all the teams Boots Athletic played against exhibited such sporting ideals, as their magazine reported ruefully. When they played the mining team Annesley Colliery in a 1927 Notts Senior cup-tie, 'the local team, realising that they could not beat us at football, played the man instead of the ball … all of our men suffered from knocks and bruises' (quoted in Phillips 2003: 35). Evidence from South Yorkshire, however, suggests a more sporting situation. From 1923–24 to 1938–39 the number of clubs affiliated to the Sheffield and Hallamshire Football Association fluctuated between 601 and 874 but at its monthly Council meetings only a tiny number of players were suspended for fighting, inciting others to fight, insulting referees, leaving the field or not being registered to play.

Spectators, decorum and sportsmanship

Sport discourses also expected spectators to behave in accordance with accepted standards of decorum and sportsmanship. The *Daily Express*, looking forward to Wimbledon, reminded spectators in 1927 that

> a sporting, impartial gallery will inspire players on court, while an ignorant one, favouring one side can often spoil a match. Never applaud a difficult get in the middle of the rally, this is apt to make a player miss his next stroke unnecessarily. The decisions of the umpire or linesman should never be questioned from the stands. These officials are in a better position to judge … Try not to leave your seat to watch another match until a set is finished.[25]

Such comments implied that the behaviour of some spectators in the previous few years had not been acceptable.

The behaviour of spectators at golf's Open Championship was sometimes condemned as unsporting and out of keeping with the game's traditions. In 1936 the golf correspondent for the *Field* found that because spectators were so 'anxious' and 'selfish' to see a particular golfer, his opponent would inevitably suffer:

> [being drawn to] play behind a popular idol, a famous champion, or even a local professional means an extra handicap, and in many cases this has ruined the chances of several promising competitors … If their 'hero' puts his ball anywhere on a big green the following clap, and as he holes his putt they never miss applauding. Such demonstrations are futile, and it is

unsporting to clap the individual who holes out in front of the opponent who still has a chance of a half ... the majority who know nothing about the game go about without thinking. At one recent championship mothers turned up with babies in perambulators, young girls from the village shops and vast numbers of schoolchildren. Not to see the golf, but to catch a glimpse of a world-famous film actor who got beaten in round number one! Let it be hoped that this may never occur again.[26]

Interviews with ex-players suggest that for county cricket crowds were usually silent during a bowler's run up and delivery and generally quieter than those in Australia or the Caribbean. Abuse of players and umpires, hooting and jeering, unruliness and unfair and boisterous behaviour were portrayed as a disgrace entirely foreign to the true spirit of the game. The MCC *Pavilion and Ground Regulations* of 1939 banned betting as well as any noise or confusion. The most detailed research thus far concludes that 'the impression which arises from consulting a wide range of sources is that in general spectators at first-class cricket did behave in accordance with what were thought to be the standards of sportsmanship'.[27] The dislike that England's cricket authorities had for the barracking by cricket spectators in Australia has been discussed in Chapter 1.

In general the press showed little concern about the behaviour of spectators at county cricket, though there were occasional examples of spectator misconduct. The Sheffield crowd in the 1920s gained a reputation for being fiercely partisan and ill-mannered, placing players and umpires under intense strain. In 1924, for example, *The Times* claimed that they 'behaved very badly indeed, making the task of the umpires almost unbearable' in the match between Yorkshire and Middlesex.[28] The *News of the World* commented that another metropolitan county could have something to say about 'certain "incidents" in the North' and that neither Lancashire nor Nottinghamshire 'carried away particularly pleasant reminiscences of their experiences at Sheffield'.[29] Perhaps because of a desire not to sully cricket's decorous image, no national newspaper gave details of this spectator misconduct. Williams, however, argues that such behaviour was untypical and that in general county cricket spectators behaved in accordance with standards of sportsmanship. In 1920, for example, Kent threatened to expel from the club one member who used abusive language in the neighbourhood of ladies. The same study suggests that even in league cricket contemporary accounts show that though crowds were fiercely partisan, unruly and unfair conduct was rare. Fighting amongst spectators at the socially prestigious Eton versus Harrow match at Lords in 1919 prompted Old Boys to demand that there should be no repetition of such behaviour in 1920. Sportsmanship among spectators may not always have conformed to the image created by the game's apologists of the game, but there was never sufficient bad behaviour to challenge the belief that cricket was an expression of sportsmanship (Williams 2003: 88).

Greyhound racing, a leading spectator sport by the mid-1930s, was often criticised by opponents of gambling but they rarely complained about crowds being unruly or unsporting. Mike Huggins has shown that flat race meetings were often local or regional festivals and that crowds were usually well-behaved. Complaints about horseracing disorder usually centred around gangs such as Birmingham's Brummagen Boys or the Sabini Boys who intimidated bookmakers and ran protection rackets at race meetings as part of wider criminality, or the pickpockets who operated in all large crowds. Huggins (2003: 142, 146–50) concludes that racing was 'a major context for convivial enjoyment of the social pleasures of ludism, laughter and liquor' and that 'little misbehaviour generally resulted'.

Middle-class commentators often condemned soccer spectators for being unduly partisan. The golfing journalist Bernard Darwin, for instance, described them as having only a 'rough and unceremonious' chivalry (1940: 25). Queens Park Rangers, Millwall and Carlisle had their grounds briefly closed in the 1930s following disturbances, and there were public concerns over crowd behaviour in 1919–22 and again in the later 1930s (Russell 1997: 100–101). Yet in comparison with the Victorian period and the last half-century, the inter-war period has been seen by sports sociologists as a relatively peaceful one in terms of crowd disturbances (Murphy *et al.* 1990: 73–76). In 1924 at an FA Cup quarter-final tie between Manchester City and Cardiff City, where its 76,166 spectators were a record for a soccer match played in the English provinces, only 66 policemen were on duty at the ground which suggests that crowd misbehaviour was not anticipated.[30] Images of football crowds on newsreels project a happy, convivial but lively picture of a relatively stable, ordered community, one in which, as Fishwick concludes, 'enthusiasm was not incompatible with restraint' (1989: 63).[31] Throwing items onto the pitch and demonstrating enthusiastic support were not uncommon, but given the political problems of unemployment and strikes, soccer crowds were comfortingly well-behaved, and disorder was treated as relatively unproblematic by the press. There was, says McKibbin, 'comparative tranquillity' (McKibbin 1998: 343).

Spectator misbehaviour at speedway meetings was reported rarely. In 1936 some spectators were banned from Harringay because they tried to shout down the announcer and had tried 'to do all they could to spoil the meeting for everybody else'. There were also disturbances at a Harringay meeting in 1938 when the spectators disagreed with the decision to abandon the meeting because of a wet track after only five races.[32] Spectators at ice hockey were more often criticised for being disorderly and unsporting. When a Great Britain team played Canada at Harringay in 1937 spectators dissatisfied with refereeing decisions threw oranges, newspapers and coins onto the rink. The publicity manager took the microphone and asked whether 'there were any British sportsmen in the house?' The national anthem was played in the hope of quieting the crowd. Cecil Headley, sports editor for the *People*, who had already castigated ice hockey spectators as likely to throw bottles at the opposing team when home players were injured. He described the Canada match as 'almost a riot' and ice hockey as 'this game we could well do without' whose spectators throw orange peel, or paper or anything they have at hand quite impartially at the players, the referee, or, to show what poor fish they are, on to the ice to stop the game ... Mind you, the bulk of these fatheads around the rinks are bits of boys and girls such as you see at speedway racing.[33]

In *Ice Hockey World* its columnist 'Indian' admitted that items had been thrown but tried to argue that this was an expression of sportsmanship. He blamed the trouble on incompetent refereeing and wrote, 'I don't blame the urge that made the crowd yell their disapproval. Their methods may have been crude but it was the cry of sportsmen, nevertheless, yelling for fair play'. Such comments indicate the sensitivities aroused by accusations of being unsporting. In 1939 the *Ice Hockey World* wrote that the 'missile throwing problem' had to be dealt with because this provided more 'material for the anti-hockey writers brigade' than even fights between players.[34]

Sport, decorum and clothing

Notions of appropriate sporting attire were very much intertwined with beliefs that correct sporting standards had to be preserved. The sports equipment manufacturer Spalding regularly reminded its readers that it sold '*Correct* [our italics] Sportswear for men and women'. Having the proper clothing signalled knowledge of what was the accepted sporting apparel, and sufficient wealth to acquire it. Notions of correct clothing helped to keep clubs playing at certain levels of a sport socially exclusive. It was acceptable for men competing at the least prestigious level of recreational cricket to play in dark trousers though some leagues insisted that bowlers wore white shirts or sweaters. It would have been unthinkable for those playing at socially exclusive clubs not to have worn white flannels. At the highest levels of league cricket in the North and Midlands, where ability rather than social standing determined team selection, all working-class players had white trousers.

Correct clothing was thought to encourage acceptance of traditional views of how sport should be played. Casual dress implied a casual approach, a lack of appropriate *gravitas* in striving to win and probably disregard for sportsmanship. The manual of *Rugby Football for Public Schools* told boys that, if only for practical reasons, 'nothing looks worse than a player to have his stockings round his ankles'. Those who read *Golf for Beginners* were told that 'clothes constitute an essential asset' and that 'the guiding principle should be moderation in all things' (Campbell 1927: 15). *Women's Cricket* contended that in 1939 'the standard of equipment and uniform were on the downgrade' and that 'players who fail in these respects only exhibit to the world, as if on a hoarding, that they personally are inefficient, lazy, thoughtless, inconsistent and quite incapable of even minding themselves'.[35] In many sports older clubs, with longer traditions, were most likely to insist on such standards. To Anglophile Rudolf Kircher, players at many of the new sport clubs wore clothing 'considerably short of English standards' (1928: 68).

Appropriate decorum in dress was especially important for women playing sports that men also played. Few women's cricket or hockey clubs had their own grounds. They had to play on municipal pitches or those belonging to men's clubs. Marjorie Pollard argued that women cricketers had to display 'dignity, circumspection, caution and submission to public opinion', by which she meant male opinion in most cases, if women players were to gain access to good pitches, ones easier to bat on (Williams 2003: 103). The Women's Cricket Association encouraged teams to play in white and ruled in 1928 that sleeveless dresses and transparent stockings were not permitted. In 1930 players were given the option of wearing regulation dresses and tunics not more than three inches above the knee when kneeling. It wanted players to wear white shoes. Trousers were certainly not allowed (ibid.: 102–03). Such guidance was not always followed. *Women's Cricket* complained regularly of the 'clothing problem'. In 1931 it lamented that in 1930 there had been 'black shoes, shoes with coloured saddles ... silk frocks, pique frocks, and all sorts of frocks – with sleeves, without sleeves and some with nearly sleeves'.[36] The Women's Cricket Federation, limited to Lancashire and Yorkshire, had a more relaxed dress code and even allowed trousers, though show photographs show most of its players wearing skirts or dresses.

In bowls, another sport where women's participation was problematical, one female commentator saw women's dress and deportment as simultaneously setting a standard for men to live up to and dressing modestly for men's eyes. 'We have shown the bowling world how to dress for the green – Avoid pitfalls like the silk dress, not sufficiently shadowed beneath ... an over-display of jewellery is also to be deprecated' (Hartley 1935: 57). The rules of hockey applied to men and women, but significantly there were specific regulations only about women's playing clothing, which would have required careful measuring to ensure they were obeyed. Women were instructed that

> all players shall wear skirts, tunics or divided skirts. Skirts shall not be less than knee length and in no case longer than fourteen inches off the ground all round. Tunics shall not be less than one and not more than four and a half inches off the ground when the player kneels. Long stockings must be worn with tunics. Divided skirts shall not be more than three inches off the ground when kneeling.
>
> (Shoveller and Pollard 1936: 126–27)

In 1930 Jacqueline Howard wrote in the *Morning Post* about appropriate clothing for women who wanted to be crew members at Cowes and for those going grouse shooting while in the same newspaper Mrs Norman Wright gave advice about what women wanting to take up gliding should wear.[37] In 1931 Patience Young wrote in the *Billiard Player* about what women players should wear when playing in the evenings. She recommended a long black dress down to the ankles with a short coatee with no trimming and a large bunch of velvet roses six or eight inches below the hips to relieve the sombreness.[38] Such articles suggest uncertainty among women players about what to wear but this could also have been linked to a desire to appear fashionable.

Clothing, especially for women, changed in some sports between the wars. A new emphasis on wearing comfortable and functional clothes could be seen, for example, in lower-middle-class leisure activities such as hiking where many women wore shirts and shorts in drab potato-colour or khaki. In 1925 the editor of *Golf Illustrated* thought that the 'evolution of *habilement*' had contributed much to the 'wonderful improvement' in the playing standard of women's golf. The female golf journalist J.E. McNair thought that women suffered a 'sartorial handicap' through 'fashion and sumptuary laws' but noted women had abandoned skirts in hunting and winter sports. She regretted that no woman seemed prepared to take the plunge and wear plus fours which gave greater freedom.[39] Gloria Miniprio in 1933 was the first woman to play in trousers at the English Ladies' Championship. *Golf Illustrated* reported that this was 'only officially frowned upon' and argued that such attire was not only warmer and more comfortable but 'most of all, they emphasise in the woman's mind the sense of her complete emancipation'.[40]

In tennis, one-piece short frocks, bandeaus, open-necked blouses, shorts and bare legs became more common in the early 1930s, providing greater freedom of movement, and symbolising some emancipatory relaxation of restraints, especially as the lower-middle classes took up the sport. It reflected too, the wider public mood, with its importation of American modes and manners. All the more élite tennis clubs continued to insist that men and women looked neat, tidy and, above all, wore white. Mrs Satterthwaite's book of tennis guidance told women to 'avoid colour of any sort (even a coloured belt) about the dress itself, but if you must break out somewhere, have a coloured silk handkerchief for your head, which you must wear well forward on your forehead, and not at the back of your head' (Satterthwaite n.d.: 65). Reports of the Hallamshire tennis tournament in 1928, however, showed that in some cases 'a brightly coloured belt matched the short tennis socks and the ribbon bandeau, while woollen pullovers to slip on after the game in soft shades of rose, blue and lemon' were being worn.[41] Visiting foreign players, such as Mlle Suzanne Lenglen, demonstrated both a more active style of play and a shockingly different mode of dress, with a short skirt (just below the knee), stockings held up with garters, and a sleeveless, collarless vest. Not only that but Lenglen was ebullient and dramatic rather than, as expected, modestly reticent. American Helen Jacobs wore knee-length shorts in 1934. White stockings were discarded by younger players, but Wimbledon remained fairly conservative. In 1928, when John Hennessy played at Wimbledon with a stripe down his white flannels, one 'old gent' described this as 'sartorial Bolshevism'.[42] Bunny Austin and a few other men played in shorts at Wimbledon in 1933 but men who played tennis on the municipal courts of the industrial town of St Helens throughout the 1930s were expected to wear full-length white flannels.[43] No instances have been found of demands for cricket to abandon playing in whites.

The significance ascribed to correct forms of behaviour in sport and the assumptions that the wealthier classes were best equipped to ensure their observance can be related to the uncertainties of the inter-war world. In such a world, one can argue, the supposed morality of sportsmanship, and especially its stress on selflessness, and persuading the working class to accept this, were all the more necessary to the wealthy as a justification of their fitness to provide social and political leadership. The constant reiteration of values of amateurism, sportsmanship and decorum were an expression of élitism, but also to a large degree a sign of anxiety.

Gaining meaning from sport
Englishness and isolationism

One of the more lasting consequences of Britain's nineteenth-century imperial and economic supremacy was following overseas for its sports. By 1914 association football was played extensively in continental Europe and Latin America. Lawn tennis had spread to much of Europe, the Empire and the United States. Modern forms of boxing, athletic races and racing were based on English models. Golf, originating in Scotland, was played in the rest of the English-speaking world. Cricket was largely restricted to the dominions and colonies as was rugby union, though this was also played to a high standard in France. Few ball sports popular before 1914 other than polo, billiards and snooker – and snooker was invented by a British army officer in India – were not invented in Britain. The ball games of other countries rarely spread beyond their boundaries. Before 1914 American football and baseball had little following outside North America. Yet by 1914 top English players were often experiencing defeat by overseas competitors in cricket, athletics, rugby and tennis, and the USA and Australia were becoming seen as leading sporting rivals.

England and America

American sporting successes fuelled broader élite concerns about American influence, fears which provided content for contemporary cultural critiques. Hollywood films, fashions in clothing, drinking, dance and popular music had a major impact on English society. They were widely popular, and often welcomed as aspects of 'modernity'. A vociferous, often high-brow minority condemned them as worryingly vulgar, commercialised, mass-produced, democratic, more equal and less restrained. In J.B. Priestley's *English Journey* (1934: 401) 'post-war England' was symbolised by cocktail bars, motor coaches, wireless, hiking, factory girls looking like actresses, greyhound racing, dirt tracks and by cheap and American Woolworths stores. American values and ethics impacted on English sports reporting, bringing more populist, personalised and brash approaches. Americanism was held back, although only in part, by the resilience of England's own sporting culture and by traditional beliefs in sportsmanship and amateurism. There was also strong BBC resistance, although British newsreels quite regularly featured imported American as well as British sports features.

American sports were steadily infiltrating too. It was a rich American, J.A. Munn, who brought greyhound racing from the USA to spread rapidly under predominantly English management from 1927. Speedway, conceived in America, began in England the same year, introduced largely through Australian riders and experts. American 'all-in' wrestling, which allowed new holds and introduced submission moves, became commercially popular in the early 1930s, with thirty-nine regular shows running in Greater London alone. Baseball received limited support in London, Lancashire and Yorkshire.

In some formerly British-dominated sports, American players increasingly won. American golf professional Walter Hagen won the British Open in 1922 and thereafter he and countryman Bobby Jones became leading figures. In golf matches between the two countries, the Walker Cup for amateurs was usually won easily by the Americans although in the professionals' Ryder Cup, founded in 1927, home advantage usually told. In tennis, at Wimbledon, the Americans, along with the French, were becoming supreme. In track, field and swimming, where Britain had once led the world, the USA won sweeping victories at the post-war Olympiads. In amateur boxing, Britain could no longer defeat the world's best, winning no boxing medals in the 1928 Olympics. In the professional ring, Americans increasingly triumphed.

Involvement with sport overseas

Despite increased American, European and colonial pressure, English sports organisations retained power in the administration of international sport. Sport was still a potent element of imperial power, supporting British authority and defusing discontent. England dominated those sports, such as cricket and rugby, which were more or less restricted to the Empire. Even though cricket lacked the formalised national structures of the Football Association or the Rugby Union, the MCC was still accepted as the chief authority for world cricket and its laws. Other national governing bodies were independent but accepted MCC changes, such as the revision of the LBW law. In 1909 the English Board of Control, which superintended Test matches in England, the Australian Board of Control and the South African Cricket Union set up the Imperial Cricket Conference (ICC) to be responsible for test match cricket. Between the wars, the ICC always met at Lord's, and the MCC provided its secretarial support. Cricket governing bodies in the West Indies, New Zealand and India joined the ICC as they started playing Test cricket but only the three founding members could veto proposals. Senior English officials on occasions represented other countries at ICC meetings. At one 1930 meeting the West Indies were represented by Pelham Warner, the former England and Middlesex captain and selector, and R.H. Mallett, president of the Minor

Counties Cricket Association, who had managed the West Indian tours to England in 1923 and 1928, while Henry Leveson Gower, the President of Surrey CCC, represented South Africa.[1] The only serious challenge to the MCC domination of world cricket came in 1933 when an Australian threat to stop playing test cricket against England persuaded the MCC to prohibit 'direct attack' bodyline bowling.

The Royal and Ancient Golf Club at St Andrews in Scotland was the controlling body for golf in Britain and most of the world, though not the United States and Canada. In 1924 the English Golf Union was established to promote golf in England, but claimed that it was not trying to usurp the authority of the Royal and Ancient Club. England's Rugby Football Union (RFU) was a founding member in 1886 of the International Rugby Football Board (IRB) which superintended international rugby. From 1931 the IRB framed the laws of the game. England had four votes on the Board, the unions of Scotland, Wales and Ireland only two each. The minute books of the RFU and of the IRB show that between the wars the Board almost always followed English recommendations. In 1920 the RFU decided that it was not the time for France to press for membership of the IRB. A year later it told representatives from the Rugby Union of New South Wales that it was not opportune for them to bring forward proposals to the IRB.[2] In 1925 the IRB rejected proposals from New Zealand and New South Wales for the establishment of an Imperial Advisory Board. It agreed that there could be imperial rugby football conferences every three years in London to consider amendments to the laws. The first was arranged for 1926 where New Zealand, South Africa and New South Wales, but not France, were to be represented and would have two votes each whereas the IRB would have ten.[3] In 1929 the dominion unions again wanted to discuss their relationship with the IRB, but the IRB decided unanimously that 'as a condition precedent to the consideration of the creation of a consultative body under the supreme control of this Board, all Dominion Unions should agree to adopt the laws of the game as framed by the International Board'.[4] The dominion unions appear to have accepted this. The IRB minutes do not indicate that any advisory conferences were held in the 1930s. In 1932 the IRB informed the President of the Federazione Italiana Palla Ovale, the Italian governing body, that his proposal for an international federation to codify rules and superintend propaganda, discipline and international matches for rugby throughout Europe was not 'workable or desirable'.[5] The RFU and IRB minute books and press reports reveal little about why such policies were adopted but they clearly indicate that the RFU had little intention of weakening its control over rugby.

English sports bodies were less dominant where sports were not restricted to the Empire. The modern Olympic movement had its headquarters in Geneva. No British representative headed the International Olympic Committee (IOC), although in the mid-1930s Lord Aberdare, Lord Burghley and Sir Noel Curtis-Bennett were members of it. No British representative was president of its Executive Committee, though in 1936 Aberdare was one of its five members. The English were however strong opponents of any weakening of amateurism. In the later 1920s the governing bodies of British Olympic sports and the British Olympic Association (BOA) took a leading role in prohibiting 'broken time' payments being made to Olympic competitors to compensate them for loss of earnings.[6] Continental IOC members were reportedly 'flirting' with introducing these for the 1932 Games, and at the Berlin Olympic Congress in 1930 Belgian delegates proposed that for each sport the definition of amateur status be left to its international federation. This could have resulted in some sports permitting broken time payments. At the Congress, the English argued that all sports should have a common definition of amateurism and that broken time payments struck at the root of the Olympic idea. A British amendment accepted that governing federations should define amateur status for their sports but only in accordance with the definition of amateurism accepted by the Olympic Congress at Prague in 1925. As the Prague Congress had outlawed broken time payments, this British amendment ensured that they would not be accepted. Even so, the British amendment was accepted by 41 votes to 11 partly through the support of the USA and a threat by the International Athletic Federation to boycott the 1932 games if broken time payments were legalised.[7]

The FA's relations with FIFA, the body established in France in 1904 to provide an international organisation for soccer, were never easy between the wars. The International FA Board (IFAB) which controlled soccer rules had been set up in 1886 by the four home football associations. The FA joined FIFA in 1906 and in 1913 FIFA was given one vote on the IFAB but the four British unions retained one vote each. As this remained the case throughout the inter-war years, the British associations, by acting together, could decide international rules. In 1920 the FA and the other home associations resigned from FIFA after unsuccessfully calling for the exclusion of the former 'enemy' nations. By 1922 the FA and the other home associations had changed their policy, agreeing to allow international and club matches against former enemies, but delayed rejoining FIFA until 1924. When FIFA agreed with the IOC that footballers receiving broken time payments could play in the Olympics, the FA believed this would destroy the basis of amateur sport, and the home nations withdrew again in 1928. In 1931 they jointly agreed to have no further discussions with FIFA about re-affiliation, though to a degree the FA acted as if it were still a member. Useful personal contacts continued between FA and FIFA officials in the 1930s and FIFA remained a member of IFAB.

England's Lawn Tennis Association (LTA) accepted a reduced role in the control and administration of international tennis in the early 1920s. When the International Lawn Tennis Federation (ILTF) was first set up in 1913, the LTA retained special privileges. It received an extra vote and the right to hold the world's championship on grass, which gave the Wimbledon championship official recognition as the world's most prestigious grass court championship. The LTA also retained the right to make the rules for tennis. But after 1918, the

American Lawn Tennis Association refused to join the ILTF. It was especially critical of the LTA's right to hold the world grass championship in perpetuity and of the LTA's additional vote on the ILTF. In 1923 an extraordinary meeting of the LTA agreed unanimously that in order to have a universal code of rules for tennis, the right of making and amending rules would be handed to an International Rules Board which in turn would soon give this power to the ILTF and then dissolve itself when the American LTA joined the ILTF. The LTA also surrendered its right to hold in perpetuity the world championship on grass and its additional vote on the ILTF. A few days later the ILTF announced that it would scrap the world championship for grass and hard courts but that instead the championships of the LTA, the United States, France and Australia would be known as the 'official lawn tennis championships of the International Federation'.[8] The American Association then joined the ILTF. This surrender of authority by the LTA seems to have been a reaction to American pressure and a reflection of America's playing power in world tennis.

England's Hockey Association remained a member of the International Rules Board that standardised and amended the rules of hockey but declined to join the Federation Internationale de Hockey, the international controlling body, established so that hockey could continue to be an Olympic sport. Although England had won the 1920 hockey Olympic gold medal, its refusal meant no team in the 1928 Olympics. English cycling also had limited international influence. In 1892 England's National Cycle Union had taken the lead in establishing the International Cycling Union but a rival body, the Union Cycliste Internationale (UCI), was created in Paris in 1900. Continental cycling was stronger so the UCI soon became the accepted international authority. The National Cycling Union joined it in 1903. In 1936 the editor of *Cycling* argued that in

> the international legislation for the sport the English activities are confined to an attendance at the congress of the Union [UCI] twice yearly, where, owing to language difficulties, our delegates sit strangely silent. The same state of affairs obtains at the world's championships, even although, in the rotation of complimentary appointments among the nations, it becomes an Englishman's turn to act as one of the commissaires or stewards.[9]

Participation in international sports competition

More international sporting contests were held between the wars. The British Empire Games, first held at Hamilton in Canada in 1930, focused on international track and field competition but included lawn bowls, rowing, swimming and diving. Cycling and women's events were added for London in 1934. England played four inter-war international rugby matches at Twickenham, against touring teams from Australia, New Zealand, and South Africa. Cricket test matches, first played against Australia in 1877 and against South Africa in

1889, were extended to the West Indies in 1928, New Zealand in 1930 and India in 1932. The last season when no touring side visited England to play test matches was in 1927. The England women's cricket team first played test matches on its tour of Australia and New Zealand in 1934–35 and against Australia in England in 1937. English women track and field athletes took part in the Women's Olympics in 1922 and in the Women's World Games of 1926, 1930 and 1934. In golf, the Walker Cup, contested by men's amateur teams representing Britain and the United States, was first played in 1922, and the Ryder Cup, for professional teams, in 1927. The Curtis Cup, played between women's amateur golf teams representing Britain and the USA, started in 1932. Its tennis equivalent, the Wightman Cup, began in 1923. The first series of speedway 'test' matches against Australia were held in England in 1930 and in each subsequent English season. Before 1914 England played only seven soccer internationals against continental countries but played nineteen in the 1920s and twenty-eight in the 1930s.

Matches between English club teams and overseas sides expanded to a more limited degree. Yorkshire's tour of Jamaica in 1936 was the only inter-war overseas tour undertaken by an English county cricket club, but the MCC regularly sent out weaker teams to play overseas tours against first-class and non first-class sides. In the early 1930s some men's hockey clubs toured the continent.[10] Some Football League clubs played summer friendly matches against continental clubs. Manchester City, for instance, played in France in 1932, France and Italy in 1934, Austria and Switzerland in 1935, Germany in 1937 and Denmark and Sweden in 1938. But hardly any calls were made in England for the establishment of international club competitions. English Football League clubs seemingly attached little importance to continental tours, and often performed poorly. Tours usually followed a hard season, and there was occasional player indiscipline. In 1929 the *Sunday Times* claimed that 'foreigners whom we have taught to play and enjoy football are complaining' that touring teams 'either cannot or will not play up to the standard expected of them', of 'regrettable incidents' and 'too often a display of mutual recrimination entirely alien to sportsmanship'.[11]

In rugby, although Cambridge University toured the USA in 1935, the RFU was suspicious of contacts outside the Empire. In 1924–25, seven English clubs had played in France.[12] England played international matches against France from 1920 to 1931, but thereafter all competition with French clubs was suspended. In 1932 the Rugby Union decided that no clubs would be allowed to tour Germany in an attempt to discourage 'the competitive element'. It also resolved to advise the German Union of the 'danger' of championships to the game.[13]

Ice hockey in the mid-1930s was probably the only spectator sport in England with a competition involving clubs from outside the United Kingdom. In 1935–36 six London clubs and the Brighton Tigers played in the National League but the six London clubs also played in the International

League, which included Francais Volants and Stade Francais, both based in Paris. In the following season the International League was scrapped. The Volants and another Paris-based club, Rapides, joined the National League, soon renamed the Ice Hockey League. Because of financial difficulties, Volants and Rapides soon dropped out but their players came to England, joining the Ice Hockey League as Southampton Vikings and Manchester Rapids.[14]

Some annual English sporting events, such as the Wimbledon tennis championships or the Henley rowing regatta, attracted the best overseas competitors, and the final of the speedway World Championship, first staged in 1936, was held annually at Wembley. Leading American golfers took part in the annual Open Championship, thought this was not held on an English course each year. Top English golfers and tennis players played in the leading American competitions, while tennis players also played in Europe. Those wishing to compete at a high level in winter sports and mountaineering over ice had little choice but to pursue these sports overseas. At a time when foreign travel was time-consuming and expensive, most overseas competition was restricted to middle-class players, though Stephen Jones has shown the extent of sporting contacts between British labour and the continental socialist movement. Left-wing Labour groups were keen to foster proletarian solidarity and peace through sport, despite the hostile response given by the British government to some of their initiatives. In the 1930s, for example, the National Workers' Sports Association organised tours to Holland, Belgium, France and Switzerland, and hosted reciprocal visits. Solidarity did not stretch to Nazi Germany. The TUC (Trades Union Congress) attempted unsuccessfully to stop England's soccer match again Germany in 1935. The communist-backed British Workers' Sport Federation regularly took part in international sport, and there were also Workers' Olympiads in 1931, 1935 and 1937 (Jones 1988: 176–78).

Some English sports bodies declined to take part in international competitions or withdrew from them. The FA refused invitations to take part in the FIFA World Cups of 1930, 1934 and 1938, although FA officials attended the 1938 World Cup final, and continued to arrange 'friendly' internationals. In 1935 Sir Charles Clegg, President of the FA, rejected suggestions for a European national championship, saying, 'Perhaps in a few years' time it will be more practicable'.[15] England's rugby union internationals against France ceased in March 1931 following a dispute over excessive violence and the flouting of amateur regulations. Some French clubs had broken away from the Rugby Federation to form a new Amateur Union. There were accusations that the French club championship masked professionalism and had led to brutal play, assaults on referees, and undue emphasis on gate receipts, and complaints about violent play in international matches. Due to the 'unsatisfactory condition of the game … as managed and played in France', England's RFU explained, there could be no further international or club matches until it was 'satisfied that the control and conduct of the game has been placed on a satisfactory basis in all essentials'. A rugby correspondent for *The Times* argued that the French 'must get away from championship methods and follow British ideas'.[16] The exclusion of French rugby from the international championship and internal divisions in French rugby union gave rugby league opportunities to expand as French players changed codes. Exhibition matches were held in France in 1933, in 1934 a French side toured Yorkshire, and in 1935 France began playing international matches against England and Wales. By 1939, 434 rugby league associations had been established in France (Dine 2001: 86–91). The game also developed further in Australia and New Zealand. No other English ball sport expanded overseas on such a scale between the wars, a growth which contrasted sharply with the failure of attempts to promote the game in England outside its northern heartland.

In the 1920s some English sports organisations were antagonistic to the Olympic movement, which was seen as over-nationalist and political. The RFU and other British unions did not compete when rugby was included in the Olympics of 1920 and 1924. In 1924 *The Times* argued that it was

> useless to attempt to create a brotherhood of sport which will react to the improvement of political relationships so long as these political relationships are permitted from the outset to embitter and demoralise the sport. Before the Olympic games can do any good, all members must learn equally to regard sport and politics as two separate and independent spheres which at present not all nations seem to do ... There are Englishmen and others who could almost weep over it.[17]

There were other complaints: biased French judgements in the boxing ring, a free fight in the France–USA rugby union match, Hungarian and Italian fencers coming to blows and perceived French hostility towards the British and Americans. Indeed the same article suggested that persistent hostility to American competitors in Paris made the treatment of British competitors seem 'almost cordial'. The Amateur Rowing Association declared in 1925 that it 'had never been in sympathy with the Olympic Games or Olympic Regattas'.[18] When track and field competitions for women were introduced at the 1928 Olympics, British women boycotted them because they were restricted to five events (Hargreaves 1984: 59). At the same time, however, the world-wide political and propagandist significance of the Games ensured Britain continued to send representatives.

Perceptions of overseas sport

What English followers of sport knew about sports overseas varied with media coverage. Top international golfers and tennis players took part in the Open Championship and Wimbledon, so most fans knew the world's leading players.

Cricket fans would have been aware of the best test players from overseas, especially those from Australia. Though England was no longer a major force in international cycle racing, the weekly magazine *Cycling* reported in detail to its enthusiasts on the annual World Championships and covered the Tour de France, an event which daily national newspapers largely ignored. Except for those with a special interest in track and field, the best overseas athletes were often featured only during the Olympics. Leading overseas rugby union and rugby league players probably became known only when they toured Britain. Even the English racing press gave limited coverage to horse and greyhound racing abroad. American world champion boxers, especially heavyweights, were known by name in England thanks to the newsreels, but American football was ignored.

As English soccer had so few competitive contacts with club football abroad, most soccer supporters in England would probably have been hard-pressed to name many foreign players or even clubs. W. Schmid-Parker, a sports journalist familiar with continental football, pointed out in 1935 that 'very little attention is paid [in England] to the progress Association Football is making in foreign countries'.[19] The lack of press interest in the defeat of England by Spain in 1929, the first time that a continental country had beaten England, suggests editors thought readers had little interest in foreign matches. *Athletic News* excused it as 'England's First Fall: hot weather a big factor in defeat'.[20] The *Daily Mail* and the *Daily Express* did not even report it. This mirrored English national press attitudes to the World Cup, which was also largely ignored. Only the *Manchester Guardian* reported the first final, in about twenty lines. It provided fifty lines on the 1934 final.

The late 1930s saw more extensive press coverage of England's overseas internationals. In 1938 the *Daily Express* sent Henry Rose, its main soccer reporter, to cover the England–Germany match in Berlin. For three days before the match, Rose wrote extensive previews of the match, accounts of previous England–Germany games and a history of German football. The day after the game, which England won 6–3, Rose's match report covered three columns of the sports page. An account of a match between Aston Villa and a German XI was the second biggest article onto the front page, though most of this was concerned with the crowd booing the Aston Villa team for running onto the pitch without giving the Nazi salute. The sports page also had a short report on Preston North End's defeat of Racing Club de Paris.

Some English sports journalists admired the achievements of overseas champions. In 1925 a *Times* tennis correspondent wrote of American Bill Tilden that Britons 'should be grateful to him for the contribution to the science of match play'. His victories were 'a triumph of mind, and he is never tired of preaching that the game is more than physical exercise'.[21] More generally foreign stars were praised if they personified qualities associated with English sport. In 1924, for example, when American Olympic athletes were allegedly victims of foul play and crowd hostility in Paris, a *Times* correspondent wanted it 'clearly … put on record that the Americans have behaved admirably … have shown nothing but good humour and generous sportsmanship'.[22] The *News of the World* claimed that 'our American friends have reached the happy state when they wish the best man to win, and when they are beaten, they admit the victor is the best'.[23] Following the British Empire–United States athletics match held in London just after the Olympics, a *Times* editorial declared that the Empire athletes 'took their beatings with perfect good humour' while the Americans were 'free from the arrogance of success'.[24]

English discourses commonly suggested that even if foreign competitors were more successful in international competitions, the English approach to sport remained superior. This explained away failure by equating it with a different form of cultural capital, a new form of national self-assertion. If an English team lost, this was because it was more 'sporting', less 'professional', thus giving England the moral high ground. English visitors to America and Europe soon recognised that Americans approached training in a far more scientific way, and employed 'an army of paid coaches' (Rudd 1938: 8). Such 'professionalism' was deemed inappropriate. To be English was to be sportsmanlike, and seemingly indifferent to winning. An English athlete, for example, according to reporter Arthur Hardy, supposedly would have 'trained as he thought fit, run whenever he had wanted a race, shown consistently good form without intense application'. British athletes 'do not apply themselves to their sports and games with the same deadly intensity of purpose as so many foreigners and Americans do' (Hardy 1934: 18–19). In 1936 an editorial in the *Observer* thought that

> the Olympic contest goes a little against our grain ... our own particular amalgam of work and play expresses a better philosophy of life than those other codes which have reaped superior honours at Berlin. We have contrived to make sport a tonic and moral support of general existence.

The English, it claimed, believed that 'sport was made for man and not man for sport'.[25] The *Field* pointed out that in Germany games were taken 'very seriously' and 'stand for all that matters in their national life'; 'many Britons have not yet been educated to regard the loss of a game or two as a national disaster'.[26]

Other defenders of amateurism claimed that English culture created all-round sportsmen, not mere 'professionals'. Horace Vachell recognised that there were 'those who consider that the loss of championships indicates national degeneracy', but argued that the ambition of our 'best' men [was] to be lovers of many games and sports rather than specialists'. While 'the specialist achieves immense publicity and a measure of fame ... he ought to be considered a professional'. He concluded that England could still be victorious – if only there were more pentathlons (Vachell 1930: 124–25). Sadly, thought another commentator, amateur sportsmen were 'most rapidly and regrettably disappearing' (Hardy 1932: 10). So, the English Davis Cup Player, G.R.C. Crole-Rees, argued, Americans succeeded because they concentrated: 'they specialise to a very marked degree … they let nothing interfere with their determination to get to the top', but 'if it were possible to arrange a lawn tennis match between the first 2,000 players in this county and the first 2,000 in any other, England would win by an overwhelming margin'. Americans had a 'deadly earnest' approach, the English a 'happy-go-lucky disposition'.[27] According to Major J.C.S. Rendall, the English, as a nation, still believed that it was

> incontrovertible that games must not be taken seriously, although those who participated in them were of course encouraged to put all possible vigour into them during play. Off the field however, no one was supposed to consider methods or strive for self improvement by detailed preparation.

But 'Americans persist in concentrating as much energy and devotion to perfecting performance at a game as we consider legitimate only when business or art is concerned'. Yet he also recognised, as the English more generally were increasingly doing, the ambiguity of such a position, accepting that 'it is out of date today' because 'amateur means second best … the highest achievements demand life-long devotion which professionals alone are able to give' (Rendall 1930: 196–97).

Criticism of foreign sport surfaced regularly in English sport discourse between the wars. Matches without time restrictions in Australia were condemned for encouraging defensive play and slow batting. When Victoria scored 1,059 in one innings against Tasmania in 1923, *Athletic News* called the total 'appalling' and commented that a 'craze for records cannot improve cricket … The passion for establishing or maintaining records is not by any means always consistent with sound sportsmanship'.[28] In 1925–26 the editor of the *Wisden Rugby Union Almanack* praised the brilliant play of the All Black tourists but added that they 'did not always play the game in quite the right spirit'. He suggested that this rubbed off on English players, with one England forward in the New Zealand match reprimanded by the Rugby Union Committee.[29] In the *Field* in 1936 the New Zealand rugby union team was criticised again for playing in a highly robust style, and rejecting open play in favour of 'keeping your line intact and hoping for blunders by your opponents'.[30]

Foreign crowds were supposedly sometimes unsporting. After the 1924 Olympics there were English complaints of 'miscellaneous turbulence, shameful disorder, storms of abuse, free fights and the drowning of National Anthems of friendly nations'.[31] The MCC dislike of barracking by Australian spectators has been mentioned earlier. Just before the 1936 Olympics, an editorial in *Cycling* complained that on 'the Continent, where international feeling has somewhat marred sporting rivalry, incidents we should call dirty … are applauded by the riders' supporters as clever tactics'.[32]

Press reports on England's soccer internationals, especially in the 1930s, often suggested that continental soccer was characterised by foul play. The fiercely contested 'friendly' in which England defeated the World Cup holders Italy in 1934 was dubbed 'the battle of Highbury'. The *Daily Express* front page accused the Italian team of 'ankle-tapping, tripping, obstruction, free punching, brawling, shoulder-shrugging, and a variety of other objectionable things that have no place in football [and] the addiction of some of the visitors to kicking opponents off their feet'. On an inside page it acknowledged the Italians' 'individual cleverness, speed, thoroughness, and deft manipulation of the ball' but did not want to see them again 'until they have acquired a newer knowledge of the original rules of football and of traditions that, unless, respected, will push all sportsmanship to the wall'. It suggested the FA should 'announce that they will have nothing more to do with the football of the Continent until the regulations of the game, and the element of any principles of sportsmanship, are properly learned'.[33] Other newspapers also condemned the Italian tactics. 'Corinthian' of the *Daily Herald* wrote that the Italians seemed to 'disregard the rules, as we read them'. Another *Daily Herald* columnist argued that 'the Italians, and every other European country for that matter, should know that dangerous fouling ... cannot be tolerated in football'.[34] In the *Daily Mail* F.M. Carruthers accepted that Italian and English interpretations of the rules differed, but the general tenor of his remarks assumed English moral superiority. He wrote that

> the English defender goes into a tackle with the intention of getting it [the ball], even if he uses his shoulders in a charge this is his purpose. The Italians, on the other hand, may apparently jump, push or barge an opponent over from behind. They may even further obstruct by grabbing a man round the neck.[35]

When England played Italy at Milan in 1939, the FA insisted that its interpretation of football rules was broadcast to the crowd before the match (Sharpe 1952: 71).

The desire for success in international sport

Governing bodies, players and fans all clearly hoped for international successes. Apologists for rugby union often argued that playing was more important than winning but the four home unions refused to send a side to New Zealand in 1927 after their 1924 South African tour had shown they would not have a side capable of extending New Zealand.[36] British and English successes in international sport were certainly patriotically celebrated. Something approaching national rejoicing surrounded England's regaining of cricket's Ashes in 1926. When England won the 1932–33 Ashes, the team received messages of congratulation from the Prime Minister and the Colonial Secretary.[37] During the tour Neville Cardus thought that 'few folk in this land seemingly want anything else out of Test cricket but victory for England'.[38] In 1933 *The Times* believed that everyone in the country welcomed the return of the Davis Cup to Britain after an absence of twenty years.[39] A 'mighty crowd' greeted Henry Segrave when he arrived at Waterloo in 1929 after setting a new world land speed record in America and winning the International Motorboat Championship.[40] Winning Olympic gold medals did not provoke celebrations on a similar scale. Most of the press gave more column inches to sport events in England than to the Olympics and much press coverage of the Olympics in the 1920s consisted of lists of results.

By contrast, English international failures did not usually cause great anguish or a sense of national calamity. Even when Scotland beat England 5–1 at Wembley and there were headlines such as 'England's Football Humiliation'; 'Our Biggest International Disaster for 46 Years'; 'Thrashed', the result was still excused. It was 'not as bad as painted', being due to 'Scots' fervour', and English lack of 'international spirit'.[41] In 1934 the *Daily Mirror* claimed that in soccer, 'we like to beat Scotland, Ireland and Wales when we meet them, but defeat does not leave us with any feeling of depression'.[42] Just before England played Italy in 1934, Trevor Wignall wrote in the *Daily Express* that an England victory by several goals would be 'the next worse thing to disaster to many Italians' but asked, 'How many people between Liverpool and Torquay will lose much sleep if we are beaten?'[43] International defeats provoked surprisingly few calls for English sport to adopt overseas methods. Between the wars no continental country won an international soccer match in England, so there was no anguish and condemnation of English practice similar to that of Hungary's victory over England in 1953. In 1932 a 'brilliant Austrian side', showing 'perfect team work', outclassed England, taught it 'how to play' and received generous press praise, but with luck against them were defeated 4–3.[44] The BOA report on the 1936 Olympics implied that copying German methods and having more competitors, more time for training and greater specialisation would improve 'our lamentable exhibition' in international athletic field events but also asked whether a 25 feet long-jumper, a 52 feet weight putter and a 230 feet javelin thrower would 'really demonstrate anything of national importance' (Abrahams 1937: 54).

England's heavy Test match defeats against Australia in 1920–21, 1921 and 1924–25 did not lead to calls for radical change. In 1926 there were press demands for England's prospects of victory to be improved by abandoning the tradition of having an amateur captain, but this was never adopted. Changes were limited, although in 1926 the professionals Jack Hobbs and Wilfred Rhodes were co-opted onto the Test match selectors' panel. A *Daily Telegraph* editorial commented in 1926 that there would be no enthusiasm in England to copy the Australian decision forbidding players' wives to leave Australia while their husbands were playing in England.[45] Press reports of the meetings of the Advisory County Cricket Committee and of the Board of Control, though brief, do not indicate that any reform of county cricket was proposed on the grounds that it would enable the England team to compete more effectively.

County cricket took precedence. Senior figures at Yorkshire CCC, for example, such as Lord Hawke, were anxious that Test matches should not supersede county cricket. This prompted the *Athletic News* to write that the 'leaders of English cricket have no viewpoint outside their own parishes. It is far more important that Yorkshire should thrash Derbyshire than that England, the home of cricket, should conquer Australia'.[46] When the Yorkshire professionals Hedley Verity and Bill Bowes reported that they were not fit to play for Yorkshire in 1932 because of the pre-tour inoculations they had received, Yorkshire captain Brian Sellers said 'Inoculations for Australia! ... Yorkshire means more than England. You should know that' (Hill 1986: 89).

There were occasional calls to emulate foreign approaches. By the 1930s, some in cycling, possibly because English riders so rarely won international competitions, argued that much could be learned from continental Europe. *Cycling's* editor called in 1936 for 'recruiting of brain on the official side, and of talent, well directed, on the racing side'. New outdoor tracks, he claimed, would 'be of assistance', but stressed that these needed to be 'designed like Continental tracks'.[47] English-born speedway riders imitated the techniques of Australian riders. In ice hockey, it was recognised that home-grown players needed to adopt Canadian playing and training practices. In 1925 Mrs R.J. McNair, who wrote for *Golf Illustrated*, praised American amateur golfers' hard practice and of leaving 'nothing to chance even at games'. While commenting that 'we do not take our games so seriously' and that 'most women golfers had a rooted objection to practising', she thought that 'it might benefit our golf if we copied them in this respect'.[48] In 1934 a *Golf Illustrated* editorial praised the American practice of having tuition to learn the game properly, but this was part of a move to boost sales by offering each new subscriber three free lessons with a professional.[49] In 1922 a *Times* editorial argued that to regain tennis supremacy, 'we will have to adopt the more aggressive methods of foreign players'.[50] A year later, however, another *Times* article, while admitting that English players would like to play as well as Tilden or Lenglen, thought they had no 'zest for imitation' of the long hours which they spent practising. The British player, it maintained, for 'good or evil ... regards that kind of drill as the average British artisan regards overtime; he will not deny that it may profit him in the long run, but he is not one of those who that distant prospect pleases'.[51] In 1928 the editor of *Tennis Illustrated* advocated special training by top-class players but accepted that some regarded American specialisation as a 'wicked practice' and inferior to preparing in 'a haphazard fashion'.[52] Another 'Candid Critic' thought that 'our overseas opponents *do* care about winning' whereas too many 'of our players don't really seem to have their hearts in the game'.[53]

Something of a watershed came during the 1936 Berlin Olympics. British athletes won only two track gold medals and did poorly in the field events. Such disappointing performances provoked great consternation. In the *News of the World* athletics reporter Joe Binns wrote of British athletes being 'outclassed', in a 'tragic position', and that 'our deplorable showing, especially in the field events, became the laughing-stock of the huge crowds'.[54] The *Daily Express* reporter argued that the British performances at Berlin were

> lamentable, not because our luck was out, but because the majority of our representatives were not good enough ... Our exhibition in Berlin was one of which we should feel ashamed ... the Americans and the Germans, and the Japs and the Finns, licked us hollow. What was worse, they made us look ridiculous.[55]

An *Observer* editorial argued that to 'be beaten into an insignificant ranking is to convince half the world that we are decadent in those qualities that were distinctive of our past'.[56]

Tennis tried to improve international performance. In 1922 a 'Reform Committee', supported by a number of so-called 'second-class players', won 28 seats on the Council of the Lawn Tennis Association but failed in its bid to unseat the treasurer. Its aims were to train 'by every means consistent with amateurism' those capable of winning the Davis Cup and Wimbledon, strengthen tennis in the public schools and raise tennis standards in public parks.[57] In 1927 Lord D'Abernon, President of the LTA, asked whether 'any sensible Englishman' could be satisfied that neither of the Wimbledon men's championships had been won by an Englishman. He argued that 'regaining supremacy in international competition had great urgency and real importance'. The LTA should devote its 'best brains' and 'an adequate portion of funds' to this task. Methodical training, coaching and team organisation should not be 'inferior to other nations'.[58]

The LTA's subsequent initiatives were far from radical. It increased coaching. In 1927, 25 county lawn tennis associations received subsidies from the LTA for coaching schemes.[59] In 1930 nearly £3,000 was spent on coaching but those receiving the coaching still contributed half the fee. In total 4,800 players were coached but only just over 1,000 were aged under 18. In 1932 the LTA Council decided that 75 per cent of any grants it gave had to be spent on the under-25s.[60] Frequent references in the tennis press to the coaching schemes of the Middlesex LTA suggest that these were more extensive than those of other associations. In 1937 it spent £165 on coaching 563 players, over 90 per cent of whom were aged under 20, but on average each player received less than one hour's coaching.[61] The LTA also made little attempt to improve Britain's international performances by broadening the social base of players. Frequent complaints about the opposition to, or limited support for, tennis in the public schools reflected assumptions that the public schools would be the source of future international champions. In 1935 an editorial in *Tennis Illustrated* argued that because of the lack of enthusiasm for tennis among public-school authorities, 'real tennis genius for the game may lie undiscovered till post-school days. Four years at least thrown away, while France or America are producing fully-fledged champions at 18'.[62] Tennis only expanded on a modest scale at public schools between the wars. In 1932 the LTA sent professionals to coach at 21 public schools.[63] The Public Schools' LTA was established only in 1937. In 1938, when the LTA spent £400 on coaching at 33 public schools, its 25 affiliated schools still did not include Eton, Harrow, Rugby, Shrewsbury or Winchester.[64]

Much discourse surrounding international sport reiterated that games were merely games. It was the spirit of the game, not winning, that was important. *Golf Illustrated* contended in 1925 that while British competitors had not won many of the major international tournaments, it was 'of far greater importance that we should maintain our reputation for being a nation of sportsmen and sportswomen, who play their game in the right spirit, and it is a reputation of which we should feel proud'.[65] An anonymous writer in the *New Statesman* wrote in 1926 that taking a game too seriously

> is to turn it from a sport into a business – and that is exactly what most of these foreigners, who have borrowed our games, do. They say we are lazy, not serious enough, too casual about 'training' and so on. Surely we may not only admit such charges, but welcome them. We invented cricket and tennis and golf as recreations, not as short cuts to newspaper fame or financial prosperity ... It is infinitely more important that we should maintain the spirit of national sport than that we should endeavour to compete for pre-eminence in those professionalised areas where the latest international 'champion' met and fight for money or fame ... If we cannot keep them as games, then let us withdraw from international contests altogether.[66]

In 1934, when Fred Perry won the Wimbledon Men's Singles Championship and Henry Cotton won golf's Open Championship, a *Times* editorial pointed out that those

> unhappy people who lament the decadence of their country whenever an Englishman or an English team is beaten in an international contest may now find it easier to recover their balance, to remember that a game is a game, and that neither the interests nor the honour of the nation hangs upon the result

It thought once the spirit of devoting lives to perfecting 'these accomplishments for the honour and glory of the country' became general, it would be 'high time to put a stop to international competitions altogether as more likely to breed bad feeling than to promote good fellowship'.[67] The underplaying of sporting success can be seen both as consolation for disappointing performances in international competition and as a tactic for resisting change in English sporting administration.

Very occasionally journalists tactfully challenged the emphasis on sportsmanship at the expense of winning international events. In 1934 F. Stacey

Lintott thought that the England footballers carried 'their spirit of chivalry a little too far'. The FA wanted them to be 'perfect little gentlemen'.[68] Joe Binns suggested in 1936 that 'many in charge of athletics in this country who say that as long as our men maintain the highest traditions of sportsmanship it does not matter where they finish' were fooling themselves.[69]

Most still hoped for English successes. Not all of them thought that international sport success measured national prestige, but trawls through national newspapers suggest that by the 1930s more writers recognised the wider ramifications of success. On the eve of the England–Italy football match in 1934, Frank Carruthers of the *Daily Mail*, hearing that the Italian team 'were fighting for Italy and that if they fail they will be disgraced', still claimed that 'no national honour is at stake. It is just a plain simple game of football'.[70] But Stacey Lintott argued in the *Daily Mirror* that a decisive England victory would mean that

> the stock of England, not merely of English football, would jump as it has not jumped for years … the combined efforts of half a dozen of the greatest politicians and business men in England cannot do more for the prestige of this country than our football team to-day.[71]

After the Berlin Olympics an *Observer* editorial argued that repeated failure would 'be punished by national second-rateness.[72] In the *Daily Express* Trevor Wignall argued that the British preparation and performance at the Berlin Olympics had been 'an insult to all Britons who live abroad'.[73] By 1938, when the English football team beat Germany 6–3 in Berlin, it was the result, not the diffident giving of the Nazi salute that mattered. The *Daily Express* described it as '1938's snappiest blow for our prestige', a magnificent achievement which announced that 'England are World Champions'.[74]

Governments and international sport

Governments did little between the wars to help élite players achieve international success. No government-funded coaching and training centres for those with an outstanding aptitude for sport were created. Governments did not subsidise the Olympic or Empire Games, although prominent politicians associated themselves with fundraising attempts. Lord Birkenhead, Secretary of State for India and former Lord Chancellor, for example, was chairman of the 1928 BOA Appeals Committee. The King was its Patron and its Vice-presidents included the Prince of Wales, the Duke of York and Prince Henry. A House of Commons Olympic Games Committee, whose patron was the Speaker and its President the Prime Minister, was also formed to raise funds.[75] Governments supported flying clubs and aeroplane sport in the hope that this would stimulate aeroplane manufacturing, air travel as a form of imperial communication and provide pilots on whom the RAF could call. The financing of the National

Fitness campaign was designed to promote the health of the general population rather than to produce successful international sports players, though Lord Aberdare, the first Chairman of the National Fitness Council, wrote in October 1936 that urgent government action was needed to 'help our country to hold its own with other nations in friendly competition ... I'm sure many share my dislike of seeing Germans, Italians, Japanese and other youth being superior to the British' (quoted in Beck 1999: 222). In 1936–37 the government put achieving friendly relations with Japan before international sporting prestige, putting tacit pressure on the BOA to withdraw its bid to host the 1940 Olympics, to allow the IOC to award the 1940 Games to Tokyo.

Sporting bodies made few requests for sports subsidies similar to those of Nazi Germany or Fascist Italy. The report of the BOA on the 1936 Olympics pointed out the difficulties of depending on public donations and governing body funds to finance Olympic competitors. While it noted that in some countries the state met such costs, it did not call for government funding, but recommended annual donations from sports clubs and sport club members (Abrahams 1937: 44, 46). After the 1936 Winter Olympics E.D. O'Brien wrote in the *Daily Telegraph* that because money was 'very nearly everything' in international skiing, British skiers might not be able to compete in subsequent Olympics. The German team had been 'maintained at their country's expense for no purpose except skiing'. British skiers, he thought, could compete against 'subsidised gladiator skiers of the Alpine countries' only if 'wealthy prodigies' were found. He did not ask for skiers to receive state funding.[76]

So few calls for government funding suggests governing bodies realised that there was little prospect of receiving this. Inter-war governments believed that keeping government expenditure low was the most effective method of promoting economic growth. For all three parties health, defence, education and unemployment relief were governmental funding priorities far higher than attempts to achieve international sporting success. Had there been more pressure from the electorate for the state to subsidise sport, some MPs would perhaps have taken this up.

Parallels can be drawn between England's position in international sport and its more general international position. By 1914 English industrial and sporting attainments had been overtaken, or were being matched, by overseas countries. Between the wars England retained much prestige both in international politics and in sport and so tended to assume that English practice and methods were superior to those of overseas. This cloaked structural weaknesses and incompetence. Few English believed that England had much to learn from foreigners. The enormous prestige accorded to sports that were largely concentrated on the Empire such as cricket and rugby union reflected the emphasis in politics on fostering imperial ties while avoiding close relationships with the European powers. Soccer's reluctance to have closer links with FIFA can be seen as having much in common with the refusal to have any binding military alliances with any European powers until 1939. In sport, as in other spheres, many of the English recognised that contacts with the overseas world were unavoidable but carried the risk of undermining what they imagined to be morally superior practices.

British governments were always ambivalent to international sport. As Peter Beck has demonstrated, nearly all British governments regarded international success as politically desirable. As international sport became increasingly politicised in the later 1930s they were increasingly aware of and affected by overseas sporting developments and slowly began to view sport as a relatively cheap way of projecting Britain. In Fascist Italy and Nazi Germany, countries which achieved independent national statehood only in the later nineteenth century, international sporting success was pursued in order to promote national unity and national self esteem. Their approaches to the 1936 Olympics led the British government to become more sensitive to the political ramifications of international sport. Yet as Beck admits, British governments for most of the period were indifferent and even hostile to international sport, lacked a coherent approach, took minimal interest in the Olympics, avoided unwelcome fiscal commitments, and tried to signal the separation of sport and politics (Beck 1999).

Sport and English nationalism

Sport, it has been argued, expressed and helped to raise national consciousness in the other home nations (Sugden and Bairner 1993; Jarvie and Walker 1994; Johnes 2002). In part such senses of nationhood were fashioned by a sense of animosity towards or perhaps of being victims of the English. Though independence from England had little support in Scotland or Wales, beating the English did. In the FA Cup Final of 1927, for example, Cardiff City represented the whole principality in a struggle against England, according to Swansea's *Sporting News*. As Anderson pointed out, nations are imagined collectivities which depend on a sense of being different from others and on taking pride in this sense of otherness (Anderson 1991). Often national awareness has stemmed from resentment at overbearing attitudes from others and a feeling of being denied full recognition of one's worth and rights. Success on the sports field was a means of emphasising that others needed to take note of a nation.

Those overseas often referred to England when it would have been more accurate to talk of Britain. Many in England, and particularly those with established wealth, often used the terms English and British interchangeably. Britishness was a 'fragile construct' between the wars (Walton 2003: 517). But Britain had been a political entity since 1707 and even though many in Scotland and Wales thought of themselves as separate nations, electoral support for political independence was little more than negligible. The Conservative Party, the most successful political party in electoral terms between the wars, was called the Conservative and Unionist Party and in some areas its candidates preferred to be known as Unionists. Yet in many sports England, Scotland and Wales fielded separate teams and had distinctive governing bodies. In cricket the England team represented Great Britain, but in sports where England, Scotland, Wales and Ireland fielded separate representative teams, hardly any called for these to be replaced by a Great Britain team. Rugby touring sides did not play against a British Isles team when they toured Britain and Ireland, although British Isles rugby union teams went on southern hemisphere tours because of financial pressures and the need to field a strong side, and there were also British teams in the Olympics.

In general English sport continued to express English national pride. One can argue that English national confidence was so firm that it was not dented by defeats in international sporting competition, though, of course, international sporting success brought great joy. As the rulers of the world's largest empire, the English, unlike other nations, did not have to use sport to assert their national worth in the face of oppression. For the English, their way of playing sport, of seeing sportsmanship as a distinctively English characteristic, a moral value that could be extended to all spheres of conduct, aided this conviction of national superiority. It is possible that the cult of sportsmanship was in part consolation for sporting defeats, but at the same time the selflessness and concern for others, modesty, honesty, courage and abiding by the rules that were involved with sportsmanship were interpreted as evidence that the English could be trusted to exercise colonial power not for their own ends but for the benefit of the colonised.

Chapter 8

Class, conflict and cohesion

Sport by its very nature engendered conflict as individuals or teams strove to defeat opponents. But team sports also required cohesion, as team members pulled together for victory or tried to avoid losing. Players and spectators imagined opponents as the 'other' even though opponents often had very similar social backgrounds and could be seen as allies in other social contexts. The conflicts and forms of co-operation found in sport were given added intensity by, and had the capacity to deepen, other forms of identities and loyalties.

Class, sport and amateurism

Inter-war England was a deeply stratified society with high levels of economic and social inequality. Movement across the faultlines of social hierarchy was usually slight and perhaps affected only a minority. Everyday discourse showed that the great majority believed that they lived in a class society consisting of an upper, middle and working class, though there was also much talk of upper and lower divisions within the middle and working classes and notions of class boundaries were often inexact. David Cannadine has pointed out that social observers used different models and language to describe social class but most contemporaries seem to have been aware of their place in the social hierarchy, and through signs such as speech, dress, occupation and residence could quickly situate the social standing of others. Whether class was the overriding form of social consciousness to which most people subscribed is debatable, since in some contexts identities of gender, religion, ethnicity and place were stronger, and specific leisure contexts often structured social roles. To an extent all classes were too divided and fractured to have real class cohesion. Some, especially those influenced by Marxism, have claimed that a class mentality involves the conviction that the interests of classes are irreconcilably opposed. The electoral strength of the Conservative Party for so much of the twentieth century suggests that many working people did not imagine that their interests were opposed to those of the upper and middle classes.[1]

Sport reflected differences between and within classes, but sporting interests that crossed class boundaries expressed and strengthened social cohesion. Few sports were restricted to one class, though some were far more associated with one class than another and in many sports those from different classes had different roles. Interest in horseracing was extensive among the working class, but no working men owned racehorses. Only the upper and wealthier sections of the middle classes participated in deer hunting or grouse shooting, although these depended on the expertise of working-class employees. Golf, tennis, rowing and rugby union had an upper- and middle-class ambience, though some clubs were more socially exclusive than others. Cricket players and spectators came from across society. Greyhound racing, association football and rugby league were often thought of as essentially working-class sports but only the better-off could have afforded the best seats at their stadiums. Soccer, the 'people's game', was still played at some public schools and at the universities.

Overt sporting expressions of class prejudice in sports were rare, although upper- and middle-class condescension towards the working classes was common. The *Illustrated Sporting News*, for example, reported one rugby club member's view of the difference between soccer and rugby supporters largely in class stereotypes, claiming that 'the soccer supporter ... goes to the ground armed with a bottle of beer, a half brick, a comic hat and a packet of fags, and proceeds to enjoy himself thoroughly'. By contrast, the rugger man 'parks his two-seater behind the stand, lights a cigar and proceeds to swap sneers with his neighbours'.[2] The cricket journalist William Pollock wrote that 'The football public is a cloth-capped, fried fish lot ... The cricket public is on an altogether higher plane' (Pollock 1934: 70). When the introduction of totalisator betting at a Frinton golf tournament was proposed in 1929, *Golf Illustrated* asked whether 'we want our golf courses crowded with a set of raucous-voiced thugs whose ideas on sportsmanship are as far removed from the ideals as the earth is from the moon' (quoted in Lowerson 1989b: 203). In 1925 'Amateur Internationalist' wrote in *Golf Illustrated* that most caddies were 'good fellows, being generally interested in the game', but that as caddies bet between themselves on the matches in which they were employed, they were 'ready to adopt a lax code of morality on points of the game if opportunity serves'.[3]

Sports clubs remained socially exclusive by having high subscriptions and blackballing those considered unsuitable for membership. Usually clubs played against clubs with members of similar backgrounds. Printing club subscription costs in the Club Cricket Conference annual handbook may have been a means of signalling a club's social tone. Rugby union possibly became more socially exclusive in the 1920s. According to supporters like Leo Murphy, 'rugby was supposedly governed unofficially by one unwritten law – observance of the spirit of sport' (1934: 94). Most rugby union writers argued that 'the troubles of amateur sport begin when gates are taken. A charge for admission implies an obligation to the public, and committees are often torn between their duty to the public and their duty to the players' (Gent 1922: 215). English amateur rugby enjoyed much success between the wars. The number of clubs affiliating to the Union was greater in the 1920s than in any other decade and the proportion of public-school educated players in the English side was at its peak. It was presented as a sport only for 'genuine amateurs'. At Blackheath, for example, even travel expenses were limited to third-class rail fare and meals to the prices of 'an ordinary London railway hotel'.[4] The social ambience of many golf and tennis clubs may have discouraged many working-class men from applying to join. Opposition to league competitions in rugby union and among cricket clubs in the South of England was usually justified on the grounds that leagues could undermine sportsmanship but there may have been fears that the need to do well in league competitions would lead to teams being selected on playing ability rather than social background.

The cult of amateurism was very much entwined with the desire to keep sports socially exclusive and to maintain class authority but this was rarely mentioned in public. In 1934 the socially élite Amateur Football Alliance, which oversaw the all-amateur Senior Challenge Cup, a competition with more entries than all but the FA and FA Amateur Cups, had about 320 clubs in membership, drawn almost exclusively from university, public and grammar schools, old boy sides, and the London hospitals, banks, assurance offices and business houses. Yet it still claimed to be 'not in any sense of the word a "class" organisation', just 'an association of men who play football for the love of the game' (Johnston 1934: 50–51). As Chapter 6 has shown, the most quoted justification for amateurism was that it was essential for the survival of sportsmanship. Definitions of amateurism varied between the sports. The Amateur Rowing Association was probably the only sport whose written rules excluded the working classes. Its constitution stated that no-one 'who is or has been by trade or employment for wages a mechanic, artisan or labourer, or engaged in any menial duty' could be considered an amateur oarsman, sculler, or coxswain. The Australian Olympic eight was not allowed to race at Henley in 1936 because it included policemen and the ARA abolished the clause in 1937. That questions were raised in Parliament suggested attitudes were shifting. The alternative National Amateur Rowing Association, formed in 1890, did allow working men to row as amateurs (Vamplew 1988: 186, 303). The Amateur Athletic Association barred anyone who had been paid to take part in any sport from its events, whereas the Rugby Union allowed those who had played other sports for money to play unless they had played rugby league, even as amateurs, or other forms of football as professionals.

Cricket permitted professionalism but still included a reasonably strong amateur presence even in England sides. England never fielded an entirely professional team between the wars, but amateur numbers generally were in decline. In 1919 amateurs made 40 per cent of all appearances in the county championship but by 1930 this had fallen to 20 per cent. County sides were nearly always captained by amateurs. England never had a professional captain between the wars but in 1938 Walter Hammond, who had just become an amateur after being a professional, was made the England captain. In 1935

Leicestershire actually appointed a professional as captain but this was for only one season. The playing ability of some captains was so low that they would probably not have been selected regularly had they been professionals. The Club Cricket Conference, the major club cricket organisation in the South of England, which had 1,148 affiliated clubs in Essex, Kent, Middlesex and Surrey in 1939, did not allow the playing of professionals. The highest levels of league cricket in the North and Midlands permitted professionalism, but usually this was restricted to one professional per club.

Few amateurs played in the Football League between the wars. A.G. Bower of the Corinthians, the last amateur to play in a full international, in 1927 against Wales, also captained the side. In the 1920s the Charity Shield was still an opportunity, like Gentlemen versus Players matches in cricket, for a leading professional side to play leading amateurs, but professional sides competed in the 1930s as the gap in standards grew. The highest levels of football outside the Football League were amateur in the London area but semi-professional elsewhere. Even in the nominally amateur Northern League, payments and inducements to 'amateurs' were privately well known, and the FA suspended 341 players during the 1927–28 season in a vain attempt to stamp it out. In racing amateur riders competed against professionals quite successfully in National Hunt events and some flat races were restricted to amateur riders, but the overwhelming majority of horses were ridden by professional jockeys.

Snobbery had some part in the exaltation of amateur sport. Condemnation of such attitudes occasionally occurred, but was more intense in some sports than others. Keeping a sport amateur helped ensure that those from wealthy backgrounds with less time for training and practice could compete at the highest level. In golf and cricket professionals had separate changing rooms and were often expected to address amateurs as 'Sir' or 'Mister'. At some county cricket grounds they had separate entrances to the field of play. Such distinctions were weakening, albeit slowly. In 1926 amateurs and professionals playing for England began to share the same dressing room. In the mid-1920s there was some discussion whether having an amateur captain increased the England cricket team's chances of winning the Ashes, and the distinctions of separate dressing rooms and entrances to the field of play were criticised, but there were no demands for first-class cricket to become entirely professional.

Few in rugby union called for the game to permit professionalism. Few argued that the major athletic and tennis competitions should offer cash prizes. Some sports did not have the funds to support professionalism. The great majority of those who played at the higher levels of sports with competitions open to professionals, such as soccer, cricket, rugby league and boxing, had working-class origins. Many recreational football and cricket teams had only working- and lower-middle-class members and probably the great majority who played knur and spell or were involved with pigeon racing were working class. Whether they would have welcomed upper- and middle-class members is unclear but they often sought the patronage of other classes.

In sports where both amateurs and professionals played at the higher competitive levels, professionals were treated with less respect, but this largely mirrored how the working classes were treated in other forms of employment. At golf clubs professionals were primarily coaches but they could supplement their earnings by selling and repairing equipment. Golf professionals may have been treated with more consideration by their employers than county cricketers because they had a professional association. Even so, at the Open Championship in 1925 the professionals had only one small dressing room and one small lavatory.[5]

Chapter 1 showed that sport enthusiasts from the privileged classes argued that playing sport promoted class harmony. What they usually meant was that playing sport would prevent socialism and encourage the working class to accept the social order. We mentioned that in 1922 the former England captain and cricket writer Pelham Warner claimed that village cricket promoted 'feelings of freemasonry, camaraderie and *esprit de corps*'. He could not imagine a cricketer becoming a Lenin.[6] Only weeks after the collapse of the general strike, a *Times* editorial advocated the provision of more playing fields as playing cricket would help to mould the working-class boy into 'a strong and happy and helpful citizen'.[7]

Yet whether sport diminished class antagonism is unclear. Support for a local team or player could create a sense of unity between those from different classes and a feeling of animosity to those from the same class who supported an opposing team. International sport could also stimulate patriotic sentiment that transcended class boundaries, but such forms of social cohesion may not have transferred to other social settings. Few sporting contests, not even cricket's Gentlemen versus Players match, seem to have been viewed in terms of a combat between classes. Class privilege in sport was not condemned strongly in public. The Labour Party showed little interest in the issue, devoting far more attention to the inequalities in incomes, education, housing and health provision. Socialists generally favoured amateur sport, viewed commercial sport with suspicion, and wanted more facilities for working-class recreational sport. Had there been a strong animosity to class distinctions in sport, it is likely that Labour politicians would have seized on this. Most national newspapers supported the existing social and political order and made little of class privileges. Even the *Daily Herald*, which supported the Labour Party, made criticisms of class distinctions in sport only rarely. While sport made class distinctions clear, the workplace and economic inequality probably did more to sharpen class mentalities.

Reactions to class divisions in cricket and horse racing have been studied more extensively than for any other sport. Both had occasional examples of professionals resenting amateur privileges but most professionals made little of them publicly. The predominant attitude may have been that class divisions were a fact of life about which little could be done and that those in sport were broadly similar to those encountered in other walks of life. Many professionals wanted to keep a social distance between themselves and amateurs. Most amateur cricketers who discussed in print the amateur/professional divide stressed that relations between amateurs and professionals were cordial and that professionals did not object to amateur captaincy, though such comments could have been wishful thinking. In order to protect their employment and earnings, professionals, may also have thought it politic to keep disapproval to themselves. The outrage that Cecil Parkin's criticisms of cricket snobbery provoked in Lord Hawke may have dissuaded other professionals from making similar comments. Perhaps those with strong views about amateur privilege chose not to take up county cricket. Amateur captains could not be too high-handed with more talented professionals, and amateurs with poor playing skills and little experience often had to seek advice, so overt snobbery was risky. When in the mid-1920s the popular press advocated England having a professional captain their arguments were not based on the grounds of class equality but because it would improve England's chances of defeating Australia. Class antagonisms in cricket, and in society at large, were not so strong as to prevent cross-class identification with England or county teams or with town clubs in regions where league cricket was played.[8]

In racing the Jockey Club remained dominated by landed aristocrats and senior military officers. Owning racehorses was very expensive so very successful owners were generally those with traditional forms of wealth or those with new money. Jockeys were overwhelmingly from the working classes and in order to be sure of getting rides, treated owners and trainers with courtesy and respect. Though the best jockeys were able to pick and choose, they still touched their caps, but only as a tradition. Owners and trainers, but not jockeys, could bet on races. Jockey Club stewards could suspend from racing those they suspected of corruption or unfair riding, and their rule was generally accepted. Public complaints from jockeys and from the public at large about the authority structure of racing were rare though this does not mean that there was no resentment among jockeys over their lack of formalised power. Racing had often been celebrated as the sport of kings which united the pleasure-seeking upper and working classes against a puritanical middle class. In reality, however, racing drew support, and opposition, from all classes. The social disagreements of racing, particularly over gambling and its supposed moral degeneracy, were not conflicts between classes but ones that stimulated social division within them (Huggins 2003).

Some sports paradoxically promoted both cohesion and animosity between the traditional landed classes and the *nouveaux riches*. Following the impact of death duties and increased taxation many rural sportsmen began noting what some saw as perhaps a 'social revolution' or 'social decay' in field sports, when great estates were broken up and sold. Horace Vachell, a prolific writer on country sports, believed that 'the impoverishment of the squirearchy and the enrichment of the many who had no affiliations with sport', meant that since the war

half the men who hunt, shoot, stalk and fish were not "entered" to those
sports in childhood … there are thousands today who hang back from
such pursuits, not from lack of means, but from lack of knowledge how to
set about being sportsmen

(Vachell 1930: 4).

Another writer, Captain H. Hardy, made a similar point, arguing that such
sports were being taken up increasingly by the *nouveaux riches* and that the 'old
order' was changing (Hardy 1932: 1–2). Stockbrokers and city squires, urbanites
with little understanding of rural society, crowded to take part, or bought land
as social decoration, but dressed, talked and acted in ways that broke 'accepted'
rules. J. Wentworth Day, an editor of *Country Life*, felt that economic changes
had 'beggared the natural leaders of the rural community', and introduced
'snobbery and avarice into sport, and a sullen class consciousness'. Family hunting packs had disappeared and hunting, fishing and other rights were bought
and sold. Day believed that 'the result has been disastrous', introducing businessmen who knew 'little or nothing of country life and customs, and even less
of the art of hunting. Their appreciation of the courtesy, understanding and
sympathy which make country life possible between rich and poor is micro-
scopic' (Wentworth Day 1934: 83–85). Field sports became increasingly
expensive, the more so as more farmers made claims against hunts. A pack cost-
ing £6,000 to maintain before 1914 cost nearly £14,000 by 1934, while
changes such as the commercial growth of chicken farming and market gardening or the growing electrification of the railways also impacted on hunting.

Yet the arrival of these new groups ensured that hunting experienced a significant resurgence, attracting large crowds to certain famous packs, while
urban spectators increasingly drove to meets using motor transport. By the
1930s even less fashionable packs were finding hunting more popular than
ever. Their defenders argued that 'blood sports' were for true sportsmen, gave 'a
much more lasting fascination and enjoyment, and build up character much
more surely and lastingly than do games pure and simple'. They had 'better,
higher, healthier aims' than other sports (Hardy 1932: 11). They argued that it
was appropriate to hunt for vermin and for food, provided such sports were
kept clean and free from unnecessary cruelty. Hunts increasingly worked hard
to ensure that local farmers were won over, and elected onto hunt committees,
and that rural communities were generally supportive.

Opposition to such sports was also growing, especially in the towns, again
often cutting across class boundaries. The RSPCA had made only spasmodic
attacks on racing and hunting and other blood sports before the First World
War, not least because much of its income was provided by participants, but
thereafter its failure to tackle such perceived animal cruelty was criticised by
more militant members. In the early 1920s Lord Lambourne and others
objected to leading steeplechases, such as the Grand National, because of their
excessive demands on horses. There was little effect except for some limitation

on entries. Indeed, Aintree's race grew in popularity. From the mid-1920s, new, more radical organisations like the National Society for the Abolition of Cruel Sports and the League Against Cruel Sports launched better-organised attacks on field sports. Stag hunting was an early target, despite or because of its rarity, since there were fewer than ten packs in the country, and an RSPCA-supported parliamentary bill was introduced but not passed in 1929. In 1930 there were militant demonstrations against the Mid-Kent Staghounds, who used carted deer, and these were followed by attacks on stag hunting packs in the South-west. Anti-blood-sport groups increasingly used the press to influence public opinion in their support, with some 140 letters and articles published in 1931 alone. Rather than a conflict between classes, debates about the cruelty of field sports were a contest between town and countryside. Urban dwellers, it was alleged, understood little of rural sports. J.B. Priestley, for example, admitted that he had 'only now and again met hunting people ... and I do not understand them' (Priestley 1984 [1934]: 91). For many townspeople, resentment of the privilege and display of wealthy participants combined with strong opposition to what were perceived as 'inhumane' practices. Anti-hunting organisations began to consider parliamentary means to ban field sports, with the *Daily Herald* taking a leading role in opposing hunting.

In response members of the Devon and Somerset Staghounds were instrumental in forming the British Field Sports Society (BFSS) in May 1930, which quickly attracted support from military men and aristocrats such as Earl Fortescue and the Duke of Beaufort. By July 1932 it had 8,548 members across Britain, with local organisations often based on hunts. Over the next seven years the BFSS organised its own 'educational' propaganda campaign, with articles sent to newspapers and magazines on field sports countering the 'outrageous' statements of the League, and explaining the Society's aims and work. It also developed a strong and well-cultivated link with government, lobbying MPs, and appearing before relevant enquiries, to head off anti-blood-sport legislation (McKenzie 1996: 177–91).

Gender conflict and cohesion in sport

Between the wars sport remained a site of male social power. Much male sport depended on family income, time and responsibilities being budgeted in their favour. Some wives and mothers resented this. Oral evidence reveals examples of men who stopped playing sport because of objections from their womenfolk but the extent of this is unclear. Our interviews showed that some wives supported their husbands playing and watching sport, and encouraged their sons to become interested. Some suggested that their husbands could have 'done much worse' than be involved with sport. By this they seem to have meant that many alternative male interests could have been more harmful to family welfare. In this respect sport seems to have expressed and consolidated cohesion between the sexes.

Chapter 4 has discussed the playing of sport by women. Jennifer Hargreaves has argued that the inter-war years, stimulated by the social changes of the First World War, were a 'remarkable period in the development of women's sport' (Hargreaves 1994: 113). Facilities for their sports became more common. Firms, factories and other voluntary clubs and organisations became more likely to include women's sports, while more socialist youth groups such as the Labour Party League of Youth introduced mixed or female sections. Middle-class women benefited, yet as Davies (1992) and Langhamer (2000) show, opportunities for working-class women to play sport remained limited. Position within the life-cycle largely determined women's leisure interests. Sport might be regarded as a 'right', like dancing and the cinema, for single women in full-time employment. It was often abandoned on marriage.

The growth of sports playing among women was a form of women's libera-tion. Sport was traditionally associated with qualities thought to signify masculinity such as physical strength, daring and the inflicting and taking of pain. Between the wars women acquired a stronger, though by no means equal, presence. Hargreaves cites the establishment of women-only sports organisa-tions such as the Pinnacle Club which allowed its members to rock climb and mountaineer without men. Independent governing bodies for women's sport such as the Women's Amateur Athletic Association (1922), the Women's Cricket Association or the All-England Netball Association (both 1926), provided 'sports separatism' which reflected and boosted women's confidence in their administrative abilities. Successful women tennis players such as Suzanne Lenglen and Dorothy Round, or golfer Joyce Wethered, who became a profes-sional in America, now attracted increased attention. Those taking part in aeroplane sports, such as the King's Cup Air Race, also received much press adulation.

Men varied in the extent to which they felt challenged by this. Although the media increasingly covered women's sport, the coverage of male sport was still significantly greater, reflecting assumptions that male sport was more important. In Burke's 1922 *Who's Who in Sport* fewer than fifty women were listed, almost all tennis or golf players, though badminton, hunting, racing, swimming, croquet, lacrosse and hockey were also mentioned. The Oxford graduate Margaret Lane, who wrote for the *Daily Mail*, felt in 1934 that women's sport was 'tucked away at the end' of sports books, and that 'the open-air girl' and other sporting women were expected by men to 'know their place' (Lane 1934: 258–68). The attitudes of male governing bodies to women play-ing their sports varied from hostile to indifferent. Hardly any women expressed any desire to play rugby, box or wrestle and the governing authorities in these sports never seem to have encouraged women's participation. Women's football enjoyed a brief flowering during and briefly after the First World War, some-times initiated by female welfare supervisors in various industries and munition works, reinforcing the culture of the 'plucky heroine'. In 1920 the most popu-lar side, Preston-based Dick Kerr's Ladies, played thirty matches, often for local charities, and attracted 53,000 spectators to a Boxing Day match at Goodison Park. By 1921 there were about 150 women's clubs, and in Lancashire and the North-east sides raised funds during the Miners' Lockout. Despite good attendances, and the guidance given by some male professionals, the all-male FA declared that 'football is quite unsuitable for females and should not be encouraged'. It called on its affiliated clubs not to lend their grounds for such games. This weakened interest though some teams survived, mainly from the working class and often based on factories and the business world, to flourish in the 1930s (Jean Williams 2003). By 1934 Woolworths and Marks & Spencer had teams.

In the late 1920s around half a dozen women took part in speedway races against each other and against men but they did not compete in the speedway leagues. Speedway racing by women was stopped in 1930 after complaints that a woman rider hurt in a crash was partially undressed in view of a grandstand so that her injuries could be treated. In horseracing women were not allowed licences as either jockeys or trainers, although a very select few trained using the names of their father or their head lad. The MCC showed no interest in women's cricket. In 1922 the Amateur Athletic Association told women athletes to set up their own governing body. The All-England Women's Hockey Association, founded in 1896, was quite separate from the Hockey Association which controlled the men's game. The LTA was the governing body for men's and women's tennis in Britain but, as we indicated in Chapter 4, its standing committees had no women members, even though more women than men played the game.

Many men belittled or derided women's sport. Jennifer Hargreaves has pointed out that in the press 'even tolerant comment was often synonymous with condescension and patronizing humour' (Hargreaves 1994: 124). When Dick Kerr's side played against a Bolton Ladies football team at Bolton Wanderers' ground in 1921, one journalist wrote that he could not remember any match at that ground which 'provoked so much hearty laughter' but added that the play was 'very far from being farcical'.[9] A *Daily Telegraph* report on a women's cricket match in 1931 mentioned with surprise that 'all the bowlers bowled overarm, and the batsmen did not long indulge in grass mowing'. But it praised the skill of the wicketkeeper and mentioned that when batsmen were given out, 'not one argued or even stamped a foot'.[10] Adrian Smith has pointed out that companies such as GEC which provided sports facilities for their employees often marginalised women, especially when they played games dominated by men. The GEC women's cricket teams, for example, were often mocked, and only women's hockey teams got some 'grudging' acceptance (Smith 2002). At golf clubs women members were often expected to play at times when few men wished to play. Chapter 2 has shown how the commentary of cinema newsreels sometimes trivialised women's sport. Such amused condescension towards women's sport does not suggest that men felt strongly threatened. Men's greater expertise in sport may well have reinforced male assumptions of their 'natural' superiority.

Both sexes often thought that sports were sometimes too strenuous for women. In 1922, after sending questionnaires to over 600 doctors, medical students and headmistresses, a committee of the College of Preceptors concluded that tennis and netball were acceptable for girls, hockey was approved but thought too rough for some girls, cricket was 'generally approved' while football received least approval.[11] The *Daily Mail* firmly believed that 'in contests of physical skill, speed and endurance they [women] must remain forever the weaker sex'.[12] Some, who believed that women were 'primarily designed as mothers', claimed that athletics were 'unsuited to women's physique, destructive of the prospects of motherhood, and ... would turn women into "an unnatural race of Amazons"'. Dr Arabella Kenealy's *Feminism and Sex Extinction* (1920) outlined the supposedly sterilising effects of sport while even less hostile commentators, including some women athletes, doctors, educators and administrators, believed that there could be long-term constitutional overstrain (Hargreaves 1994: 133; Williams 2003: 35). Harold Abrahams, the Olympic sprinter, sports journalist and administrator, did 'not consider that women are built for really violent exercise of the kind that is the essence of competition', and that they were 'awkward' in the running track (quoted in Birley 1995: 213). The Arsenal manager Leslie Knighton feared that if women were injured playing soccer, 'their future duties as mothers would be physically impaired' (quoted in Melling 2002: 324–29). Not all, however, shared this view. The *News of the World*, the *Sporting Life* and the *Daily Mirror* gave financial support to the Women's International and British Games in 1924. The higher standards achieved by women between the wars may have caused assumptions about sports being too demanding for them to fade. By the beginning of 1934 eight of the eighteen authenticated Channel swims had been by women. Press responses to the achievements of women in aeroplane sport mixed admiration with awe.

Many feminists have argued that the emphasis on physical attraction thwarted the emancipation of women. It led women to prioritise their sexual appeal for men as the measure of their social worth and caused men to regard them as sex objects. When women ceased regarding male notions of feminine appeal as important, they were challenging a mindset helping to uphold male social power. Between the wars apologists for women's sport were still eager to stress that playing sport did not masculinise women and that it would not diminish their physical appeal for men. The Women's League of Health and Beauty, founded in 1930, stressed the importance of physical culture, healthy living and gymnastic callisthenic displays, although its title implied the need to convince people that exercise was not inimical to physical attractiveness. In soccer, women's clubs emphasised their femininity, wearing smart dresses or skirts when going to matches, and dressing up for celebrity functions. When Miss E. W. Edwards of Middlesex Ladies Athletic Club challenged the 'oft repeated statement that athletics tend to make women masculine', she argued that the idea that women cannot take part in athletic contests without losing their feminine charm is absurd .... We girls take our training seriously, in fact more seriously than men, but we do not let it interfere with our feminine interests .... The sports girl is prettier and more healthy than the pampered woman of yesterday, a much fitter companion of men and a better mother to her children ... none of the girls believe that sport makes a woman mannish .... They are all keen on their training but take as great an interest in dainty clothes as breaking records.

(*Daily Express* 18 January 1927)

In 1928 Lady Heath, the first woman to loop the loop, a founder of the Women's Amateur Athletic Association and a javelin thrower for Great Britain at the Women's International Games in 1926, argued that 'health and beauty go hand in hand' and athletic exercise helped factory, city and shop girls to become 'more upright of carriage, and brighter of eye and talk, and clearer of vision and manner'. In her view, the 'beauty of women is not beauty alone of face. Beauty of form, beauty of courage, and beauty of character all go together to make the most perfect woman'.[13]

Women who played sport between the wars rarely claimed in public that they were challenging men. Women made few public calls to have a bigger say in bodies such as the LTA or to be admitted to membership of the MCC or the Jockey Club. Much women's sport was played in accordance with the norms of male sport. The Women's Cricket Association (WCA), for instance, which was stronger in the South and whose members tended to be from the upper and middle classes, followed the practice of club cricket in the South and discouraged leagues although, unlike the Club Cricket Conference, it did not refuse membership to clubs that formed leagues. Athletics for women were restricted to amateurs. In hockey, tennis and golf women played to the same rules as men. Few women's sport clubs had their own grounds and if they wished to use men's grounds, members knew that they could not offend men's clubs. Much of women's sport also reflected the class divisions that were found in men's sport. Golf and tennis tended to be sports for the better off. In the North the numbers of church and factory rounders teams suggest that this sport was played mainly by working-class women and girls. In Lancashire and Yorkshire the Women's Cricket Federation, established and run by men, was an alternative organisation to the WCA, and had more working-class players than the WCA clubs in those counties. Because it did little to bridge class divisions among women, sport's potential to challenge men was weakened.

Women who played sport rarely argued that they saw women playing sport as a form of emancipation. By far the most common reason that women gave for playing sport was that they liked its fun. Marjorie Pollard believed that most women who played hockey and cricket enjoyed playing team games with other women. She denied that the WCA prohibition on matches against men's teams or teams including men was 'anti-men' (Pollard 1934). Her reply to Neville

Cardus' contention that women 'cannot follow … into the great and true province of the game', was that 'we will go to the province our own way, and it will not be lonesome, neither will it be without fun, gaiety and achievement'.[14] Interviews show that some women thought it important that they were allowed to decide for themselves what sports they took up. Sport did not figure prominently in feminist discourse in the 1920s and 1930s which suggests that women's activists did not consider that it was a very great priority.

Between the wars sport does not seem to have provoked deep gender divisions. The support that women provided for male sport was a form of social harmony although it tended to strengthen assumptions that domestic activities were the natural sphere for women, a form of thinking which, as feminists have argued, upholds male social power by implying that the world outside the home is the natural province of men. The increased playing of sports by women extended the range of women's social activity but few women or men perceived this as a deliberate challenge. Sports separatism or women having separate governing bodies for their sports expressed and boosted women's confidence in their administrative abilities but were not intended to rival those of men. Sport provided opportunities for the liberation for women; it was not often a cause of conflict between the sexes.

Racial conflicts in sport

Examples of racial prejudice are not difficult to find in English sport between the wars. Professional boxing was the only sport with a formalised colour bar. The British Boxing Board of Control did not allow black boxers to contest British titles although they could compete for British Empire championships. Few protested about this policy. Black boxers occasionally fought against whites in England but this caused unease. In 1919 the Home Secretary prohibited a fight between the British heavyweight champion and Battling Siki, the black Senegalese world light-heavyweight champion, because 'the colour issue might awaken grave partisan passions and animosities among the spectators' (quoted in Jones 1985: 154). Boxing writer Andrew Soutar claimed in 1934 that 'in England … the idea of a black man meeting a white man wasn't acceptable to the general public' (1934: 237). Few if any complained about the West Indian cricket team being captained only by white players or about the South African cricket team choosing only white players. In the late 1930s an invitation for Learie Constantine, the black Trinidadian, to play for Lancashire was withdrawn following objections from the players but in the 1920s Lancashire players had not opposed the white Australian Ted McDonald being engaged by the county (Bearshaw 1990: 271). Conversely there were almost no public protests about the Asians Duleepsinhji and the Nawab of Pataudi being selected for England or Duleepsinhji being made captain of Sussex. No instance has been found of white cricketers refusing to play against black players in first-class cricket in England, though Duleepsinhji believed that he was not selected for a Gentlemen versus Players match in 1929 because a good performance would have made his selection for England certain and some South African politicians could not face the risk of a black man scoring a century against South Africa (Constantine 1946: 90).

Racist assumptions recur in inter-war sport discourse. Whites often attributed the achievements of black athletes to their race, often couching them in language that stressed 'the noble savage' and a primitive, animalistic source for their sporting prowess. Neville Cardus (1948: 31) wrote of Constantine that

> we know at once that he is not an English player ... that his cuts and drives, his whirling fast balls, his leaping and clutching ... are racial; we know they are the consequences of impulses born in the blood, heated by the sun, and influenced by an environment and a way of life much more natural than ours – impulses not common to the psychology of the over-civilised quarters of the world.

The leading English amateur athlete and journalist Captain Webster saw Jesse Owens as 'lithe, leopard-like, determined, a black thunderbolt', who showed 'a spontaneity of spring which is still the heritage of the native not yet too untrammelled by the filters of civilisation'.[15] Comments by white players sometimes reveal assumptions of white supremacy, though these probably reflected views that were held widely in England at that time. Jack Hobbs, almost universally regarded as one of nature's gentlemen and one who would not knowingly hurt the feelings of others, described the white Middlesex player Patsy Hendren as 'cricket's Prime Minister of mirth .... Perhaps his speciality is his nigger stories' (1981 [1935]: 140). Hobbs (1931) had written that West Indian cricketers were 'very high up in the air one minute, very down in the mouth the next. They were just big boys. Which explains why they bowled fast and could not play slow bowling. All boys want to bowl fast' (p. 140).

Sport also reflected the anti-Semitism of English society. Tennis and golf were popular among better-off Jewish families but some clubs excluded Jews from membership. Very wealthy Jewish families like the Rothschilds and Sassoons had become leading racehorse owners, although only the Rothschilds were members of the Jockey Club, and Jewish trainers or jockeys were very rare. Jewish boxing promoters were common in London, as were Jewish members of the bookmaking profession, especially in the East End. Despite traditional values that shunned physicality, boxing and table tennis were perhaps the most popular sports in Jewish boys' clubs. Playing football or cricket was more problematical, since observant Jews could not play on the Jewish Sabbath, but Tottenham and Manchester City reputedly had substantial numbers of Jewish supporters. London's East End halls with large Jewish followings produced prominent Jewish boxers – Ted 'Kid' Lewis and Jack 'Kid' Berg were both British champions. Covert anti-Semitism existed in a variety of contexts. Although criminal extortion gangs could be found in Leeds, Birmingham and elsewhere, it was the 'racecourse' gangs with predominantly Italian and Jewish members based at Aldgate and Saffron Hill in London which attracted most press publicity. In London and Manchester, Jews from the Communist Party were often singled out by the press and judiciary. At the trial of three Communist-inspired working-class leaders of the Kinder Scout trespass of 1932 a hostile judge deliberately called attention to their Jewishness before warning the jury of landowners and army officers not be influenced by their origins and names. The press often mentioned the Jewish origins of boxers such as Berg and Lewis but rarely did so for successful Jews in more middle-class sports. The Jewish background of the Olympic gold medal athlete Harold Abrahams was rarely acknowledged. The brothers M.D. and B.H. Lyon were Oxbridge cricket Blues and county captains but the cricketing press did not mention their Jewish backgrounds. When Lionel van Praag won the first speedway world championship at Wembley in 1936, national newspapers mentioned his Australian, but not his Jewish, origins.

The England–Germany soccer international at Tottenham in 1935 was an occasion when a sporting event with a racist dimension provoked political conflict in inter-war England. Opponents of Nazi racial policies and trade unions, who also objected to the Nazi attacks on trade unions in Germany, called for the match to be banned as a means of demonstrating opposition in Britain to Nazism. The FA and the football world very much wanted the match to take place. Editorials in the *Football Pictorial and Illustrated Review* wrote of the 'ill-timed objections' to the match and that the 'introduction of politics or trade unionism into sport must not be tolerated for one minute. International sport – in the widest sense of the word – is one of the finest movements for peace that can be conceived.'[16] At the post-match banquet Charles Clegg saw no justification for the TUC intervention. 'These TUC people', he said, 'seem to forget that this is a sport – a sport free of political influence ... they will never succeed in dragging politics into the great game of football' (Sharpe 1952: 75). The government refused to prohibit the match. The Home Office tried to avoid any impression of giving in to left-wing and trade union pressure while the Foreign Office felt that the match could be 'advantageous' to Anglo-German relations.[17] In 1936 some feared that the Nazis would use the Olympics to validate their political regime but there was no widespread movement in Britain sport for the Games to be boycotted as a protest against the Nazis' racism.

Responses to the West Indian Learie Constantine when he played in the Lancashire League show that sport could promote racial harmony. Few public protests were made when his appointment was announced. He experienced some racial prejudice in Lancashire but recalled later that for every insult, there were '10,000 expressions of warmth and friendship towards me'.[18] His exciting style of play and engaging personality had huge spectator appeal. He was very much a hero in Nelson and great pleasure was taken in the fame which he brought to the town. Other West Indian and Indian test cricketers played as professionals for league clubs in Lancashire in the 1930s. None had the same popular appeal as Constantine but they seem to have generated more acceptance than resentment. As so few blacks played other sports in England, other sports did not have such a capacity to promote racial harmony but no black player experienced animosity from whites on a scale similar to that of the black world heavyweight boxer Jack Johnson in the United States before the First World War.

Sport, Christianity and sectarian divisions

Religion remained a source of social division in England between the wars. Sectarian prejudices had not disappeared and religious affiliation remained an important form of social identity. Sectarian hostilities, however, surfaced rarely in English sport. Some football clubs such as Everton and Manchester United were often thought to have strong Catholic followings but English football had no equivalent to the sectarian rivalries of Glasgow Rangers and Celtic. The press hardly ever referred to the religious affiliations of prominent players. Newspapers often stated that Dorothy Round was a Sunday school teacher and that she had refused to play in the French championship on a Sunday but they did not mention her religious affiliation. There were sometimes complaints that players were discriminated against because of their social class but hardly ever because of their religion.

To a modest degree sport weakened sectarian animosity, and there was a strong church presence, especially of Anglicans and the larger Methodist sects, at the lower levels of recreational sport, particularly in the North and Midlands. Sunday school leagues were usually inter-denominational though the strength of denominations in recreational sport varied between towns. Teams from a variety of denominations also played in leagues that did not restrict membership to church-affiliated clubs. Sectarian suspicions were rarely sufficiently intense to preclude participation in interdenominational sport, although Catholic teams were reluctant to join interdenominational leagues and this helped to emphasise the distinction between Catholics and Protestants. The decline in the number of church teams in the late 1930s as grounds were lost to housebuilding somewhat diminished the capacity of sport to provide interdenominational contact.

In general terms the churches encouraged social cohesion. Clerics could be found among supporters of all three major political parties but leaders of all denominations advocated co-operation between classes and between capital and labour on social questions. Understanding between individuals and groups was advocated as the means of solving society's problems. Church sports clubs usually required their members to attend church regularly and oral evidence indicates that the great majority did. The presence of young men at churches helped to attract young women whose presence in turn encouraged other young men to attend. In this way church sports clubs helped to uphold the cultural significance of an institution committed to social harmony. At the same time churches may have enhanced respectability as a source of social division.

The churches also deepened conflicts in sport, since opposition to gambling came largely from them. Religious condemnation, especially from nonconformists, was a major reason why pre-paid off-course betting was not legalised. The churches were also prominent in the conflicts surrounding the playing of sport on Sundays. Hardly any mass spectator sport was held on Sundays and few public calls were made for this. Denominations were divided in their attitudes to the playing of sport on Sundays. Nonconformists in almost all regions were opposed but Anglican opposition was stronger in the North than the South. In the South some Anglican clerics argued that playing sport on Sundays would be a distraction from leisure interests harmful to religion such as drinking. The extent of Sunday play varied between sports. The FA refused to sanction it, but many tennis and golf clubs, as private clubs with their own grounds, played on Sundays. In 1927 only 82 English golf clubs did not allow Sunday play. By 1939 their numbers had fallen to 27. The fiercest battles were over whether local authority land could be used for Sunday sport. London County Council in 1922 was the first major local authority to permit Sunday sport on its grounds but until 1934 no game could be part of a league or cup competition. Few other authorities followed the LCC's lead. Those that did were mainly from the South.

Sport, geographical loyalties and conflict

Sport in inter-war England was linked to social identities based on place. At times loyalties of place could transcend identities based on gender and class. Pride in England could stand above local patriotisms centred on the region, county, town or village. The structures of sports, however, meant that different sports expressed, and perhaps created, differing forms of geographical loyalties. Professional league football, with its teams representing towns, tended to foster town identities whereas first-class cricket expressed support for counties. The highest levels of league cricket, on the other hand, helped to sustain identification with towns and villages.

Sports could draw together those who lived in an area closer. Many sports encouraged a local dimension. In cricket and rugby union only those born in the county or who had lived there for a specified number of years could be selected for county teams. In league cricket players often had to reside within a few miles of the club ground. It has already been mentioned that sporting success in regional and national competitions encouraged ritualised local celebrations in which the official leaders of local society such as mayors were expected to participate. The naming of sports clubs after places was partly convenient but also suggests the importance of place in sporting consciousness. In almost all team sports, clubs playing at the highest levels of competition were named after places. In recreational football and cricket, teams not named after churches or firms were invariably named after places, sometimes even a street. Most Football League clubs eventually took titles incorporating the name of a town, at least partly in the hope of gaining more support by drawing on existing town identities. This process was more or less complete by 1914, though Everton and Aston Villa, two of soccer's giants, retained their district names, and the Wednesday became Sheffield Wednesday only from the 1929–30 season. London clubs had names based on districts within London, though Arsenal, which ironically took its name from an institution, Crystal Palace and Thames FC were exceptions. St Helens Recs, the works club of the Pilkington Brothers glass manufacturers, played in the Rugby League between the wars but chose not to be called Pilkingtons' Recs. Football and rugby clubs occasionally moved their grounds from one part of a town to another, but rarely moved further. Rugby league's Broughton Rangers moved from Salford to Belle Vue in Manchester but kept the title of Broughton Rangers until after the Second World War. Chapter 4 has mentioned how Wigan Highfield moved to London and then to Liverpool.

Individuals could feel different geographical loyalties in different sports. Nine of the twelve clubs in the Bolton Cricket League came from the urban districts that fringed the county borough of Bolton and expressed, and helped to boost, localised patriotisms which emphasised their separateness from Bolton. At the centenary celebration sports day of the Eagley Cricket, Bowling and Tennis Club in 1937, Mass-Observation was told that 'if a good cricketer shows up locally, they find him a job around the place in United Thread Mills. It's "a bit of prestige, you know, for the village." There is a definite local feeling and Bolton is another place'.[19] Yet during the football season those from these surrounding districts identified with Bolton Wanderers football club. Cricket enthusiasts could also identify with a village or town team and also with the county club, although in Lancashire relations between the county club and the leading leagues were not so cordial as in Yorkshire.

Intense rivalry meant that county cricket matches between Lancashire and Yorkshire were fiercely competitive and often played in a dour, slow style, expressions of what one chairman of Lancashire called 'northern doggedness'.[20] Many in Lancashire and Yorkshire believed that the true worth of their cricket was not respected in the South. Matches between Yorkshire and Middlesex were often particularly tense. After the match at Sheffield in 1924 there were fears that Middlesex might refuse to play Yorkshire again.[21] In Lancashire and Yorkshire it was often claimed that test selectors often overlooked northern players. In 1931, for instance, Neville Cardus claimed that England selectors gave preference to London amateurs over professionals from the North, Midlands or West, a contention hotly denied by Pelham Warner.[22] In 1935 the cricket correspondent of the *Yorkshire Sports and Cricket Argus* wrote that it was

only ungraciously, and only because England couldn't very well do without them, that Yorkshire players were tolerated in Test matches by some of their caustic critics who … were badly bitten by jealousy of a county that couldn't be "held down" for any length of time in the championship.[23]

It is not clear whether regional animosities in other areas of life strengthened sporting antagonisms. Many in rugby league seem to have been proud of the game's Northern roots but in 1922 the sport adopted the name by which it was known in Australia. Attempts were made to give the game a broader profile by launching teams in other parts of England and by promoting the game in France.

Local solidarity and hostility to others may have been most intense when neighbouring teams played each other. In league cricket 'the chronic, long-standing rivalry' between Colne and Nelson was 'more like a bloody civil war'.[24] Most football and rugby supporters of clubs for both codes wanted to win most matches against neighbours. Surprisingly little research has been conducted into whether in towns or cities that had two football teams, supporting one implied hatred of the other, which seems to be the case today. In Manchester matches between City and United usually had nearly twice as many spectators as the average number which suggests that the two clubs had different sets of supporters. In interviews some have claimed that in Manchester in the 1930s there was a sense that belonging to Manchester which involved supporting either City or United and wanting the other club to do well, but how many shared this attitude is unclear. Attendances at the rugby league matches between St Helens and St Helens Recs were not much higher than those of other matches which could mean that the two clubs shared the same supporters.

The inter-war period, like the twentieth century in general, has often been seen as a time of when the influence of the provinces in national life declined. Centralising forces that enhanced the role of London included the expansion of Fleet Street national newspapers, BBC radio, the decline of older manufacturing industries in the North and the continued growth of the London-based financial sector (Read 1964: sec. v). But sport in many ways bucked this trend. Success in national or even regional competition not only stimulated local pride but showed that the provinces could still outstrip London. Arsenal may have been the most successful football club but every season a provincial club won the League or the Cup. Yorkshire or Lancashire won cricket's County Championship in seventeen of the twenty-one inter-war seasons. The holding of the FA and Rugby League Cup Finals, England–Scotland soccer internationals, the speedway World Championship and the greyhound Derby at Wembley emphasised the growing importance of London as the capital city, but success in London allowed the provinces to show that they could still be national leaders. The provincial could still outdo the metropolitan in sport and reinforce a sense of local self-worth.

Conclusion

The rationale for this book has been that sport provides valuable insights into the nature of society in England between the wars. We have shown that social divisions existed in sport and that sport helped to make clear inequalities of income and education. Sports which only the wealthy could pursue such as staghunting, grouse shooting, yachting or polo emphasised social privilege. The social ambience of golf, tennis and rugby union clubs expressed middle-class identities and at the same time stressed the 'otherness' of the working class. In sports with a strong following across the social spectrum, such as horseracing, cricket and football, those from different classes often had different roles. Stadium social zoning reflected economic differences between spectators. Authority in sport, especially when linked to the cult of the amateur, was in the hands of the middle and upper classes. The playing and watching of sport demonstrated the greater social power of men and showed how male interests usually took precedence in the budgeting of family income and time. Gambling and to a lesser degree cruelty in sport created and reflected social divisions though over notions of morality, not gender or class. Village, town, county and regional loyalties associated with sport involved animosity to those from other locations.

But the overwhelming impression that arises from the examination of sport in inter-war England is that it was characterised more by social harmony and co-operation than by conflict. Sport enthusiasts from all classes and both sexes tended to attach the same values to sport. They agreed that primarily interest in sport was pleasure, a means of having fun. Those from the wealthier classes often imagined that they were the ones most committed to sportsmanship and linked this with the cult of amateurism to justify their control of so much sport. Yet many working-class players and spectators also accepted the notion of sportsmanship, which remained the dominant discourse. The sheer volume and weight of cultural references to sportsmanship, their almost universal presence, show its significance, status, cultural power and impact. Sporting heroes from all backgrounds were expected to be modest and unassuming and to be sportsmanlike. There may have been elements of hypocrisy and self-delusion in all classes about this, but one can argue that even the widespread paying of lip service to sportsmanship was a recognition that very many accepted its importance. Adopting sportsmanship had broader resonances. It suggested to the working classes that they should play by the rules themselves. The wealthier were expected to live up to such standards.

Of course, there were also counter-currents. Sportsmanship was never universal and its power may have been waning even in golf, but only to a minor extent. Soccer may have been relatively peaceful, but as we have seen, sections of the crowd at professional football matches were often aggressively vocal against the visiting team and referee, and Queens Park Rangers, Millwall and Carlisle all had their grounds closed for a period following disturbances in the 1930s. Anglophile Rudolf Kircher saw soccer crowds as being 'un-English' in 'vulgarly' shouting, and being 'happily, drunkenly enthusiastic' (Kircher 1928: 4). Most professional soccer teams included at least one hard man, or 'killer', and some sides had the reputation of adopting excessively rough play. Cricket was concerned that Australian-style barracking might spread, and there were occasional crowd problems here too. Crowds at boxing matches could equally be aggressive, especially when home-town rivalries were involved, while the new sport of all-in wrestling exploited and distorted notions of sportsmanship by introducing heroes and wrestling villains at whom crowds could direct their barracking and aggression.

The attitudes of politicians reflected the capacity of sports to promote social cohesion. Sport rarely caused party political conflict and was never a major issue at general elections. No prominent parliamentary politician argued in public that sport should be an arm of the state, used to validate a political system as in Nazi Germany or Fascist Italy, although in the late 1930s Neville Chamberlain and others claimed that the National Fitness Campaign would illustrate that democracies could match dictatorships in promoting physical culture. Gambling on sport provoked political controversy but because any changes in the betting laws were potentially divisive, most politicians tried to avoid becoming too strongly involved. One can argue that had sport been a source of deeply felt social resentments, parliamentary politicians would have been obliged to pay more attention to it.

This book has also shown that sport was used to promote social harmony, though often this was seen in terms of persuading the working class to accept the prevailing social order. Sportsmanship, and particularly the putting of others before oneself, was often seen as an application of Christian morality. The strong church presence in recreational cricket enhanced the respectability of team ball sports and provided interdenominational contact, especially among Anglicans and nonconformists. By encouraging church attendance, the church presence in sport helped to bolster the influence of a cultural institution that advocated social co-operation and goodwill. Had sports been viewed as tending to create and exacerbate social divisions, it is unlikely that clerics and Sunday school leaders would have permitted the formation of so many church-affiliated sport clubs. Oral evidence reveals that the favoured treatment of talented players at firms with sport clubs could cause resentment and sometimes make industrial relations more awkward. On the other hand the management of so many firms would not have permitted the establishment of company sport clubs had they expected that this would not promote co-operation from labour. Interviews have shown that sometimes employers started sport clubs because of pressure from workers. Had industrial relations been characterised by a strong sense of animosity between management and labour, workers would probably not have made such requests. The small number of sport clubs based on trade unions, institutions whose existence assumed that the interests of workers were opposed to those of employers, also suggests that sport was not thought to promote conflict between classes. It also possible, of course, that sport may have been for the working class a distraction from economic and social grievances, perhaps part of a culture of consolation, but even if sport helped people to bear what they ought not to have accepted, this does not gainsay that it was promoting social harmony, or at least discouraging social confrontation.

While the playing of sport by women can be regarded as a form of liberation because it broadened their sphere of social activity, women did not usually see this as challenging male social power. Many men and some male sports organisations dismissed and disdained women's sport, but they do not seem to have felt threatened by it. Women usually played in accordance with the rules and customs of sport devised by men and often felt the need to seek approval from the male sporting world. The geographical identities expressed in sport crossed class and gender boundaries and, as was shown in Chapter 8, individuals and groups subscribed to different loyalties of place in different sports.

As social harmony tended to be stronger than social conflict in sport, one can argue that this demonstrates that society in general in England was generally cohesive and not divided into mutually hostile groups. There can be no doubt about the depth of economic and social inequalities in England, and particularly in some areas during the years of mass unemployment, but this did not lead to extensive support for political extremism. The Labour Party eclipsed the Liberals but did not win a general election. It advocated a moderate form of socialism. Acceptance of the declaration of war in 1939 was more or less total across society. Hardly any instances can be found of sport in England being a site for conflicting social antagonisms as were the Rangers and Celtic sectarian animosities in Glasgow. Sporting contests were not usually thought of as opportunities to express class antagonisms. In very general terms cricket's Gentlemen versus Players matches were matches between those with upper- and middle-class backgrounds and those with working-class origins but they were not usually regarded as class conflicts. Reports of spectator behaviour at these matches do not mention a class dimension and those playing in them seem to have regarded them more as test trials (Williams 2003: 125). Likewise, although geographical faultlines in England surfaced in images of North and

South, with a supposedly more amateur, middle-class South, and there were parochial rivalries between cities and regions, these loyalties never challenged the dominant values of sport. Had social relations in England been riven by deeply felt antagonisms, it seems implausible that so much social harmony would have been found in sport. The nature of sport in inter-war England registers the cohesion of English society.

Such cohesion prompts the question of how far sport in England expressed an English identity, a sense that those who called themselves English believed that their shared values and assumptions set them apart from other peoples. How far was there an English identity that transcended divisions of gender, class, religion and locality? Did sport provide another way of manifesting national consciousness? Did the sporting media merely create what sociologist Michael Billig (1995) calls 'banal nationalism'? Was sport really part of the 'national character'? Only in recent years have historians begun to consider how the English have defined themselves but few have discussed the role of sport in expressing and shaping English national consciousness, even though, as Grant Jarvie (1993: 79) has pointed out, sport 'whether it be through nostalgia, mythology, invented or selected traditions, contributes to a quest for identity'. No work on sport and English national identity similar to *Ninety Minute Patriots*, the volume of essays on sport and the shaping of Scottish national consciousness edited by Jarvie and Walker, has been published, although Williams has looked at why cricket was thought to express how the English wished to perceive themselves.[1] Roger Scruton (2001: 44) has argued that the English thought of themselves and were seen by others as a 'distinct human type'. Few in inter-war England spoke ideologically of English 'nationalism', though the term 'the English nation' was used. Nationalism in Ireland, Italy and Germany was perhaps easier to define because of its association with campaigns for political independence. A sense of nationality has often been connected with one group feeling that it is the victim of another, but this was hardly the case with the English between the wars. The English may have felt burdened by imperial responsibilities but they believed themselves to be the top dogs of the largest empire the world had seen. The extent of English speaking across the globe meant that language could not be used as a measure of Englishness as occurred with German and Italian.

One problem when considering what sport reveals about English character is that talking about sport in general overlooks differences between sports. Not all sports stressed the same values to the same extent. Sports in general, however, show that the English were patriotic. Indeed in sport the English often displayed a national pride which assumed a superiority over other nations. Delight was taken in England's sporting successes. Widespread celebration surrounded England's regaining of the cricket Ashes in 1926 and in 1932-33. Segrave and Campbell were national heroes for setting land speed records. The year 1934 was regarded as an *annus mirabilis* because Henry Cotton won golf's Open Championship and Fred Perry and Dorothy Round won the

Wimbledon singles titles. On the other hand victory over England by Scotland at soccer or by Wales at rugby union seems to have meant more in Scotland and Wales than winning these matches meant to the English. Defeat in international sport did not create a sense of great disaster in England. Few sports considered root and branch reforms of their structures or launched massive coaching schemes to achieve international success. Rather defeats were taken as evidence that English approaches to sport, such as not taking sport too seriously and observing sportsmanship, were superior to those of other countries.

Sport provided myths to live by. It reinforced and mobilised values associated with Englishness. England might not always win but the English told themselves that they played sport in the 'right' way. Convictions about the superiority of English approaches to sport probably owed something to so many sports having been invented in England. To foreigners, English beliefs in their supposed sporting superiority may have seemed expressions of self-satisfaction and smug self-righteousness. Confidence in English approaches to sport reflected convictions of English superiority in economic or imperial contexts. Many in England imagined that the British Empire was morally superior to all other empires and that the rest of the world envied political institutions such as Parliament and the common law.

Cricket was often described, particularly by those from the wealthier classes, as the sport which most encapsulated the English national character. It was often claimed as England's 'national' sport even though more played and watched soccer. Cricket was a narrative through which the English told themselves what being English meant. It symbolised both England and English moral worth. A *Times* editorial summed up the belief of many that cricket was 'the foundation of Imperial and manly virtue, and is the source of that spirit of unselfish teamwork which has undoubtedly made England what it is'.[2] For Horace Vachell, writing in 1930, cricket was 'a national convention, an institution, almost unintelligible to foreigners and to Americans of a get-there-quick complexion who refuse to sit still for three days' (p. 10). Sir John Simon, Foreign Secretary from 1931 to 1935, claimed that cricket and the House of Commons were the two institutions most 'characteristic of the English spirit' (Beck 2003: 455). Even if E.M. Forster prayed that 'God preserve us from cricket in heaven', for most people cricket was still 'the great national game' which supposedly stood for broader features such as sportsmanship, concerted action, team play, discipline and recognition of authority (Lago and Furbank 1985: 62). Neville Cardus had his own test, claiming he 'would challenge the Englishness of any man who could walk down a country lane, come unexpectedly on a cricket match, and not lean over the fence and watch for a while'. He argued that 'wherever cricket is taken, England and the flavours of an English summer go with it' (1930: 6).

The exaltation of cricket was very much related to how the English wished to perceive themselves. The levels of sportsmanship in cricket were thought to be higher than those of other sports and it was often assumed that this resonated with an English sense of fair-mindedness and that all English sport expressed a higher respect for sportsmanship than that found in other countries. Though soccer was often criticised in England for being deficient in sportsmanship, those involved with English football saw foreign football as less sporting. Cricket discourses stressed that cricket was essentially a rustic sport. Village cricket was presented as the truest form of the game. This emphasis on the rural nature of cricket harmonised with a more general respect for the rural in English culture that was also expressed in the pastoral poetry and painting and the revival of English country song and dance. A majority of the English lived in towns, but the notion that the Englishman was at heart a countryman persisted. The inter-war growth of suburbia and the cult of gardening can be seen as in part attempts to recreate rural values in an urban setting, a form of *rus in urbe*. The rural dimension of other English sports such as horseracing, cross country-running, hunting, shooting, angling and rowing was also stressed. All athletic sports, being in the fresh air, were presented as escape from the urban environment.

The representation of sporting heroes as modest men or women who respected their opponents and practised sportsmanship suggest that such qualities were thought of as part of the English national character. Most leading players felt it necessary to present themselves as unassuming and as gracious to their opponents, though success in sport may have called for a self-confidence and single-mindedness that did not sit easily with modesty. Jack Hobbs, the biggest star of English cricket in the 1920s and a man widely admired, was often praised for personifying sportsmanship, good manners, modesty and concern for others. Part of cricket's esteem in the 1920s and 1930s was related to how Hobbs conducted himself. Hobbs' humble origins – his father was a Cambridge college servant – showed that English people of any background could display the characteristics expected of English sporting heroes. The footballer Stanley Matthews and the jockey Gordon Richards displayed similar characteristics.

Sport also shows what respect for tradition, formality and of the importance of observing accepted customs meant to the English. Earlier chapters have shown that all sports had their rituals and forms of decorum. The correct form of attire was especially important in the sports of middle and upper classes. Women's sports placed particular emphasis on what was thought appropriate dress. Many working men who played cricket could not afford white flannels but some tried to make acceptable substitutes from white overalls. Coaching manuals often stressed the correct form of clothing for sport and emphasised the spirit in which sport should be played. Cricket, tennis and golf had conventions about the right and wrong way to play shots. Respect for sportsmanship can be seen in observance of sporting etiquette. New sports such as speedway and greyhound racing were eager to show that they conformed to what were considered the conventions of sport. The respect for decorum in sport suggests the importance of conformity to the English.

Conformity implied acting and thinking like others linked to a disregard, almost a disdain, for the individual. In part this explains why team sports were held in higher esteem than individual sports but even in individual sports, players were not expected to display a flamboyant individualism.

Many in inter-war England imagined that emotional restraint was a defining characteristic of the English. Maintaining the stiff upper lip was often thought to be encouraged by playing sport. Sport, it was argued, fostered resolution, physical courage and being prepared to accept hard knocks without flinching, qualities, which it was imagined, promoted emotional self-control. Extravagant displays of joy in winning were thought incompatible with the modesty that society expected. Yet sport provided only partial support for this assessment of English character. Admittedly victory in top-class sport was celebrated with less exuberance than is the case today. Spectators seem to have been more orderly than their present-day counterparts but, as has been pointed out, playing and watching sport were also liminal zones where the usual forms of behaviour were relaxed. Although there were exceptions, most sport crowds were orderly and conformed to what was thought acceptable forms of behaviour, but shouting and other forms of boisterous conduct that would have been out of place in other settings were permitted. It may well be that the emotional release of sport may have made it easier to behave with more emotional restraint in other areas of life.

Sport also suggests that deference and a respect for social hierarchy were features of Englishness. Sport made social privilege and economic inequality obvious. Amateur authority in sport reflected the power of the upper and middle classes in wider society. A gentlemanly amateurism was still prized, especially amongst the public-school educated, the Conservative party, and gentlemen's clubs. Characterised by a sporting spirit and the virtues of fair play, this gentlemanly image was sometimes seen as intrinsic to the English way of life, a national ideal: tolerant but complacent, insular but pro-imperial, cultured yet conservative, sentimental yet possessing a stiff upper lip.

The social inequalities of sport provoked relatively little protest. Few called for root and branch reforms of sports organisations such as the Jockey Club or for the scrapping of amateurism. New sports tried to conform to the values and customs of older sports. In sports where amateurs captained professionals, the professionals seem to have accepted this as more or less a fact of life, as something over which they did not expect to have any say. Trade unionism made little headway among professional sportsplayers between the wars. The impression that the study of sport provides of England between the wars is that it was a society characterised by cohesion and harmony which in turn reflected that its people were characterised by a conservative frame of mind. Sport suggests that the English were a people largely at peace with themselves and each other.

Notes

Chapter 1

1 *Sunday Graphic*, 6 July 1933.
2 *Golf Illustrated*, 30 January 1930.
3 *Ice Hockey World*, 16 October 1935.
4 *Speedway News*, 4 June 1936.
5 *The Times*, 17 August 1927.
6 *The Times*, 4 June 1927.
7 *Buff*, 29 June 1929.
8 *Cricketer Annual*, 1922–23, p. 24.
9 *The Times*, 25 June 1938.
10 *The Times*, 8 January 1938.
11 *The Times*, 1 June 1929, shows that eighteen elementary schools used college grounds in 1928. There had been an earlier London scheme where secondary schools provided facilities for elementary schools.
12 *The Times*, 26 July 1926, 17 August 1935.
13 *Field*, 19 June 1915, 9 March 1918, 17 January 1920.
14 *Cricketer*, 18 June 1932.
15 *Cricketer*, December 1922.
16 *The Times*, 9 February 1924.
17 *Buff*, 26 May 1928.
18 Membership of the Conference was restricted to clubs not playing in leagues, but league cricket was not strong in the Home Counties.
19 *The Times*, 12 June 1939.
20 *The National Fitness Campaign* (n. d.) London: National Fitness Council, page 9.
21 *National Fitness Council for England and Wales: Report of the Grants Committee to the President of the Board of Education for the Period Ended 31st March 1939*, London: HMSO, 1939, p. 9.
22 *The Times*, 1 May 1933.
23 *The Times*, 12 June 1939.
24 *The Times*, 29 June 1938, 12 June 1939.
25 P. Hick (1971) 'A Study of the Development of Physical Education and Recreation in the City of York from 1900 to the Present Time', Newcastle University M.Ed. thesis, p. 163.
26 Surrey County Council (n. d.) *Surrey for Health, Sport and Residence*, Leatherhead: Surrey C.C., *c*.1932.
27 D. Crook, (1979) 'The Development of Physical Training in Coventry 1933–44', Liverpool University M.Ed. thesis, p. 78.
28 *The Times*, 21, 22, 26 April 1926.
29 *The Times*, 21 August 1922.

30   *Speedway News*, 13 April 1935, 27 March 1937, 28 May 1938, 1 April 1939.
31   *Bolton Corporation Yearbook 1930*: D.C. Jones (ed.) (1934) *The Social Survey of Merseyside, Volume Three*, London: Hodder & Stoughton, 1934, p. 290.
32   *29th Report of the Commissioners of Customs and Excise for the Year Ended March 31, 1938*, (1938–39) London: HMSO, p. 102.
33   *Kinematograph Year Book 1949* (n. d.) London: Kinematograph Publications, p. 50.
34   *The Times*, 14 September 1926.
35   *Liverpool Echo*, 20 July 1932.
36   *The Times*, 22 November 1927.
37   *The Times*, 24 September 1927.
38   *The Times*, 4 April 1932.
39   *The Times*, 7 November 1922.
40   *Athletic News*, 10 February 1930.
41   *Field*, 23 November 1918.
42   *Athletic News*, 4 August 1919.
43   K. Jones (1983) 'Physical Education in four North West public schools from 1920 to 1930', Liverpool University M.Ed. thesis, pp. 135–39.
44   *The Times*, 5 March 1920.
45   *Empire News*, 25 January 1925.
46   *The Times*, 2 February 1928.
47   *Golf Illustrated*, 30 January 1930.
48   *The Times*, 8 April 1932.
49   *The Times*, 11 November 1932, 13, 14 June 1933.
50   *Daily Telegraph*, 8 January 1926.
51   *Sunday Graphic*, 6 July 1933.
52   *The Times*, 7 January 1933.
53   *New Clarion*, 24 September 1932.
54   *The Times*, 15 June 1937.
55   *National Fitness Campaign*, p. 13; *National Fitness Council for England and Wales: Report of the Grants Committee to the President of the Board of Education for the Period Ended 31st March 1939*.
56   *The Times*, 3 October 1936.
57   *The Times*, 2 July 1937.
58   *The Times*, 24 January 1938.
59   *The Times*, 14 October 1936.
60   *The Times*, 9 February 1937.
61   *The Times*, 19 October 1936.

Chapter 2

1   For circulation figures and statistics on the penetration on national daily newspapers by different income groups in 1935, see J. Tunstall (1980) 'The British press in the age of television' in H. Christian (ed.) *The Sociology of Journalism and the Press*, pp. 20–4.
2   Investigated Press Circulations, quoted by R. McKibbin (1998) *Classes and Cultures England 1918–1951*, p. 552.
3   *Radio Times*, 25 March 1927.
4   *Daily Herald*, 26 May 1930; *Daily Mail*, 24 May 1930.
5   For a discussion of the variety of books published on cricket, see J. Williams (2003) *Cricket and England: A Cultural and Social History of the Inter-war Years*, pp. 68–71. A. Bateman (2003) '"More mighty than the bat, the pen…": culture, hegemony and the literaturisation of cricket', *Sport in History*, 23, 27–44 discusses how cricket sought literary authorisation.

6   For a discussion of the features of racing literature, see M. Huggins, (2003) *Horseracing and the British 1919–39*, pp. 48–49.

7   For the notion of 'active audiences', see J. Fiske (1987) *Television Culture*, and J. Fiske (1990) *Reading the Popular*.

8   Annual Report of the British Board of Film Censors, 1933 quoted in S.C. Shafer (1997) *British Popular Films 1929–1939: The Cinema of Reassurance*, p. 230.

9   For women's attitudes to sport see J. Gammie, 'Women are interested in newsreels', *Film Weekly*, 18 November 1932.

10   L. McKernan (ed.) (2002) *Yesterday's News: The British Cinema Newsreel Reader*, London, although not strong on sport, provides a very useful introduction to the topic.

11   *Pictorial Weekly*, 31 March 1934. For similar strategies in 1935 see Huggins (2003) *Horseracing and the British*, p. 54.

12   *Rugby Union Finance and Emergency Committee Minutes*, 17 September 1926, 20 September 1929, 18 September 1931.

13   *Gaumont British News*, 4 June 1936.

14   *Universal News*, 11 December 1930.

15   *Universal News* 31 July 1930.

16   *The Times*, 10 July 1940.

17   H. Fyfe, 'The way they have in America II: broadcasting football', *Radio Times*, 7 January 1927.

18   *Radio Times*, 28 January 1927.

19   *Manchester Guardian*, 24 January 1927; *The Times*, 24 January 1927.

20   *Radio Times*, 8 April 1927.

21   *Radio Times*, 15 April 1927.

22   *Radio Times*, 8 April 1927.

23   'Confessions of two commentators', *Radio Times*, 10 April 1931.

24   *Radio Times*, 28 March 1930.

25   For detailed analysis see R. Haynes (1999) 'There's many a slip 'twixt the eye and the lip', *International Review for the Sociology of Sport*, 34, 2, pp. 143–56.

26   *Radio Times*, 17 April 1931.

27   *Radio Times*, 24 March 1939.

Chapter 3

1   *Golf Illustrated*, 3 July 1925.

2   *Gaumont British News*, 4 December 1937; 14 December 1939.

3   In examining 'celebrity' and stardom, R. Dyer, *Stars* (1998) and C. Rojek (2001) *Celebrity*, provide useful background. E. Cashmore (2001) *Beckham*, explores contemporary celebrity. See also R. Holt (1998) 'Introduction', in J. Huntington-Whiteley, *The Book of British Sporting Heroes*. For Victorian sports stars see M. Huggins (2004) *The Victorians and Sport*, pp. 167–90.

4   *Topical Budget*, 14 July 1930; *British Movietone Gazette*, 18 August 1930.

5   *British Movietone News*, 4 September 1930.

6   *Golf Illustrated*, 26 November 1938.

7   *Gaumont British News*, 31 March 1938.

8   *Pathe Gazette*, 28 June 1928.

9   *Nelson Leader*, 2 February 1934.

10   *Daily Mail*, 10 July 1934.

11   *Football Pictorial and Sports Review*, 14 March 1936.

12   *Barnsley Chronicle*, 14 April 1928; 11 April 1928.

13   For a discussion of the qualities attached to English batsmen up to the 1960s, see R. Holt (1996a) 'Cricket and Englishness: the batsman as hero', *International Journal of the History of Sport*, 13, March 1996.

14   *Field*, 10 June 1933.
15   *People*, 21 March 1937.
16   *The Times*, 10 November 1936.
17   *Topical Budget*, 15 January 1923.
18   *Topical Budget*, 1 March 1926.
19   *Universal News*, 22 November 1934.
20   *Daily News*, 13 August 1928.
21   *Barnsley Chronicle*, 14 April 1928.
22   *The Times*, 14 June 1930; *Daily Express*, 14 June 1930.
23   *Daily Telegraph*, 14 June 1930; *Daily Mail*, 14 June 1930.
24   *Daily Mail*, 7 July 1934.
25   *News of the World*, 8 July 1934.
26   *Daily Mail*, 9 July 1934.
27   *Gaumont British News*, 9 July 1936.
28   *Weekly Dispatch*, 11 January 1925; *Daily Mail*, 21 January 1925; *Daily Herald*, 22, 23, 24 January 1925.
29   *Sunday Times*, 14 April 1929.
30   J. Hobbs (1981 reprint of 1935 edition) *My Life Story*, London: Hambledon, pp. 69–70.
31   *Women's Cricket* Vol. 1, May 1930, p. 13.
32   *Observer*, 10 February 1923; *Tennis Illustrated*, January 1928.
33   *Tennis Illustrated*, February, March 1935.
34   *Golf Illustrated*, 26 November, 3, 10 December 1938.
35   *Daily News*, 27 May 1930.
36   *Daily Express*, 18 June 1930.

Chapter 4

1   L. Murfin (1990) *Popular Leisure in the Lake Counties*, pp. 89–130 provides a useful review of sport in Cumbria.
2   *Pathe Gazette*, 5 June 1922.
3   *Gaumont British News*, 11 February 1937.
4   *The Times*, 19 November 1924; *Tennis Illustrated*, November 1928.
5   A Wisden rugby union almanac was published but it never achieved the status of the Wisden cricket almanac.
6   *Speedway Express*, 16 August 1932.
7   *Rochdale Observer*, 8 July 1936, 5 August 1939.
8   *Buff*, 1 August 1936.
9   Belle Vue (Manchester) Limited Monthly Statements, Manchester Public Library Archives M491/2/1/1, November 1934–October 1935.
10 *Football Pictorial and Baseball Review*, 21 March, 4 April 1936.
11 *Football Pictorial and Baseball Review*, 4, 11 April 1936.
12 *The Times*, 26 April 1935.
13 *Greyhound Racing Yearbook 1933*.
14 *Greyhound Express*, 18 June 1938.
15 National Archives, HO45/158590, police replies to Home Office enquiry, January 1934.
16 *Greyhound Tracks Review*, 23 March 1935.
17   National Archives, HO45/15853/663749/29, letter from chair of Brighton and Hove Stadium, 21 Nov. 1933.
18 *The Times*, 17 August 1927.
19 During the course of the building of an athletics stadium at Belle Vue, it was decided that this would be used for speedway.
20 *Ice Hockey World*, 10 March 1937.

21 *The Times*, 21 May 1930.
22 *The Times*, 9 August 1922.
23 *The Times*, 19 February 1930.
24 *Universal News*, 26 May 1932.
25 For a full list of the grants made by the National Fitness Council, see *National Fitness Council: Report of the Grants Committee to the President of the Board of Education for the Period Ended 31st March 1939* (1939) London: HMSO.
26 *Field*, 29 December 1927; Reverend Henry Carter (1928), *Facts About Greyhound Racing*.
27 *Final Report on the Fourth Census of Production (1930)*, Part I (1933) London: HMSO, p. 356; Part IV (1935) London: HMSO.
28 *Annual Statement of the Trade of the United Kingdom with Foreign Countries and British Countries 1925*, Volume I (1926) London: HMSO, pp. 58, 97; *Annual Statement 1933*, Volume III (1934) London: HMSO, p. 379, *Annual Statement 1934*, Volume I (1935) London: HMSO, pp. 136, 348.
29 For an opposite view of British culture and industrial decline, see W. D. Rubinstein (1993) *Capitalism, Culture and Decline in Britain, 1750–1990*; H. Berghof (1990) 'Public schools and the decline of the british economy 1870–1914', *Past & Present*, 129. For assessments of this debate, see N. McKendrick (1986) '"Gentlemen and Players" revisited: the gentlemanly ideal in English literary culture' in N. McKendrick and R.R. Outhwaite (eds), *Business Life and Policy: Essays in Honour of D.C. Coleman*; B. Collins and K. Robbins (eds) (1990) *British Culture and Economic Decline*; J. Raven (1990) 'Viewpoint: British history and the enterprise culture', *Past & Present* 129.
30 *Stalybridge Reporter*, 15 Jan 1923.
31 Joint meeting of the County Cricket Advisory Committee and the Board of Control, 23 November 1933, Meetings at Lord's Minutes, January 1927 to October 1934, London, MCC Library at Lord's.
32 Meeting of Seven Umpires with the Secretary and Assistant Secretary of the MCC, 11 October 1934, Meetings at Lord's Minutes, January 1927 to October 1934, MCC Library; *Cricketer Spring Annual 1935*, pp. 6–7.

Chapter 5

1 *Sport and Pleasure*, Vol. 1 no. 1, January 1936.
2 N. Elias and E. Dunning (eds) (1986) *The Quest for Excitement*, argue that in sports spectatorship, pleasurable excitement and gratification are major dynamics. S.G. Jones (1988) *Sport, Politics and the Working Class*, p. 1, has likewise stressed that sport is also 'fundamentally about play, fun and amusement'. P. Bailey (1999) 'The politics and poetics of modern British leisure', *Rethinking History* Vol. 3, p. 150 has argued that an obvious limitation of leisure historiography was its reconstruction 'as a set of activities rather than the locus of pleasure'. N. Tranter (1998) *Sport, Economy and Society in Britain 1750–1914*, p. 52 and J. Hill (2002) *Sport, Leisure and Culture in Twentieth Century Britain*, p. 26 both stress the immense enjoyment derived by so many people from watching sports.
3 *The Times*, 14 June 1925.
4 *Speedway News*, 13 April 1935.
5 *Ice Hockey World*, 16 October 1935.
6 *South Wales Football Echo*, 23 April 1927.
7 *Yorkshire Herald*, 16 April 1936.
8 *Sunday Sun*, 24 April 1932, quoted in R.J. Morris (2000) 'Structure, culture and sport in British towns', in Martin Daunton (ed.) *Cambridge Urban History of Britain* vol. III *1840–1950*, p. 420.
9 *Daily Express*, 17, 19 February 1936.
10 *Daily Telegraph*, 7 June 1928.

11   *Lancashire Daily Post*, 2 May 1938.
12   Royalty mounted a strong and largely successful defence of hierarchy at this time. See D. Cannadine (1998) *Class in Britain*, New Haven: Yale University Press, pp. 137–43.
13   *Daily Telegraph*, 20 June 1928.
14   *Daily Express*, 13, 15 June 1927.
15   *Football and Sports Favourite*, 12 February 1927.
16   *Radio Times*, 15 April 1927.
17   *Field*, 28 April 1927.
18   *Daily Dispatch*, 25 April 1927.
19   For a discussion of the origins of such celebrations, see J. Williams (1997)' "One could literally have walked on the heads of the people congregated there": sport, the town and identity', in K. Laybourn (ed.) *Social Conditions, Status and Community 1860–c.1920*.
20   *Yorkshire Herald*, 11 May 1936.
21   *Empire News*, 7 May 1933.
22   *The Times*, 1 June 1938.
23   K. Roberts (2000) *The Leisure Industries*, p. 173. He quotes the National Opinion Research Centre (1999) *Gambling Impact and Behavior Study*, Chicago: University of Chicago Press, as estimating that in the USA it was about 2.5 per cent of all gamblers.
24   *The Times*, 14 November 1923.
25   *Golf Illustrated*, 2 January 1925.
26   *Suffolk County Bowling Association Handbook, 1937; Bedfordshire County Bowling Association Official Handbook 1939*.
27   *Golf Illustrated*, 13 February 1925
28   *Golf Illustrated*, 21 August, 20 November 1925.
29   Interview with Mr S. Greenhalgh (retired league club professional cricketer).
30   *Little Hulton Cricket Club Minute Book 1934–1944*.
31   *Northamptonshire Lawn Tennis Association Official Handbook*, p. 17.
32   *Blackheath Rugby Annual 1929–30* p. 20.
33   *Suffolk County Bowling Association Handbook*, 1937, p. 123.

Chapter 6

1   *Tennis Illustrated*, March 1931.
2   Quoted in H.J. Savage (1926) *Games and Sports in British Schools and Universities*, pp. 20–1. The first six of these points were also given as the definition of 'a Cricketer and a Sportsman' in the 1925 handbook of the London and Southern Counties Cricket Conference.
3   *The Times*, 13 January 1925.
4   *Sheffield Daily Independent*, 23 July 1928.
5   'Gimcrack dinner speech', *Bloodstock Breeders' Review*, XXII, 1933, p. 263.
6   *Amateur Sport and Athletics*, Vol. 1 No. 3, August 1935.
7   *Blackheath Rugby Annual,* 1925–6, p. 23
8   *Golf Illustrated*, 29 May 1925.
9   *Sheffield Daily Independent*, 13 May 1938.
10   *Cricketer Annual 1922–23*, p. 24.
11   *John Wisden's Rugby Football Almanack for 1925–26*, London: John Wisden, n.d., p. 100.
12   *Daily Express*, 31 December 1930.
13   D. Winner (2005) *Those Feet: A Sensual History of English Football*, London: Bloomsbury Publishing, 2005, p. 246. Winner argues that such values lay at the root of later World Cup failures.
14   *Cricketer Annual 1922–3*, London: Cricketer Syndicate, 1922, p. 24.
15   *Field*, 13 February 1932.

16 *Tennis Illustrated*, March 1928.
17 *The Times*, 7 March 1929.
18 *Athletic News*, 10 December 1928.
19 For a full account of bodyline and its repercussions, see R. Sissons and B. Stoddart (1984) *Cricket and Empire: The 1932–33 Bodyline Tour of Australia*, London: Allen and Unwin, 1984.
20 *Golf Illustrated*, 30 July 1938.
21 *Tennis Illustrated*, March 1931.
22 *Football Illustrated and Pictorial Review*, 19 October 1935.
23 *Daily Express*, 20 March 1936.
24 Auto-Cycle Union Minute Book 1938–1947, 27 July 1939.
25 *Daily Express*, 20 June 1927.
26 *Field*, 11 January 1936.
27 The following paragraph is largely based on Williams (2003) *Cricket and England*, p. 88.
28 *The Times*, 21 July 1924, quoted in Williams (2003) *Cricket and England*, p. 86.
29 *News of the World*, 27 July 1924.
30 *Athletic News*, 10 March 1924.
31 M. Johnes (2002), *Soccer and Society: South Wales 1900–1939*, Cardiff: University of Wales, pp. 130–2 comes to similar conclusions.
32 *Speedway News*, 1 August 1936; *Daily Mirror*, 20 May 1938.
33 *People*, 7 February, 7 March 1937.
34 *Ice Hockey World*, 3 March 1937, 1 March 1939.
35 *Women's Cricket*, May 1939.
36 *Women's Cricket*, May 1931.
37 *Morning Post*, 2, 9, 14 August 1930.
38 *Billiard Player*, March 1931.
39 *Golf Illustrated*, 23 January, 8 May 1925.
40 *Golf Illustrated*, 9 November 1934.
41 *Sheffield Daily Independent*, 23 July 1928.
42 *Tennis Illustrated*, July 1928.
43 Interview with Mr E. Tatlock, glass manufacturer's warehouse labourer.

Chapter 7

1 *The Times*, 21 May 1930.
2 *Rugby Football Union Minute Book (RFUMB)* 1920 to 1934, 24 September 1920, 11 February 1921.
3 *RFUMB*, 3 March 1925, 19 March 1926; Minutes of the Meetings of the International Rugby Football Board (IRFB), 24 July, 11 August 1924, 20 March, 18 August 1925.
4 IRFB, 15 March 1929.
5 IRFB, 10 December 1932, 18 April 1933.
6 *Sunday Times*, 5 May 1929.
7 *The Times*, 27 May 1930; D. Birley (1995) *Playing the Game: Sport and British Society, 1910–45*, Manchester: Manchester University Press, p. 235.
8 *The Times*, 6, 21 March 1923.
9 *Cycling*, 8 July 1936.
10 *Tennis Illustrated*, April 1931.
11 *Sunday Times*, 9 June 1929.
12 *John Wisden's Rugby Football Almanack for 1925–26* (1926), London: John Wisden, n. d., pp. 53, 535.
13 *RFUMB* 1920 to 1934, 19 August 1932.
14 *Ice Hockey World*, 11, 18 November 1936.

15   *Football Pictorial and Illustrated Review*, 14 December 1935.
16   *The Times*, 3,4 March, 21 October 1931.
17   *The Times*, 22 July 1924.
18   *British Rowing Almanack 1925*, p. 191, quoted by Birley (1995) *Playing the Game*, p. 201.
19   *Football Pictorial and Illustrated Review*, 5 October 1935.
20   *Athletic News*, 20 May 1939.
21   *The Times*, 22 September 1925.
22   *The Times*, 22 July 1924.
23   *News of the World*, 27 July 1924.
24   *The Times*, 22 July 1924.
25   *Observer*, 16 August 1936.
26   *Field*, 1 August 1936.
27   *All Sports Weekly*, 7 May 1927.
28   *Athletic News*, 12 February 1923.
29   *John Wisden's Rugby Almanack for 1925–26*, p. 100.
30   *Field*, 11 January 1936.
31   *The Times*, 22 July 1924.
32   *Cycling*, 8 July 1936.
33   *Daily Express*, 15 November 1934.
34   *Daily Herald*, 15 November 1934.
35   *Daily Mail*, 15 November 1934.
36   *John Wisden's Rugby Almanack for 1925–26*, p. 101.
37   *The Times*, 17 February 1933.
38   *Field*, 25 February 1933.
39   *The Times*, 31 July 1933.
40   *Sunday Times*, 14 April 1929; *The Times*, 16 April 1929.
41   *Sporting Chronicle*, 2 April 1928.
42   *Daily Mirror*, 14 November 1934.
43   *Daily Express*, 13 November 1934.
44   *Daily Herald*, 8 December 1932.
45   *Daily Telegraph*, 8 January 1926.
46   *Athletic News*, 6 February 1922.
47   *Cycling*, 18 August 1934; 8 July 1936.
48   *Golf Illustrated*, 2 January 1925.
49   *Golf Illustrated*, 25 May 1934.
50   *The Times*, 13 July 1922.
51   *The Times*, 14 November 1923.
52   *Tennis Illustrated*, March 1928.
53   *Tennis Illustrated*, April 1928.
54   *News of the World*, 16 August 1936.
55   *Daily Express*, 14 August 1936.
56   *Observer*, 16 August 1936.
57   *The Times*, 8, 12 December 1922.
58   *The Times*, 13 December 1927.
59   *The Times*, 26 October 1927.
60   *Tennis Illustrated*, April 1931; *The Times*, 16 November 1932.
61   *Tennis Illustrated*, June 1938.
62   *Tennis Illustrated*, September 1935.
63   *The Times*, 19 October 1932.
64   *The Times*, 12 January 1938; *Tennis Illustrated*, March 1938.
65   *Golf Illustrated*, 29 May 1925.
66   *New Statesman*, 3 July 1926.

67 *The Times*, 7 July 1934.
68 *Daily Mirror*, 14 November 1934.
69 *News of the World*, 16 August 1936.
70 *Daily Mail*, 14 November 1934.
71 *Daily Mirror*, 14 November 1934.
72 *Observer*, 16 August 1936.
73 *Daily Express*, 14 August 1936.
74 *Daily Express*, 16 May 1938.
75 *The Times*, 25 May, 21 July 1927.
76 *Daily Telegraph*, 15 February 1936.

Chapter 8

1 For a discussion of the historiography of class in Britain, see D. Cannadine (1999) *The Rise and Fall of Class in Britain,* New York: Columbia University Press.
2 *Ilustrated Sporting and Dramatic News*, 21 April 1928.
3 *Golf Illustrated*, 16 January 1925.
4 *Blackheath Rugby Annual*, 1925–26, p. 47.
5 *Golf Illustrated*, 3 July 1925.
6 *Cricketer*, December 1922.
7 *The Times*, 19 June 1926.
8 For further discussion of attitudes to class in cricket, see J. Williams (1999a) *Cricket and England*, chapter 6.
9 *Bolton Evening News*, 21 April 1921.
10 Quoted in *Women's Cricket*, September 1931.
11 *The Times*, 9 August 1922.
12 *Daily News*, 6 August 1926, quoted by D. Birley (1995) *Playing the Game*, p. 210.
13 *Daily News*, 13 August 1928.
14 M. Pollard, 'Where are we going?', *Women's Cricket*, July 1930.
15 *Amateur Sport and Athletics*, August 1935, pp. 58–9.
16 *Football Pictorial and Illustrated Review*, 7 December 1935.
17 P.J. Beck (1999) *Scoring for Britain: International Football and International Politics, 1900–1939*, p. 199. Beck provides the best examination of the political dimension to the England–Germany match.
18 *Lancashire Evening Telegraph*, 11 July 1989.
19 Mass-Observation Worktown Survey: Box W2: File D: Worktown: Cricket.
20 *Buff*, 6 July 1929.
21 D. Russell (1996a) 'Amateurs, professionals and the construction of social identity', *Sports Historian*, 16 and D. Russell (1996b) 'Sport and identity: the case of Yorkshire County Cricket Club, 1890–1939', *20th Century British History*, 7, 2, discuss how the sense of Yorkshire identity fostered by county cricket involved animosity to the South.
22 *Field*, 8, 29 August 1931.
23 *Yorkshire Sport and Cricket Argus*, 22 June 1935.
24 *Lancashire Evening Telegraph*, 13 June 1989.

Conclusion

1 See G. Jarvie and G. Walker (eds) (1994) *Scottish Sport in the Making of the Nation: Ninety Minute Patriots?* Leicester: Leicester University Press; Williams (2003) *Cricket and England.* R. Colls (2002) *Identity of England;* Oxford: Oxford University Press. Shows great insight into representations of Englishness but says little about sport between the wars.

2 *The Times,* 5 August 1925.

References

There is a huge volume of official government material on inter-war sport such as, for example, the evidence collected by the Home Office on various varieties of betting. Many sports organisations now deposit their club minute books, accounts and other records in county archive departments. We have consulted much of this material in the course of our studies, and have also drawn on oral evidence. However, for reasons of space, the references include only those works referred to in the text.

Newspapers and Periodicals

All Sports Weekly
Amateur Sport and Athletics
Athletic News
Barnsley Chronicle
Billiard Player
Bloodstock Breeders' Review
Bolton Evening News
[Bolton Evening News] Buff
Cricketer
Cycling
Daily Dispatch
Daily Express
Daily Herald
Daily Mail
Daily Mirror
Daily News
Daily Telegraph
Empire News
Field
Film Weekly
Football Pictorial and Sports Review/Baseball Review/Illustrated and Pictorial Review
Football and Sports Favourite
Golf Illustrated
Greyhound Express
Greyhound Tracks Review
Ice Hockey World
Illustrated Sporting and Dramatic News
Lancashire Daily Post
Lancashire Evening Telegraph
Liverpool Echo
Manchester Guardian
Morning Post
Nelson Leader
New Clarion
New Statesman.
News Chronicle
News of the World

Observer
People
Pictorial Weekly
Radio Times
Rochdale Observer
Sheffield Daily Independent
South Wales Football Echo
Speedway Express
Speedway News
Sporting Chronicle
Sports Dealer
Stalybridge Reporter
Sunday Graphic
Sunday Sportsman
Sunday Times
Sunderland Echo
Tennis Illustrated
The Times
Weekly Dispatch
Wigan Observer
Women's Cricket
Yorkshire Herald
Yorkshire Sport and Cricket Argus

Annuals and yearbooks

BBC Annual Report
Blackheath Rugby Annual
Bolton Corporation Yearbook
Cricketer Annual
Cricketer Spring Annual
Greyhound Racing Yearbook
John Wisden's Rugby Football Almanack
London and Southern Counties Cricket
    Conference Handbook
Merseyside Rugby Union Handbook
Mitchell's Newspaper Press Directory
Northamptonshire Lawn Tennis
    Association Official Handbook
Who's Who
Willing's Newspaper Press Directory

Newsreels

British Movietone Gazette and News
Gaumont British News
Pathe Gazette
Topical Budget
Universal News

Sources

Abrahams, H.M. (1937) (ed.) *British Olympic Association: The Official Report of the XIth Olympiad Berlin 1936*, London: British Olympic Association.
Anderson, B. (1991) *Imagined Communities: Reflections on the Origin and Spread of Nationalism* London: Verso.
Annual Statement of the Trade of the United Kingdom with Foreign Countries and British Countries, London: HMSO for years 1920 to 1939.
Arlott, J. (ed.) (1975) *The Oxford Companion to Sports and Games*, London: Oxford University Press.
Auto-Cycle Union Minute Book 1938–1947.
Bailey, P. (1999) 'The politics and poetics of modern British leisure', *Rethinking History*, 1999.
Bakhtin, M. (1984) *Rabelais and the World*, Bloomington Ind: Indiana University Press.
Barnett, C. (1986) *The Audit of War*, London: Macmillan.
Barratt Brown, A. (1934) *The Machine and the Worker*, London: George Nicholson & Watson.
Barthes, R. (1977) *Introduction to the Structural Analysis of Narratives*, London: Fontana.
Bateman, A. (2003) '"More mighty than the bat, the pen…": culture, hegemony and the literaturisation of cricket', *Sport in History*, 23, 1, Summer, 27–44.

Bearshaw, B. (1990) *From the Stretford End: The Official History of Lancashire County Cricket Club*, London: Partridge.

Beck, P. (1999) *Scoring for Britain: International Football and International Politics, 1900–1939*, London: Cass.

Beck, P.J. (2003) 'Leisure and sport in England 1900–1939', in Wrigley, Chris (ed.) *A Companion to Early Twentieth Century Britain*, London: Blackwell, pp. 453–69.

Belle Vue (Manchester) Limited Monthly Statements, Manchester Public Library Archives, M491/2/1/1, November 1934–October 1935.

Berghof, H. (1990) 'Public schools and the decline of the British economy 1870–1914', *Past & Present*, 129, 148–67.

Billig, D. (1995) *Banal Nationalism*, London: Sage.

Bingham, A. (2004) *Gender, Modernity and the Popular Press in Inter-War Britain*, Oxford: Clarendon.

Birley, D. (1995) *Playing the Game: Sport and British Society, 1910–45*, Manchester: Manchester University Press.

Bowman, B. (1937) *On the Ice*, London: Arthur Barker.

Boyes, G. (1993) *The Imagined Village: Culture, Ideology and the British Folk Revival*, Manchester: Manchester University Press.

Briggs, A. (1965) *The Golden Age of Wireless*, London: Oxford University Press.

Burnett, J. (1999) *Liquid Pleasures: A Social History of Drinks in Modern Britain*, London: Routledge.

Campbell, G. (1927) *Golf for Beginners*, London: C Arthur Pearson.

Cannadine, D. (1998) *Class in Britain*, New Haven: Yale University Press.

Cannadine, D. (1999) *The Rise and Fall of Class in Britain*, New York: Colombia University Press.

Capper, B. (1923) *Licensed Houses and their Management*, Vol. 3, London: Caxton, quoted in T. Collins and W. Vamplew (2002).

Cardus, N. (1930) *Cricket*, London: Longmans, Green and Co.

Cardus, N. (1948) *Good Days*, London: Hart-Davis.

Carr, A.W. (1935) *Cricket with the Lid Off*, London: Hutchinson.

Carter, Reverend H. (1928) *Facts About Greyhound Racing*, London: National Emergency Committee of Christian Citizens.

Cashmore, E. (2001) *Beckham*, Cambridge: Polity.

Clapson, M. (1992) *A Bit of A Flutter: Popular Gambling and English Society, c.1823–1961*, Manchester: Manchester University Press.

Clegg, B. (1993) *The Man Who Made Littlewoods*, London: Hodder and Stoughton.

Collins, B. and Robbins, K. (eds) (1990) *British Culture and Economic Decline*, London: Weidenfeld and Nicolson.

Collins, T. and Vamplew, W. (2002) *Mud, Sweat and Beers: A Cultural History of Sport and Alcohol*, Oxford: Berg.

Colls, R. (2002) *Identity of England*, Oxford: Oxford University Press.

Colls, R. and Dodd, P. (eds) (1987) *Englishness: Politics and Culture 1880–1920*, London: Croom Helm.

Constantine, L. (1933) *Cricket and I*, London: Allan.

Constantine, L. (1946) *Cricket in the Sun*, London: Stanley Paul.

Cook, T. (1927) *Character and Sportsmanship*, London: Williams and Norgate.

Crisell, A. (1997) *An Introductory History of British Broadcasting*, London: Routledge.

Cronin, Mike (2002) 'Arthur Elvin and the dogs of Wembley', *The Sports Historian*, 22, 1, 100–14.

Customs and Excise, *29th Report of the Commissioners of Customs and Excise for the Year Ended March 31, 1938,* London, 1938–39.

Darwin, B. (1932) 'Games with a Ball', in *Fifty Years Memories and Contrasts: A Composite Picture of the Period 1882–1932,* London: Thornton Butterworth.

Darwin, B. (1940) *British Sport and Games,* London: Longmans Green.

Davies, A. (1992) *Leisure, Gender and Poverty: Working Class Culture in Salford and Manchester 1900–1939,* Buckingham: Open University.

Dine, P. (2001) *French Rugby Football: A Cultural History,* Oxford: Berg.

Donoghue, S. (1923) *Just My Story,* London: Hutchinson.

Donoghue, S. (1938) *Donoghue Up: The Autobiography of Steve Donoghue,* London: Collins.

Dyer, R. (1998) *Stars,* London: British Film Institute.

Elder, S. (1930) *The Romance of Speedway,* London: Warne.

Elias, N. and Dunning, E. (1986) *The Quest for Excitement,* Oxford: Basil Blackwell.

Elvin, H.H. (1938) 'Workers' leisure', *Industrial Welfare,* quoted in S.G. Jones (1986), 'Work, leisure and unemployment in Western Europe between the wars', *British Journal of Sports History,* 3, 1, 55–81.

Fairfax-Blakeborough, J. (1927) *The Analysis of the Turf,* London: Philip Allan.

Fishwick, N. (1989) *English Football and Society 1910–1950,* Manchester: Manchester University Press.

Fiske, J. (1987) *Television Culture,* London: Methuen.

Fiske, J. (1990) *Reading the Popular,* London: Unwin Hyman.

Frost, D. (1996) *Wally Hammond: The Reasons Why,* London: Robson.

Gammie, J. (1932) 'Women are interested in Newsreels', *Film Weekly,* 18 November.

Geertz, C. (1973) *The Interpretation of Culture: Selected Essays,* New York; Basic Books.

Gent, D.R. (1922) *Rugby Football,* London: George Allen and Unwin.

Gent, D. R. (1933) 'Rugby football', in *The Aldin Book of Outdoor Games,* London: Eyre and Spottiswoode, 11–218.

Gifford, D. (1973) *The British Film Catalogue, 1875–1970: A Guide to Entertainment Films,* Newton Abbott: David and Charles.

Gilbey, Q. (1970) *Fun Was My Living,* London: Hutchinson.

Giuseppe, U. (1974) *A Look at Learie Constantine,* London: Nelson.

Gordon, H. (1939) *Background of Cricket,* London: Barker.

Halladay, E. (1990) *Rowing in England: A Social History,* Manchester: Manchester University Press.

Harding, J. (1985) *Football Wizard: The Story of Billy Meredith,* Derby: Breedon.

Hardy, A. (1934) 'Athletics', in Miles, C.W. (ed.), *They're Off; A Journalistic Record of British Sports,* London: Denis Archer, 17–36.

Hardy, Captain H.F.H. (1932) *English Sport,* London: Country Life.

Hargreaves, J. (1984) 'Women and the Olympic Phenomenon' in A. Tomlinson and G. Whannel (eds) *Five-ring Circus: Money, Power and Politics at the Olympic Games,* London: Pluto, 53–70.

Hargreaves, J. (1986) *Sport, Power and Culture,* Cambridge: Polity.

Hargreaves, J. (1994) *Sporting Females: Critical Issues in the History and Sociology of Women's Sports,* London: Routledge.

Harrison, T. and Madge, C. (1986) *Britain by Mass-Observation,* London: Cresset.

Hartley, James (1935) *Bowlers' Complete Guide to the Crown Green and Link Games,* Preston: British Pictorial Press.

Haworth, D. (1986) *Figures in a Landscape: A Lancashire Childhood,* London: Methuen.

Haynes, R. (1999) 'There's many a slip 'twixt the eye and the lip', *International Review for the Sociology and Sport*, 34, 2, 143–156.

Hendren, P. (1934) *Big Cricket*, London: Hodder & Stoughton.

Hill, A. (1986) *Hedley Verity: A Portrait of a Cricketer*, London: Guild.

Hill, J. (1996) 'Rite of spring: cup finals and community in the North of England', in J. Hill and J. Williams, *Sport and Identity in the North of England*, Keele: Keele University Press, 85–111.

Hill, J. (1999) 'Cocks, cats, caps and cups: a semiotic approach to sport and national identity', *Culture, Sport, Society*, 2, 2, 1–21.

Hill, J. (2002) *Sport, Leisure and Culture in Twentieth-Century Britain*, Basingstoke: Palgrave.

Hilton, J. (1936) *Why I Go In for the Pools*, London: Allen and Unwin.

Hobbs, J.B. (1931) *Playing for England! My Test-cricket Story*, London: Gollancz.

Hobbs, J.B. (1981) *My Life Story*, London: Hambledon (reprint of 1935 edition).

Hobsbawm, E.J. and Ranger, T. (eds) (1983) *The Invention of Tradition*, Cambridge: Cambridge University Press.

Hoggart, R. (1958) *The Uses of Literacy*, Harmondsworth: Penguin.

Holt, R. (1996a) 'Cricket and Englishness: the batsman as hero', *International Journal of the History of Sport*, 13, 1, 48–70.

Holt, R. (1996b) 'Heroes of the North', in J. Hill and J. Williams, *Sport and Identity in the North of England*, Keele: Keele University Press, 137–164.

Holt, R. (1998) 'Introduction', in J. Huntington-Whiteley, *The Book of British Sporting Heroes*, London: National Portrait Gallery Publications, 10–25.

Holt, R. and Mangan, J.A. (1996) 'Prologue: heroes of a European past', *International Journal of the History of Sport*, 13, 1, 1–13.

Holt, R. and Mason, T. (2000) *Sport in Britain 1945–2000*, Oxford: Blackwell.

Hoskins, J. (1977) *Speedway Walkabout*, Ipswich: Studio.

Huggins, M. (2003) *Horseracing and the British 1919–1939*, Manchester: Manchester University Press.

Huggins, M. (2004) *The Victorians and Sport*, London: Hambledon and London Press.

Inge, W.R. (1938) 'Religion' in Kingsmill, H. (ed.) *The English Genius: A Survey of the English Achievement and Character*, London: Eyre and Spottiswoode.

International Rugby Football Board, Minutes of the Meetings, 1924–1934.

Jardine, D.R. (n.d.) *In Quest of the Ashes*, London: Hutchinson.

Jarvie, G. (1993) 'Sport, nationalism and cultural identity', in L. Allison (ed.) *The Changing Politics of Sport*, Manchester: Manchester University Press, 58–83.

Jarvie, G. and Walker, G. (eds) (1994) *Scottish Sport in the Making of the Nation: Ninety Minute Patriots?* Leicester: Leicester University Press.

Johnes, M. (2002) *Soccer and Society: South Wales 1900–1939*, Cardiff: University of Wales Press.

Johns, C. (1995) *Cheer like Mad for Cornwall: The Story of Cornish Wrestling*, St Austell: C. Johns.

Johnston, F. (ed.) (1934) *The Football Encyclopaedia*, London: Associated Sporting Press.

Jones, D.C. (ed.) (1934.) *The Social Survey of Merseyside, Volume Three*, London: Hodder and Stoughton.

Jones, S.G. (1985) 'Sport Politics and the labour movement: the British Workers' Sports Federation, 1923–1935', *British Journal of Sports History*, 2, 2, 154–78.

Jones, S.G. (1986) *Workers at Play: A Social and Economic History of Leisure 1918–1939*, London: Routledge and Kegan Paul.

Jones, S.G. (1988) *Sport, Politics and the Working Class*, Manchester: Manchester University Press.

Kinematograph Year Book 1949, London: Kinematograph Publications, n.d.

Kircher, R. (1928) *Fair Play: The Games of Merrie England*, London: Collins.

Lago, M. and Furbank, P.N. (eds) (1985) *Selected Letters of E.M. Forster Vol 2, 1921–70*, London: Collins.

Laird, D. (1976) *Royal Ascot*, London: Hodder and Stoughton.

Lane, M. (1934) 'Women in sport', in C.W. Miles (ed.) *They're off: A Journalistic of British Sports*, London: Denis Archer, 258–66.

Langhammer, C. (2000) *Women's Leisure in England 1910–1960*, Manchester: Manchester University Press.

Larwood, H. and Perkins, K. (1965) *The Larwood Story*, London: W.H. Allen.

Little Hulton Cricket Club minute book.

Lomas, R. (2002) *Grasmere Sports: The First 150 Years*, Kendal: MTF Publications.

Low, R. (1985) *Film Making in 1930s Britain*, London: George Allen and Unwin.

Lowe, F.G. (1924) *Gordon Lowe on Lawn Tennis*, London: Hutchinson and Co.

Lowerson, J. (1989a) 'Sheffield triumphant – some news on sport and the regions', *BSSH Bulletin*, 9, pp. 2–13

Lowerson, J. (1989b) 'Golf' in T. Mason (ed.) *Sport in Britain: A Social History*, Cambridge: Cambridge University Press, 187–214.

Lowerson, J. (1993) *Sport and the English Middle Classes 1870–1914*, Manchester: Manchester University Press.

Lowerson, J. (1995) 'Stoolball: Conflicting values in the revival of a "traditional" Sussex game', *Sussex Archaeological Collections*, 133, 263–74.

Lowerson, J. (1996) 'Stoolball and the manufacture of "Englishness"', in G. Pfister, T. Neuwerth and G. Steins (eds) *Games of the World between Tradition and Modernity: Proceedings of the 2nd ISPHES Congress*, Sankt Augustin: Academia Verlag, 410–11.

Lyle, R.C. (1934) *Brown Jack*, London: Putnam.

Lyon, M.D. (1933) 'Cricket', *The Aldine Book of Outdoor Games*, London: Eyre and Spottiswoode, 507–695.

McKendrick, N. (1986) '"Gentlemen and Players" revisited: the gentlemanly ideal in English literary culture' in N. McKendrick and R.R. Outhwaite (eds) *Business Life and Policy: Essays in Honour of D.C. Coleman*, Cambridge: Cambridge University Press, 98–136.

McKenzie, C.C. (1996) 'The origins of the British Field Sports Society', *International Journal of the History of Sport*, 13, 2, 177–91.

McKernan, L. (ed.) (2002) *Yesterday's News: The British Cinema Newsreel Reader*, London: British Universities Film and TV Council.

McKibbin, Ross (1990) *The Ideologies of Class*, Oxford: Oxford University Press.

McKibbin, Ross (1998) *Classes and Cultures: England 1918–1951*, Oxford: Oxford University Press.

Mangan, J.A. (2001) *Athleticism in the Victorian and Edwardian Public School*, London: Cass.

Marshall, H. (1936) 'What rugger means to me', in H.B.T. Wakelam (ed.) *The Game Goes On*, London: Arther Balcer, 108–115.

Mason, T. (1990) 'Stanley Matthews' in R. Holt (ed.) *Sport and the Working Class in Modern Britain*, Manchester: Manchester University Press, 159–178.

Mass-Observation (1987) *The Pub and the People: A Worktown Study*, London: Cresset.

Matthews, H.C.G. and Harrison, B. (2004) *The Oxford Dictionary of National Biography*, Oxford: Oxford University Press.

Matthews, S (1948) *Feet First*, London: Ewen and Dale.

MCC, Minutes of Meetings at Lord's, January 1927 to October 1934, MCC Library.

Melling, A. (1998) 'Ray of the Rovers; the working-class heroine in popular football fiction, 1915–25', *International Journal of the History of Sport*, 15, 1, 97–122.

Melling, A. (2002) 'Women and football', in R. Cox *et al.*, *An Encyclopaedia of British Football*, London: Cass.

Morris, R.J. (2000) 'Structure, culture and society in British towns', in M. Daunton (ed.) *Cambridge Urban History of Britain Vol. III 1840–1950*, Cambridge: Cambridge University Press.

Murfin, L. (1990) *Popular Leisure in the Lake Counties*, Manchester: Manchester University Press.

Murphy, L. (1934) 'Football' in G.W. Miles (ed.) *They're Off: A Journalist Record of British Sports*, London: Denis Archer, 94–109.

Murphy, P., Williams, J. and Dunning, E. (eds) (1990) *Football on Trial: Spectator Violence and Development in the Football World*, London: Routledge.

National Archives, HO45/15853/663749/29, letter from chair of Brighton and Hove Stadium, 21 November 1933.

National Archives, HO45/158590, police replies to Home Office enquiry, January 1934.

National Fitness Council for England and Wales. *The National Fitness Campaign, National Fitness Council for England and Wales: Report of the Grants Committee to the President of the Board of Education for the Period Ended 31st March 1939*, London: HMSO.

Naylor, L. (2004) 'Up for t'Cup: Preston North End fans at Wembley in 1937 and 1938', *Soccer History*, 9.

Nicholas, S. (2000) 'All the news that's fit to broadcast: the popular press versus the BBC', in P. Catterall, C. Seymour-Ure and A. Smith (eds) *Northcliffe's Legacy: Aspects of the British Popular Press 1896–1996*, Basingstoke: Macmillan, 121–47.

Nicholas, S. (2002) 'Being British: creeds and cultures', in K. Robbins (ed.) *The British Isles 1901–1951*, Oxford: Oxford University Press, 103–35.

O'Prey, Paul (ed.) (1982) *In Broken Images: Selected Letters of Robert Graves 1914–46*, London: Hutchison.

Oxford Dictionary of National Biography (2004), 'Howard Marshall', Oxford: Oxford University Press.

Patterson, N.H. (1921) *Lawn Tennis by Tyne and Wear*, Newcastle: T. and G. Allen.

Perry, F. (1934) *My Story*, London: Hutchison.

Phillips, S. (2003) 'Boots Athletic FC and works football', *Soccer History*, 5, 33–8.

Pickford, W. (n.d.) *A Glance Back at the Football Association Council 1888–1938*, Bournemouth: Bournemouth Guardian.

Pollard, M. (1934) *Cricket for Women and Girls*, London: Hutchison.

Polley, M. (1998) *Moving the Goalposts*, London: Routledge.

Pollock, W. (1934) *The Cream of Cricket*, London: Methuen.

Priestley, J.B. (1929) *The Good Companions*, London: Heinemann.

Priestley, J.B. (1984) *English Journey*, London: Heinemann.

Raven, J. (1990) 'Viewpoint: British history and the enterprise culture', *Past & Present*, 129, November, 178–204.

Read, D. (1964) *The English Provinces c. 1760–1960: A Study in Influence*, London: Arnold.

Reid, D.A. (2000) 'Playing and Praying', in M. Daunton (ed.) *Cambridge Urban History of Britain Vol 3*, Cambridge: Cambridge University Press, 745–807.

Rendall, Major J.C.S. (1930) *Things that Matter in Lawn Tennis*, London: Besant and Co.

Richards J. and Sheridan, D. (eds) (1987) *Mass-Observation at the Movies*, London: Routledge & Kegan Paul.

Roberts, K. (2000) *The Leisure Industries*, Basingstoke: Palgrave McMillan.

Rojek, C. (2001) *Celebrity*, London: Reaktion.

Rowntree, S.B. (1941) *Poverty and Progress: A Second Social Survey of York*, London: Longman, Green and Co.

Royal Commission on the Press 1947–9, (1949) London: HMSO, 1949.

Rubinstein, W.D. (1993) *Capitalism, Culture and Decline in Britain, 1750–1990*, London: Routledge.

Rudd, B.D. (1938) *Athletics (by the Achilles Club)*, London: Dent.

Rugby Football Union Minute Book, 1920 to 1934, Museum of Rugby.

Rugby Union Finance and Emergency Committee Minutes, 1921–31, Museum of Rugby.

Russell, D. (1996a) 'Amateurs, professionals and the construction of social identity', *Sports Historian*, 16, 64–80.

Russell, D. (1996b) 'Sport and identity: the case of Yorkshire County Cricket Club, 1890–1939', *20th Century British History*, 7, 2, 206–30.

Russell, D. (1997) *Football and the English*, Preston: Carnegie.

Satterthwaite, Mrs (n.d) *Lawn Tennis for Women*, London: Renwick.

Savage, H.J. (1926) *Games and Sports in British Schools and Universities*, New York: Carnegie Foundation.

Scannell, P. and Cardiff, D. (1991) *A Social History of British Broadcasting: Volume One 1922–1939: Serving the Nation*, Oxford: Blackwell.

Scruton, R. (2001) *England: An Elegy*, London: Pimlico.

Seddon, P.J. (1999) *A Football Compendium*, London: British Library.

Shafer, S.C. (1997) *British Popular Films 1929–1939: The Cinema of Reassurance*, London: Routledge.

Sharpe, I. (1952) *40 Years in Football*, London: Hutchinson.

Shoveller, S.H. (1936) and Pollard, M. (1936) *Hockey*, London: Sir Isaac Pitman and Sons.

Sissons, R. and Stoddart, B. (1984) *Cricket and Empire: The 1932–33 Bodyline Tour of Australia*, London: Allen and Unwin.

Smith, A. (2002) 'Cars, cricket and Alf Smith: the place of works-based sports and social clubs in the life of mid-20th century Coventry', *International Journal of the History of Sport*, 19, 1, 137–50.

Smyth, Ian (1993) 'The development of baseball in Northern England 1935–9', *International Journal of the History of Sport*, 10, 2, 252–8.

Soar, P. and Tyler, M. (1983) *Encyclopaedia of British Football*, London: Willow.

Soutar, A. (1934) *My Sporting Life*, London: Hutchison.

Stevenson, J. (1984) *British Society 1914–45*, Harmondsworth: Penguin.

Studd, Stephen (1998) *Herbert Chapman: Football Emperor*, London: Souvenir.

Sugden, J. and Bairner, A. (eds) (1993) *Sport, Sectarianism and Society in a Divided Ireland*, Leicester: Leicester University Press.

Surrey County Council (n.d.) *Surrey for Health, Sport and Residence*, Leatherhead: SCC.

Swanton, E.W. (1985) *Gubby Allen: Man of Cricket*, London: Hutchinson/Stanley Paul.

Tabner, B. (1992) *Through the Turnstiles*, Harefield: Yore.

Tanner, M. (2003) *The Legend of Mick the Miller*, Compton: Highdown.

Tilden, W. (1933) *Lawn Tennis for Club Players*, London: Methuen.

Tranter, N. (1998) *Sport, Economy and Society in Britain, 1750–1914*, Cambridge: Cambridge University Press.

Tunstall, J. (1980) 'The British press in the age of television' in H. Christian (ed.) *The Sociology of Journalism and the Press*, Keele: Keele University Press, 19–36.

Turner, E.S. (1957) *Boys Will Be Boys*, London: Michael Joseph.

Urry, J. (1990) *The Tourist Gaze: Leisure and Travel in Contemporary Societies*, London: Sage.

Vachell, H. (1930) *The Best of England*, London; Faber and Faber.

Vamplew, W. (1988) *Play Up and Play the Game: Professional Sport in Britain 1875–1914*, Cambridge: Cambridge University Press.

Walker, G.W. (1930) 'A National Asset', in J.S. Hoskins, *Roarin' Round the Speedways with John S. Hoskins*, London: McCorquodale, 94–6..

Walton, J.K. (2003) 'Britishness', in C. Wrigley (ed.) *A Companion to Early Twentieth Century Britain*, Blackwell, 517–33.

Walton, J.K. (2000) 'Towns and consumerism', in M. Daunton, (ed.) *The Cambridge Urban History of Britain Vol. III, 1840–1950*, Cambridge: Cambridge University Press, 715–744.

Walvin, J. (1975) *The People's Game*, London: Allen Lane.

Warner, O. (1935) 'In Praise of Woolley', *National Review*, 104, June, 785–8.

Wentworth Day, J. (1934) 'Field Sports' in C.W. Miles (ed.) *They're Off: A Journalistic Record of British Sports*, London: Denis Archer, 33–8.

Wethered, J. (1993) *Golfing Memories and Methods*, London: Hutchinson.

Whannel, G. (1992) *Fields in Vision: Television and Cultural Transformation*, London: Routledge.

Wiener, M.J. (1981) *English Culture and the Decline of the Industrial Spirit*, Cambridge: Cambridge University Press.

Williams, Jack (1996) 'Churches, sport and identities in the North, 1900–1939', in J. Hill and J. Williams (eds) *Sport and Identity in the North of England*, Keele: Keele University Press, 113–36.

Williams, Jack. (1997) '"One could literally have walked on the heads of the people congregated there": sport, the town and identity', in K. Laybourn (ed.) *Social Conditions, Status and Community 1860–c.1920*, Stroud: Sutton.

Williams, Jack (2003) *Cricket and England: A Cultural and Social History of the Inter-war Years*, London: Cass.

Williams, Jack (1999) '"A Wild Orgy of Speed": responses to Speedway in Britain before the Second World War', *Sports Historian*, 19, 1, 1–5.

Williams, Jean (2003) *A Game for Rough Girls: A History of Women's Football in Britain*, London: Routledge.

Winner, D. (2005) *Those Feet: A Sensual History of English Football*, London: Bloomsbury.

Theses

Crook, D. (1979) The Development of Physical Training in Coventry 1933–44, Liverpool University M.Ed. thesis.

Hick, P. (1971) A Study of the Development of Physical Education and Recreation in the City of York from 1900 to the Present Time, Newcastle University M.Ed. thesis.

Jones, K. (1983) Physical Education in Four North West Public Schools from 1920 to 1930, Liverpool University M.Ed. thesis.

Index

eBooks – at www.eBookstore.tandf.co.uk

A library at your fingertips!

eBooks are electronic versions of printed books. You can store them on your PC/laptop or browse them online.

They have advantages for anyone needing rapid access to a wide variety of published, copyright information.

eBooks can help your research by enabling you to bookmark chapters, annotate text and use instant searches to find specific words or phrases. Several eBook files would fit on even a small laptop or PDA.

NEW: Save money by eSubscribing: cheap, online access to any eBook for as long as you need it.

Annual subscription packages

We now offer special low-cost bulk subscriptions to packages of eBooks in certain subject areas. These are available to libraries or to individuals.

For more information please contact webmaster.ebooks@tandf.co.uk

We're continually developing the eBook concept, so keep up to date by visiting the website.

www.eBookstore.tandf.co.uk

LIBRARY, UNIVERSITY OF CHESTER